TRACING YOUR ANCESTORS THROUGH LETTERS AND PERSONAL WRITINGS

FAMILY HISTORY FROM PEN & SWORD

TRACING YOUR ANCESTORS THROUGH LETTERS AND PERSONAL WRITINGS

A Guide for Family Historians

Ruth A. Symes

Pen & Sword
FAMILY HISTORY

First published in Great Britain in 2016
PEN & SWORD FAMILY HISTORY
an imprint of
Pen & Sword Books Ltd
47 Church Street,
Barnsley
South Yorkshire,
S70 2AS

ISBN 978 147385 543 4

A CIP catalogue record for this book is
available from the British Library.

Typeset in Palatino by CHIC GRAPHICS

Printed and bound in England by
CPI Group (UK), Croydon, CR0 4YY

Pen & Sword Books Ltd incorporates the imprints of Pen & Sword
Archaeology, Atlas, Aviation, Battleground, Discovery, Family History,
History, Maritime, Military, Naval, Politics, Railways, Select, Social History,
Transport, True Crime, Claymore Press, Frontline Books, Leo Cooper,
Praetorian Press, Remember When, Seaforth Publishing and Wharncliffe.

For a complete list of Pen & Sword titles please contact
PEN & SWORD BOOKS LTD
47 Church Street, Barnsley, South Yorkshire, S70 2AS, England
E-mail: enquiries@pen-and-sword.co.uk
Website: www.pen-and-sword.co.uk

CONTENTS

DEDICATION

To my sister Naomi – for the longest of family relationships.

ACKNOWLEDGEMENTS

With thanks to: Mr Colin Daniels, The National Archives, the staff of Cheshire Record Office, Alex Miller at Wigan Archives Service, Dr Helen Rogers of the Writing Lives Project at Liverpool John Moore's University (www.writinglives.org), Special Collections at Brunel University, Stockport Postcard Fair, Mr Zainul Sachak, Miss Ruby Sachak, Mrs Olive Symes, Mr Philip Watts, and Mrs Lois Wilkinson.

Introduction

GETTING UP CLOSE TO PERSONAL WRITINGS

Amongst their possessions and official paperwork, our ancestors might have left a whole raft of personal writings, from a name etched into the top of an old box, to an appointment diary, a shopping list, a recipe or remedy book, a sheaf of letters or a collection of postcards. Some may have gone further, leaving a trove of intimate detail in letters, a holiday journal, a full-blown but unpublished manuscript of an autobiography or novel, or even a fragment of original poetry.

Whilst we might easily assume that our upper and middle-class ancestors left some written evidence of their lives, it is a common misconception that our working-class ancestors probably did not. Historians of ordinary people have tended to focus on sources that record their spoken words, including stories passed down through a family's oral history, transcriptions of what was said in court, or spoken words quoted in a newspaper. In fact, however, many ordinary people with low levels of literacy left personal *writings* which may profitably be analysed by family historians. As one recent commentator, Martin Lyons, has put it: 'Our ancestors' writings are there if we care to look for them. The problem is not that ordinary writings are scarce and ephemeral: rather there is such an abundance of ordinary writing that the historian hardly knows where to begin' (Martyn Lyons, *The Writing Culture of Ordinary People in Europe, c. 1860-1920*, C.U.P., 2014).

You will probably have particular favourites amongst your ancestor's personal writings: a Victorian book with pencilled marginal markings, a half-kept 1920s appointments' diary, a typed manuscript of a life history, a telegram sent for a wedding during the interwar period, or even a glib postcard in ballpoint pen from the 1950s. This book will make you aware that whatever pieces of writing have taken your

1

interest, they were not written in a vacuum. The writer, your ancestor, was a member of a family, a community, a class, a country and most probably a religion. He or she was the product of numerous educational, reading and cultural experiences which might be reflected in the words he or she produced. And he or she wrote for a purpose – to manage time, to keep in touch, to preserve information, to express identity or to register emotion. The piece of writing itself was created with the physical materials that came to hand at the time, using the elements of spelling, grammar and punctuation with which your ancestor was conversant, to express a meaning that had resonance on that particular day in history. If it was not written for your ancestor's own reference or self-satisfaction, the piece might have been received, enjoyed and even acted upon by a person or people with broadly similar frames of reference to him or her. Less likely, but just possible, it might have been written directly for posterity, for the eyes of a descendant just like you.

Given all this context, it is little wonder that the personal writings of our ancestors have been of interest to specialists from a wide variety of fields, from palaeographers to educationalists, to specialists in literacy, literature, poetry, penmanship, papermaking and publishing. Such writings might intrigue engineers and scientists as much as cultural historians and sociologists. Really, the number of different lenses through which we might look at these personal writings from the past is huge – far too numerous to be covered in their entirety here. The main purpose of this particular book, **however**, is to make the findings of academics working in some of these fields relevant and useful to the family historian. What is of primary interest to those researching their ancestors, of course, is how personal writings might assist in the quest better to understand the worlds and lives of those who created them. With this to the forefront, this book aims to give you some useful background to the different kinds of writing that your ancestors might have produced and some practical ideas about how to analyse such writing in order to enhance your family history research.

HOW MIGHT I LOCATE THE PERSONAL WRITINGS OF AN ANCESTOR?
1. Amongst Family Papers
Personal writings by ancestors often turn up amongst family papers.

When conducting oral history interviews with relations, it is essential always to ask whether any evidence of what they are telling you has been written down anywhere. Often this query will lead you to official or published sources about an ancestor, a certificate or newspaper article, for example. But sometimes a memory might be jogged about the existence of a piece of personal writing: 'Great-grandfather wrote a poem about that'; 'Aunt Matilda once tried to draw up a family tree'; 'I think a distant cousin kept a diary about his experiences in France during the War', and the like. The challenge then is to find out whether such papers are still in existence and whereabouts they might have ended up amongst the possessions of a family who might now be widely dispersed.

Be sure to ask relatives whether they have any letters or other notes written by your ancestor that they can make available to you. If they are unwilling to part with the originals ask for a photocopy, or better still a digitally-scanned copy. The latter is far better since it can be enlarged and enhanced for closer inspection. Always be careful to note any other factors which might help you to date or otherwise interpret the writing, and ask pertinent questions of it. What kind of storage was it kept in? What other kind of materials were found alongside it?

2. In National and Local Archives and Local Studies Centres

Since the 1920s – and the expansion of archival record office provision – a vast number of personal papers have been deposited in national and local archives by ordinary people who have not had the space or expertise to keep hold of them. Archives have also taken over collections of papers held by solicitors and other professional trustees which might include items of personal writing. Although there are rules about which kinds of official papers must be preserved in archives (such as those required by central government agencies), there are no fixed rules governing which personal papers should be so kept; collections have, therefore, grown at the discretion of the archivists in charge. Provided that the papers related to people who lived within the geographic province of the archive, and that they held any degree of interest at all, they will most probably have been welcomed by the archives and preserved. In particular, any material offered to an archive detailing an individual life, especially diaries and letters (regardless of the gender, social class or ethnicity of the writer), is likely to still be there, neatly catalogued and just waiting to be discovered. If it is particularly interesting, the archive might have invested money in having some of this writing digitized and making it available to view via a computer.

To find the location of archival items of interest (kept nationwide) you may search within the 'Discovery' section of the National Archives website (www. discovery.nationalarchives.gov.uk) by the name of your ancestor as well as by the type of writing (diary, poem, letter and the like) or by keyword (such as place). Bear in mind the obvious but sometimes overlooked fact that since many kinds of personal writing are communications sent from one person to another, you might need to search for them using the information relating to the recipient rather than the sender. For instance, if you are seeking letters written by your great-grandfather to his married daughter, they are likely to remain with the papers of the daughter and be catalogued under her surname, not his.

The National Archives website will tell you which archive or local studies centre houses the documents you might be interested in. The degree of detail given about these personal papers will vary. If their potential for wider significance was noted at the time that they were deposited then you might find extra information. On the whole, however, descriptions might amount to no more than a sentence. Once you have a reference number for an archival item in which you are interested, you can contact an on-site archivist by email or telephone and arrange to go and view the documents. Be aware, however, that some documents are subject to Data Protection Laws (specifically the Data Protection Act 1998 and the Freedom of Information Act 2000). Additionally in some cases, the depositors of the papers might have expressed a wish that their material be closed to public view for a certain length of time. Make sure that you check whether you will actually be able to view the material before you make your visit.

You may access archives and take notes of the writings free of charge. If you wish to take photographs of the documents for private use, you can usually do so with your own photographic equipment, but there is usually a nominal fee. Archives tend to charge higher rates only if you wish to make your findings public by publishing them in a magazine or book.

3. In Specialist Libraries and Museums
Sometimes personal writings turn up in libraries or museums which are dedicated to certain kinds of people or certain topics. For example, some manuscript poetry by miners is preserved at the National Coal Mining

Museum in Wakefield (www. ncm.org.uk). Thousands of papers relating to significant women in the Women's Movement and other significant females are stored at The Women's Library at the London School of Economics (www.twl-calm.library.lse.ac.uk). There are many other such repositories across the country and all are putting more and more handwritten documents online in digital format.

4. In Specialist Digitized Projects
More and more projects are starting up to digitize handwritten records of many different kinds. One of the most exciting of these, which is as yet in its early stages, is The Archive of Working-Class Writing Online (www.writinglives.org/uncategorized/archive-of-working-class-writing-online) which will eventually include thousands of manuscripts written from 1700 onwards including poetry, broadsheets, songs, prose fiction, autobiographies, diaries, letters, journalism, petitions, pamphlets and polemics. This project is currently being undertaken by researchers and students at four different UK universities: Brunel, Liverpool John Moore's, The Open University and Sheffield Hallam University. The first part of this project, The Writing Lives Project (www.writinglives.org) is already well underway and is further described in Chapter 10.

Another interesting project to digitize handwritten documents is an online exhibition of the Irish in Britain, 1916 (see the Inspiring Ireland website www.inspiring-ireland.ie, part of the Irish Government's 1916 Centenary Project). Members of the public with handwritten material relating to this topic were asked in 2016 to take it to the Irish Embassy in Britain where it could be digitized and placed online. No doubt there will be many other such projects to retrieve and make available primary documents by ordinary ancestors in similar ways in the years to come.

5. Via Commercial Sites on the Internet
Commercial websites such as Ebay (www.ebay.co.uk) often advertise texts of personal interest such as old family Bibles with handwritten genealogies, collections of letters or memorandum books for sale. Auction houses too with similar material now often post their catalogues online (see for example, www.ukauctioneers.com and www. the-saleroom.com). There are also sites dedicated to old postcards and letters. These include www.oldpostardsetc.co.uk; www.postcardworld. co.uk; wwww.oldcards.co.uk; www.britishpostcardsonline.co.uk and

www.ebay.co.uk/bhp/old-letters. Some of these sites have sections specifically dedicated to family history and all can be searched by keyword. You never know, something might just turn up with your ancestor's handwriting upon it.

WHY DID MY ANCESTOR WRITE?

Our ancestors of the nineteenth and early twentieth centuries wrote more than any generation that had preceded them and had many more reasons to do so. During the period from 1860 to the 1920s, a number of historical changes took place in Britain which transformed families and the way in which they operated, and which concomitantly led to a vastly increased output of personal writing. They include the processes of industrialization and secularization, compulsory education with its attendant improvement in literacy, emigration and social and geographical mobility of all kinds. The two World Wars (1914–18 and 1939–45) created situations in which soldiers separated from their families often wrote home literally to register their continuing existence in the face of previously unimaginable circumstances. There were also huge technological advances related to the practice of writing. Improved techniques for printing, of course, revolutionized the publishing industry which meant that there were far more texts around for our ancestors to read, emulate and borrow from. Numerous other changes in the manufacture of paper, pencils, pens and ink, together with the introduction of telegrams and typewriters, all had a dramatic impact on the numbers of people who wrote and the frequency with which they wrote.

By the end of the nineteenth century, what had once been an unusual capability, the capability to write, had become a daily necessity, 'an integral and banal part of daily existence' (Lyons, *The Writing Culture of Ordinary People in Europe*, p. 3). The period was witness to millions of acts of writing that might never have taken place in other circumstances. Many of these acts were, of course, communications and transactions with the increasingly complex and bureaucratic public world of the Victorian age and its aftermath. Our ancestors might have had to petition courts or military authorities, contest wills, request financial assistance, or apply for jobs at a distance, to name but a few 'official' purposes for taking up their pens. At the same time, however, there were many new reasons for our ancestors to write *personally*, primarily for the benefit of their families, friends or themselves. The most important of these reasons are briefly discussed below. They will be developed further as they become relevant in ensuing chapters of this book.

1. To Maintain Family Networks

In an age when it became more common for many of our ancestors to move across the country and even to other countries to find work and establish better lives, long-distance communication between the different branches of a family became crucial to holding the unit together and managing its collective affairs. People wrote between towns and across continents to conduct love affairs, to transmit news and to manage family affairs of all kinds. They wrote to keep in touch with family members who were temporarily away travelling, on business or serving in the army; and they wrote to those who had permanently settled elsewhere. And the satellite members of families wrote back home with news of their new worlds, but also to maintain their identities as members of the original family group.

2. To Manage Time

Industrialization and modernization brought a new structure and rhythm to our ancestors' lives and, in particular, more of an emphasis on time. The mechanized world required regular working hours, and the coming of the railways brought a new standardization of time across the country from 1840. Writing was one way that people could attempt to take control of time. Busy working lives conducted mostly away from the family home required organization. Calendars and diaries were a useful – even essential – way of keeping track of official, domestic and social obligations in the future. In the thrusting, purposeful world of the Victorians and the early twentieth century, there was a sense of change and possibility; a feeling of the drama of life between birth and old age. Into this mêlée, our ancestors increasingly wanted to keep an account of what had happened to them in the past, to write their own self-histories, to chart their own progress, development and improvement.

3. To Develop Expertise

In a busy, changing world full of new ideas, but still lacking affordable printed material on many topics, our ancestors recorded anything and everything that might improve their individual lives and the lives of those in their families. Recipes and remedies, tips for saving money, cleaning silver, feeding children or fixing machines might all be jotted down in notebooks kept especially for that purpose. Such information was treasured, catalogued, referred to and acted upon. And even fragmentary writings concerned merely with the pragmatic details of household management, can reveal something of the way in which a writer saw him or herself, or his or her family.

4. To Express Identity and Register Emotion

The period in question saw gradual but significant shifts in the way people saw themselves in relation to each other, to nature, to society, to the state, to the class system, to the country and to history itself. The Victorian period is often described as having been marked by sentimentality and patriotism, social awareness, religiosity and a rising sense of individualism; the twentieth century by new depths of alienation, emptiness, anxiety and secularism. Some of our ancestors' personal writings sent to close contacts and, even more so, those written for their own consumption only, reverberate with these ideas. Personal writings such as letters and poetry helped our ancestors forge a sense of their own identity, and acted as psychological therapy of a kind, even in an age when such ideas had not yet been fully investigated and such terms had not yet been invented.

HOW DID MY ANCESTOR DEVELOP WRITING SKILLS?

You might be wondering if your ancestors could even write at all. More information about the likelihood that your ancestor was at all literate is provided in Chapter 1 which looks at various ways and circumstances in which people left a mark of their identity in terms of initials, a signature, or a name. But, of course, simply being able to sign his or her name – which was the extent of the literacy of very many people in the nineteenth century – was no guarantee whatsoever that he or she would ever need, desire or be capable of writing anything any longer and more complex. The kinds of writing analysed from Chapter 2 onwards required more than the basics of literacy. They involved writing sentences, constructing paragraphs, organizing thoughts lineally, and (where self-histories and poetry are concerned), raising the level of writing to something that might be called 'literary'. In order to achieve any of these outcomes, our ancestors will need to have marshalled all

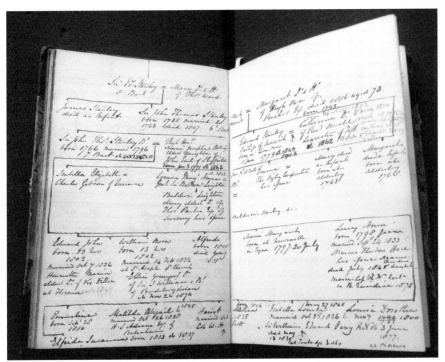

Personal writing of the most illuminating kind: Pedigree of the Stanley family of Alderley, Cheshire, by William Owen Stanley (1802–84). There was a vogue amongst upper middle-class Victorians for compiling their family tree by hand. (Document DSA105/4 held in Cheshire Record Office and reproduced with the permission of Cheshire Archives and Local Studies and the owner/depositor to whom copyright is reserved)

their resources. His or her schooling, the reading matter that he or she had been exposed to and a collection of other miscellaneous cultural factors will all have played their part in shaping your ancestor as a writer. As a family historian, you are in the fortunate position of possibly being able to find out more about some of these factors in respect of your ancestors.

Schooling
To find out more about your ancestor's level of education, remember first that children of different social classes were schooled differently to each other in the past, as were girls differently to boys. Ask yourself whether it is likely that your ancestor reached a primary, secondary or tertiary level of education? A child leaving school at the age of ten or eleven is unlikely to have tackled more than the basics of the so-called

3Rs: Reading, Writing and Arithmetic. Some poor children might have received their education as half-timers (working half the week in factories and the other half at school), others might have been educated at the opposite extreme and attended public schools or grammar schools and universities. Do you have any idea whether your ancestor might have received a religious or a secular education? Is he or she likely to have been taught the classics? Or was the school that he or she attended more modern in its outlook favouring science and languages? Attendance at school was not compulsory for our ancestors before 1870. Many did, however, attend a school of one kind or another before that.

Upper (and later) middle-class boys might have attended one of the ancient public schools or an increasing number of grammar schools. Their sisters might have been tutored by governesses at home or in small privately-run academies. In the late nineteenth century they might have been sent to one of a small number of grammar schools especially founded for their sex. Public schools occasionally published their registers in book form. If the books include brief posthumous biographies of students, you may find that you are furnished with a complete potted life history of your ancestor at the click of a button. At the subscription website, www. thegenealogist.co.uk, you may view the content of a large number of such books including, for example, the Registers of St Paul's School, London, 1748–1876 (which gives the dates of admission of individual students, their ages and the names and occupations of their fathers). The Registers of Charterhouse (1872–1910) and Westminster (up to 1927). Some other such schools can be searched at www.ancestry.co.uk under the section 'Occupations and Education'. The public schools of ancestors who fought in the World Wars are mentioned in Military Rolls of Honour now available for a subscription on the main commercial genealogical websites.

But for most of our ancestors in the early part of the nineteenth century, education, if they had access to it at all, took place in one of a miscellany of non-compulsory types of establishment: Dame Schools, Sunday Schools, Industrial Schools, Charity Schools, Ragged Schools, Non-denominational British and Foreign Schools (from 1808), and National Schools (from 1811). The location of the records of some of these places of education might be found via the National Archives website (www.discovery.nationalarchives.gov.uk) but many have been lost to time or are incomplete or unhelpful.

Happily for family researchers, however, things changed from 1870 onwards when Forster's Elementary Education Act created a framework for compulsory state-sponsored schooling (Board Schools) for children between the ages of five and twelve in England and Wales. There were some exceptions to this (at the discretion of individual School Boards) including those children in rural areas who were exempted from attendance whilst they helped with bringing in the harvests and other agricultural tasks. The Education Act (Scotland) made similar provision north of the border in 1872 for children from five to thirteen years. Ten years later a Second Elementary Education Act (1880) tightened these rules, finally making education compulsory for those of our ancestors aged between five and ten. From 1891, parents could no longer begrudge the money spent on their children's education, as schooling became free of charge. Girls, in particular, probably benefitted from this change. In 1893, The Elementary Education (School Attendance) Act raised the minimum leaving age to eleven, and a later amendment, in 1899, raised it to twelve. The Fisher Education Act of 1918 (implemented in 1921) raised the leaving age to fourteen, and Rab Butler's Education Act of 1944 (in force from 1947) saw it go up again to fifteen. It was only in 1972 that the school leaving age was finally raised to sixteen.

If family papers fail to reveal certificates or bookplates (for academic or sporting achievement) which name an ancestor's school, try old postal directories or even telephone directories of the local area. Many of these can be searched online by keyword at www.specialcollections. le.ac.uk/cdm/landingpage/collectionp16445coll4 where digitized trade directories from the past will mention local educational establishments. Archives and libraries local to the area in which your ancestor lived should also be able to help with the names of possible local schools. In 1862 (1873 in Scotland) the so-called 'Revised Code' for State Education was introduced. Amongst other academic matters, the Code stipulated that, in return for government grants, school heads must keep an admissions register as well as a log book of activities.

Admissions registers for state schools potentially include the names of individual pupils, dates of birth and the names and addresses of their parents or guardians. They may also contain the date of admission to the school, the name of the last school attended, the date of leaving the school, the reason for leaving and sometimes the name of the school to which the pupil had been transferred. Most school admissions registers remain in hard copy in local archives (check at www.discovery. nationalarchives.gov.uk for their exact location. Starting out with blank books (with no guidance about how they were to be completed), some head teachers made entries in their school log books every day, others produced a weekly digest, some limited to themselves to recording official matters, while others (to the joy of today's researchers) treated themselves to the occasional personal observation. School log books are less likely to include the name of your specific ancestor but they do occasionally mention those children who have been awarded school prizes, or who have been noted for matters of discipline, absenteeism, ill health, difficult family circumstances and even death. Log books also record general information about the functioning of the school which can give a fascinating insight into the world in which your ancestor was educated.

Sadly, of course, some school log books were lost or deliberately destroyed when schools closed down or came under new administration. To find out whether they have deposited in local archives check the discovery section of the National Archives (www.discovery. nationalarchives.gov.uk) using the name of the school as a keyword. Some of the commercially-run genealogy sites such as www.findmy past.co.uk, www.ancestry.co.uk and www.thegenealogist. co.uk now have a selection of directly accessible school records online. One of these is Find My Past's Manchester Collection (www.findmypast.co. uk) which includes school admissions registers and logbooks from Manchester and the surrounding area. Ancestry (www.ancestry.co.uk) currently has a similar resource on London schools (1840–1911) and Perthshire schools (1869–1902). In some areas, there have also been small projects to digitize school records. In September 2011, for example, the log books of schools on the Scottish islands of St Kilda (1910–30) and Mingulay (1875–1910) were digitized in a joint project between the National Records of Scotland and the Hebridean Archives. Selections from these can be viewed at www.scottishten.org/. If the records of the school in which you are interested do not appear to be in the archives, it's worth checking to see if they are still on the school premises themselves. Some schools have selections from their historical records on their own websites and others appear in published book form, so it's always worth checking under the name of the school on www. amazon.co.uk.

To improve your understanding of your ancestor's educational opportunities, you should also consult one of a number of excellent recent history and family history books which include valuable information on the possible components of our ancestors' school curricula. These include: Sue Wilkes, *Tracing Your Ancestors' Childhood*, Pen and Sword, 2013; Mark Peel, *The New Meritocracy: A History of UK Independent Schools 1979-2014*, Elliott and Thompson, 2015; Pamela Horn, *The Victorian and Edwardian Schoolchild*, Sutton Publishing, 2013; and Marion Aldis and Pam Indler, *The Happiest Days of Their Lives? Nineteenth-Century Education Through the Eyes of Those Who Were There*, Chaplin Books, 2016. If you can find something in records or books about the sort of education your ancestor probably had you will certainly be better placed to understand the early influences on their writing.

Reading

Another major influence on our ancestors' propensity to write would have been the books or other reading material to which they had access. Whilst the upper and middle classes had always had the time and the finances to read, industrialization brought regulated and increased amounts of free time to some poorer sectors of the population. Philanthropists and politicians strived to ensure that some of this time was used profitably by the working classes in reading and rational recreation rather than drinking and sport.

Few records tell us exactly what our ancestors read, though some interested individuals did keep reading lists or noted books that they had read or that they aspired to read in diaries. Very few people, however, bothered to write down all the myriad of other texts that might have passed before their eyes such as newspapers, magazines, advertisements and the like. But if the specifics of the books read by your ancestor elude you, you can have an educated guess at the sorts of material to which your ancestor might have been exposed by reading more about the general availability of books and other reading materials in the late nineteenth and early twentieth centuries (See for example, Andrew Bennett, ed., *Readers and Reading*, Longman, 1995; Alberto Manguel, *A History of Reading*, Flamingo, 1997; and James Raven, Helen Small and Noami Tadmor, eds, *The Practice and Representation of Reading in England*, Cambridge U. P., 1996).

Be aware particularly that there was an explosion of print media at this time, facilitated by a number of matters including the abolition of newspaper tax in 1855, the development of high-speed rotary presses, and the availability of cheaper kinds of paper in the 1860s. An existing provision of subscription and circulating libraries was greatly improved upon from the middle of the nineteenth century onwards by a system of public libraries. The Public Libraries Act (1850) (extended to Scotland in 1853 and accompanied by The Public Libraries Act Scotland in 1854) allowed cities with a population exceeding 10,000 the possibility to levy taxes for the support of public libraries provided that there was enough support from local ratepayers. These were libraries that were free and accessible to all and from which books could be borrowed. As the *New Weekly Messenger* of 17 February 1870 commented approvingly: 'Public libraries are an indispensable adjunct to any system of national education worthy of the name. They would go far even as a substitute for such a system. Gibbon truly said that the best and most important part of a man's education is that which he gives himself.'

The great and the good hoped that these new libraries would steer poorer people with newly-acquired leisure time away from the vices of gambling, drinking and crime and into more moderate habits. By 1877, seventy-five cities across Britain had established free public libraries; by 1900, that number had increased to 300. In the new libraries, and in an increasing number of institutions specifically set up to educate the poor in adulthood, such as working-men's clubs, our ordinary ancestors could pursue interests of all kinds, from science and engineering to poetry and fiction. In their own personal writing, your ancestors might make reference to some of the published writers they had read. But consider also as you read their words just how sophisticated the writing sounds. Traces of all sorts of miscellaneous works read by your ancestor might appear in the content, the style or the wording of the particular piece of personal writing in which you are interested.

Other Cultural Influences
The other influences circulating around an ancestor as he or she put pen to paper might be many and various. It is a useful exercise to note down the different fields of experience (and therefore language) to which a writer might have been exposed. These might include his or her regional background, country of origin (if not British), profession or employment, social class, sporting and social interests, religious

convictions, travel and other known hobbies and activities. The language, sentence structure and general level of formality of your ancestor's writing might have been shaped by all manner of language experiences from hymns and music-hall songs, to technical processes with which he or she was involved. A young girl who writes in her autobiography of 'the warp and weft' of her life experiences might be drawing on her experiences of working in a weaving shed, for example.

There might indeed be certain 'buzz' words in a piece of writing which help to first identify aspects of your ancestor's background. If he refers to 'chapels' rather than 'churches', for example, he is likely to have been a Nonconformist rather than a member of the Church of England, a Quaker might mention 'meeting houses'; or a Catholic 'Mass'. For more on such influences on the language of our working-class ancestors see, for example, Jonathan Rose, *The Intellectual Life of the British Working Classes* (Yale U.P. 2010); and Joanna Bourke, *Working-Class Cultures in Britain, 1890-1960: Gender, Class and Ethnicity*, Routledge, 1994.

WHAT DID MY ANCESTOR WRITE WITH?

The nineteenth century saw enormous advances in the making of paper, pencils, pens and other associated writing implements. In addition to your ancestors' writings themselves, you might have inherited additional stationery, pens, ink wells or writing desks. It is worth paying some attention to these physical clues to your ancestor's writing proclivities. In the first instance, they might help you to date undated pieces of writing. Secondly, they might provide clues to an ancestor's social status.

Paper

The paper upon which your ancestor wrote can be dated, though this is a complex process best undertaken by experts. Take a look at the website of the British Association of Paper Historians at www.baphorg.uk. Small samples of paper can be compared with paper sheets for which the provenance is already known **and** watermarks in paper can be compared with those noted in old catalogues or trade listings. A specialist will be able to spot distinct marks on the surface of the paper that might determine both the age of the paper and the location in which it was made.

In 1800, all paper production in Britain was done by hand in hundreds of paper mills dotted around the country. Paper at this point was made from fibre sources such as hemp, linen and cotton, collectively known as 'rags'. By 1821, a new process of papermaking, invented by T. B. Crompton, meant that large continuous sheets of paper could be made by machine. The major revolution in paper production took place in 1843 with the introduction of a process to make paper using wood pulp (rather than rags) and powered by steam-driven papermaking machines patented earlier in the century. The fewer paper mills in the second half of the nineteenth century were much larger and more efficient and the price of paper dropped significantly.

Cheaper paper fed the growing newspaper and book publishing industries, but, it also provided a portable, flexible and convenient surface upon which our ancestors could write. Sold not only as loose sheets, but increasingly in crisp wedges bound in leather or other durable materials, paper probably became the biggest game-changer in the history of written expression. In his diary entry for New Year's Day, 1858, actor John Pritt Harley recorded that, 'I gave my Dear Sister Betsy a new Pocket Book' (Heather Creaton, ed, *Victorian Diaries: The Daily Lives of Victorian Men and Women*, Mitchell Beazley, 2001, p. 46). Harley did not make it clear for what use the book was intended but there were many possibilities. And, as the century moved on, publishers rose to the demand for these pocket and desk books in multifarious shapes and sizes, some no longer filled simply with blank pages but specifically designed for particular purposes: 'almanacs', 'miscellanies', 'birthday books', 'memoranda,' 'commonplace books', 'appointment diaries' and 'holiday journals', to name but a few types.

Pencils

The graphite used in British pencils was discovered in Cumbria as early as the sixteenth century, but it was only in the nineteenth century that pencil-making there became big business with the foundation of the Cumberland Pencil Company in 1832. Take a look at the website of the pencil museum at www.pencilmuseum.co.uk for more information. Pencils continued to be made from this pure graphite – which shed no dust and marked the paper very well – until the 1860s. Meanwhile, cheaper pencils made with a mixture of graphite and a clay binder, pioneered in France in the Napoleonic period, also became popular. It's worth bearing in mind that writing with pencil in the nineteenth and early twentieth centuries was seen less as a poor alternative to writing with ink than it is today. Writers knew that pencil markings were not subject to destruction by moisture, sunlight or aging and that, rendered thus, their ideas would still have some degree of permanence. Pencils remained a popular tool for writing, especially amongst the lower classes, even after the late nineteenth-century invention of fountain pens which made writing in ink more of an affordable option.

Here is how one particular maker's Memorandum Book and 'metallic' (i.e. lead-graphite) pencil were described in *The Morning Chronicle* in 1838.

> We have been highly pleased with Harwood's improved Patent Memorandum Book and metallic pencil, and glad to hear that a Book which promises to become so useful to the public may be obtained for almost any purpose. The Paper is of a very close smooth surface, and purposely adapted to receive a clear and perfect impression from the slightest touch of the pencil, and when one made is indelible. The Pencil itself is a clever, ingenious and complete model of what a pencil should be; and in its use retains to the fullest degree that beautiful softness which has rendered the lead of Cumberland so justly celebrated, besides combining the additional advantage of durability . . .
> (*The Morning Chronicle*, reproduced in *The Bolton Chronicle*, 14 April 1838)

Erasers

Raw rubber as a method of erasing pencil marks was first mentioned by scientist Joseph Priestley in 1770, 'I have seen a substance excellently adapted to the purpose of wiping from paper the mark of a black lead pencil' (Joseph Priestley, *A Familiar Introduction to the Theory and Practice of Perspective*, J. John and J. Payne, 1770, p. xv). It was not, however, until after the development of vulcanisation by Charles Goodyear in 1839 that erasers became widely used. In 1858, the American Hymen Lipman received a patent (later withdrawn) for attaching an eraser to the end of a pencil.

Ink Pens

People had long written in ink using quill pens, but in the nineteenth century, the new invention of a steel-tipped pen on a wooden shaft was to revolutionize writing in ink. These new pens were advertised in British newspapers from 1792, but patents were not issued until the early nineteenth century and it was not until 1822 that John Mitchell started to mass produce metal-nibbed pens in Birmingham. These pens, dipped into ink wells, were the implements used by the would-be professional writers of the early nineteenth-century such as the Brontës. Here is how *The Morning Chronicle* reported upon the new kind of ink pens produced by Harwood's in 1838.

> HARWOOD'S LONDON BANK PENS
> These Pens are manufactured from the best-tempered Steel combined with the greatest care and skill in the workmanship. They possess the flexibility of the quill, with the preservation of the elasticity to a much greater degree; and are so remarkable for producing beauty and clearness in writing as to render them distinguished in numerous public offices, which is the greatest testimony of their excellence. In order to protect the Public from numerous imitations of these pens, none are genuine unless bearing their signatures JNO and Fred Harwood.
>
> In order that the purchasers of the pens may ensure the kind most particularly suited for their writing, they are made to possess different characters, which are distinguished by the following letters and each Pen is stamped, 'Harwood's London Bank Pen'.
> 'F' for Fine or Running Hand
> 'M' for Middling or Round Hand
> 'B' for Broad or Text Hand.
> (*The Morning Chronicle*, reproduced in *The Bolton Chronicle*, 14 April 1838)

Steel-tipped pens might have improved upon quills, but they still required dipping in ink at frequent intervals, a process that could be frustrating and messy. Whilst one Bartholomew Folsch received a patent in England for a pen with an ink reservoir as early as 1809 and Romanian Petrarch Poenaru patented a fountain pen in France in 1827,

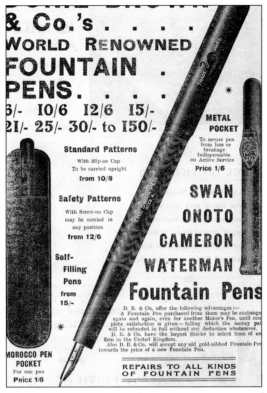

An advertisement for a fountain pen from the Post Office National Directory 1918. (Wikimedia Commons)

it wasn't until the end of the nineteenth century that pens which included a reservoir to carry their own ink were mass-produced and commonly used.

Ink

In the early part of the nineteenth century our ancestors wrote with ink commonly made from oak gall and vinegar. Any personal writing that you find amongst family papers made from this sort of ink might well have deteriorated considerably since this mixture has a corrosive effect over time. Later in the nineteenth century, ink was more commonly created from lampblack or soot plus a binding agent such as 'gum arabic' or 'animal glue'. Documents written with such ink which does not corrode or fade in sunlight – provided they have been kept dry – are quite likely still to be legible.

Ballpoint Pens

If your ancestor's personal writing is in ballpoint pen, it must have been written during or more probably after the Second World War. The first patent on such an item was issued on 30 October 1888, to John J. Loud who was trying to design a pen that would write on rough surfaces such as wood and wrapping paper. Whilst he did manage to develop a pen that could write on leather, it was too coarse for ordinary paper and the patent was allowed to lapse, without the pen ever taking off commercially. Other attempts at early ballpoints resulted in pens which worked very imperfectly, either the ink was not delivered evenly, or the pen got clogged, leaked or smeared. It was not until some fifty years later that Hungarian newspaper editor László Biró, with the help of his brother George, a chemist, began to work on the design for a new type of pen which would include a tiny ball in its tip that was free to turn in its socket. The idea was that as the pen moved along the paper, the ball would rotate, picking up ink from the ink cartridge and leaving it on the paper. With new developments in precision manufacturing and some chemical refinement in terms of the ink used, this would be a cleaner, more reliable alternative to the fountain pen. Bíró filed a British patent for the pen on 15 June 1938. In 1940 the Bíró brothers and their friend, Juan Jorge Meyne, fled the Nazis to Argentina and on 10 June of that year they filed another patent, and formed Bíró Pens. By the summer of 1943 the first commercial ballpoint pens were available. Some of the first users were British RAF crew who found that the pens worked well at high altitudes. The market for ballpoint producers such as Papermate, Bic and Parker, in the 1950s was now wide open.

Writing Desks

A familiar inherited item from a wealthy or middle-class Victorian ancestor is the writing box (also known as a lap desk, writing case, dispatch box and dispatch case). This was a portable box which opened out and often included a slope upon which to write. Part of both the personal and the professional worlds of our ancestors, such boxes were

A bureau-style writing desk very popular with the middle classes at the end of the Victorian period. This one appeared in an edition of The Girl's Own Paper *of 1885. (*The Girl's Own Paper*, Vol. VI, No. 283, 30 May 1885)*

perhaps used more than any other item of furniture in well-to-do homes of the past.

The convenience of a writing desk must have been extraordinary. In the way that laptops have recently extended the usage of desktop computers, writing desks extended the usage of the writing bureau. Now, for the first time, people could write comfortably in different locations. The slopes could be carried from room to room and were

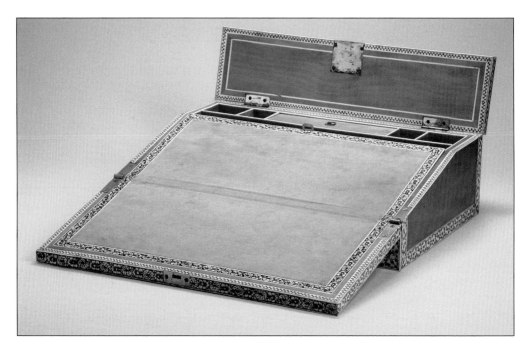

Elegant writing slopes such as this one were transported to the outposts of Empire by British officials and their wives. This one (made in England but used in Vishakhapatnam, Andhra Pradesh, India, between 1850 and 1875), is of sandalwood, with ivory and bone veneer and metal fittings and a velveteen interior. It is now kept in the Los Angeles Museum of Art. (Wikimedia Commons)

designed to be used either on a table or on a lap. Compartments were included for sealed inkwells to prevent spillages. With a writing desk, users could, for the first time, write comfortably on journeys. Such desks were carried by army men or ship's captains – or rather by their servants – to the furthest-flung outposts of the Empire.

Our ancestors' writing desks came in different shapes and sizes, made from different materials and had different extras depending on the pocket of the user. On 12 June 1862, the *Edinburgh Evening Courant* ran an advertisement that distinguished between three sizes of writing desk in four different types of wood: rosewood, mahogany, coromandel and walnut. The prices ranged from three shillings and sixpence to 55 shillings. Extras might include compartments in which to store paper and copies of letters sent, bottles of ink, pens, nibs, penwipers (made of black felt), blotting pads, postage stamps, sealing wax and seals. Occasionally writing boxes also included light wells (for matches), spaces for candlesticks and a reading stand. These new-fangled personal possessions might have been particularly attractive to our ancestors because in a bustling, urbanizing world, they provided a place of privacy and, where necessary, secrecy. Many boxes had hidden drawers and could be locked with a key. Sometimes writing desks were cleverly constructed to enable other uses; a lady's writing box might double up as a sewing box, for example, or include sections for the storage of items connected to her toilette. A gentleman's box might include similar compartments for shaving or grooming items.

Typewriters
Whilst typed documents don't feature much in this book, they might still count as examples of personal writing. The first Remington typewriters appeared in 1872, though it was not until the first decades of the twentieth century that they came into widespread use – and then more so in the office than at home.

WHAT DIFFICULTIES MIGHT MY ANCESTOR HAVE FACED IN WRITING?
For our ancestors writing could be a taxing, even a deeply nerve-wracking, business. A semi-literate adult sending a letter for the first time might well have been anxious about its possible reception. To communicate, for example, with a family member in America, so far

away in terms of both space and time, must have seemed like an extraordinary feat for people unfamiliar with using a pen. Many are the letters (but also all sorts of other kinds of writing) which open with or include abject apologies for writing that is inadequate or poor in some way.

In the first place our ancestors needed to find a quiet place to write where paper could be balanced safely. This was not always easy in crowded, noisy homes where every flat surface was in constant use. And when away from home, finding a writing space might have been even more difficult. Transport – even after the coming of the railways – was notoriously rickety unless you had the advantage of a portable writing desk. And accommodation might be entirely unsuitable to the essentially peaceful pursuit of letter or diary writing. Soldiers in the First World War, for example, might have written when they were in hospital or resting behind the lines, but less often when they were actually in the trenches themselves.

The very physicality of writing and potential mess of writing in the past particularly distinguishes it from the same practice today. Writing requires the motor coordination of multiple joints in the wrist, elbow and shoulder in ways very different from that for any other activity. To move the pen successfully across the paper, a writer must coordinate sensory impulses from the skin, joints and muscles. The business of learning to write properly might have taken years for someone who had not had the right training in childhood. Additionally, pencils required regular sharpening (often with a knife), pens needed to be regularly dipped in (or later filled with) ink to prevent writing petering out as it crossed the page, and paper sometimes had to be cut to the right size and used sparingly.

A writer in the magazine *Household Words* in 1852 looked back at some of the physical difficulties of writing in the early part of the century: 'remember the bulky pocket-book, with its leather strap (always shabby after the first month), and its thick cedar pencil, which always wanted cutting; always blackening whatever came near it; always getting used up; the lead turning to dust at the most critical point of a memorandum' (*Household Words*, 31 January 1852).

Other physical aspects of writing (that we literate descendants take for granted) all but floored some of our ancestors. 'Holding a straight line was always a problem for inexperienced writers' (Lyons, *The Writing*

Culture of Ordinary People in Europe, p. 41); since ruled paper was difficult to come by, writers often ruled a sheet themselves and then placed this underneath the plain writing sheet. Another common issue was the misjudging of space, 'Often the handwriting started confidently but became smaller and more ragged as the author tried to fit more words into an ever-diminishing space on the page' (Ibid., p. 41). There was also no easy way to correct a mistake made in ink other than by crossing it through. Some writers resorted to literal cutting and pasting, covering erroneous words, sentences or even whole paragraphs with strips of paper that they glued into their pocket books.

Academic Deborah Lutz explains how even frequent and accomplished writers could find the whole business of putting pen to paper difficult:

> Emily [Brontë] found the pen troublesome . . . Blots dropped onto the page penetrating through to the other side and interfering with the poem on the verso. She dug her nib into the paper, her pen ran out of ink as she wrote. Her nib would become clogged with sediment from the dregs of the ink bottle, and she cleaned it by dragging it along the page. Her blotting paper has holes in it from hasty nib cleaning (Deborah Lutz, *The Brontë Cabinet: Three Lives in Nine Objects*, W. W. Norton, 2015, p. 174).

But of course, far greater than the physical barriers to writing, were the potential intellectual ones – the difficulties of shaping meandering thought-patterns into 'rational linear patterns' of meaning. If we consider some of the differences between speech and writing, it is easy to understand why an ancestor from a class background where writing was an unusual rather than an habitual occurrence might find the whole business intimidating. Whereas a speaker might gain confidence from the immediate reaction of those around him or her, a writer cannot. Whilst speech can be immediately and repeatedly corrected, writing is just about permanent once written down. Where writing is used primarily for communication purposes (rather than simply for the writer's own emotional gratification) it needs to meet a higher than usual standard of clarity. When composing with a pen, our ancestors did not have at their disposal any of the tricks that they might otherwise have used in speech to convey meaning, such as timing, pauses and intonation, pitch, rhythm, stress and bodily gestures. Instead they had to rely for perspicuity on their own choice of vocabulary, and on a system of grammar and punctuation with which they might not have been entirely conversant.

Ancestors from the provinces were anxious that regional vocabulary and grammar might cause confusion when letters were sent to the metropolis or to other distant parts of the country. Women, often less skilled than men in the written arts and less conversant in general with the experience of public life, frequently expressed a lack of confidence in their own abilities. Older people, especially at the end of the nineteenth century, often deferred to the younger members of their families (who had benefitted from state-funded educational provision after 1870) to act as scribes when they were required to undertake writing tasks. Newly-arrived immigrants, such as those from Italy and Germany who came to live and work in the manufacturing districts of big cities such as Manchester, worried about their lack of facility in the English language. The physically and mentally impaired had no aids to help them write and would have been wholly reliant on others for any written communication necessary.

Our ancestors' concerns about their own writing were well-founded. Victorian society could be censorious and even cruel in its treatment of those who didn't match certain standards of literacy. The young lower middle-class girls who wrote into the *Girl's Own Paper* for advice, for example, were often reprimanded by their editors for their handwriting, grammar and punctuation even when their enquiry to the magazine had nothing to do with those matters. 'Butterfly's writing does not show any character at present. She ought to write careful copies daily. Her spelling is bad especially in writing "girld" for "girl"' ('Answers to Correspondents', *Girl's Own Paper* Vol. VIII, No. 391, 25 June 1887).

All this considered, it is perhaps surprising that so many of our ancestors put pen to paper at all. It seems, however, that the joys, pleasures and satisfaction of writing and receiving written communications generally outweighed the fear and embarrassment. Many of our ancestors, it seems, would rather break all regulations (sometimes using no punctuation at all, for example) and risk a negative reception, if it meant that they achieved their writing aim of making contact with a loved one. As Martin Lyons has commented 'written communication was a necessary to which semi-literate writers devoted

Painting entitled 'Woman Writing in An Interior' by Felix Emile-Jean Vallotton, 1904. Women's relationship with writing was a complex one. Many lower-class women were unable to write or very unconfident about doing so. On the other hand, writing was a quiet, private business very much tied up with the running of a household, so, amongst the literate classes, women's personal writings actually abound in the Victorian period and beyond. (Wikimedia Commons)

themselves with trepidation but also with passion' (Lyons, *The Writing Culture of Ordinary People in Europe*, p. 52). Both 'trepidation' and 'passion' are likely to be present in any personal writing that you find by your ancestors.

If you have several examples of writing by a particular ancestor over a number of years or a lifetime, it's worthwhile tracing how his or her writing confidence might have grown. Letters written later in life, for instance, might have been produced more regularly or might have been longer and better structured with clearer paragraph breaks and better spelling and punctuation. Vocabulary might have improved or have become more specialized as a writer developed in his or her career. Don't view your writing ancestor as a static character, but always one who might have developed his or her writing prowess with time and experience.

HOW CAN I LEARN TO READ AND UNDERSTAND MY ANCESTOR'S WRITINGS BETTER?

Before you can start to analyse and properly understand your ancestors' writings, you need to be able to read them. This may not be as straightforward as it sounds: handwriting may be difficult to decode, punctuation may be unusual, erratic or just plain wrong, the overall style of a piece may mystify rather than elucidate. Your first concern as a family historian might be whether or not the handwriting was in fact produced by one of your ancestors rather than somebody else altogether or indeed how to identify exactly which ancestor it was.

Nowadays, thankfully, there is a great deal of advice on the internet about how better to make sense of – and by extension identify – writing by ancestors, usually in official documents. You need to approach the business on two levels: first how better to understand the technicalities of your ancestor's handwriting (palaeography), and secondly how to employ a whole range of tools to find out more about the document in its historical context (i.e. as a product of its times).

The Technicalities of Handwriting

In terms of handwriting, most of our ancestors in the nineteenth and early twentieth centuries used a version of modern cursive writing generally known as copperplate. This is a round-hand that finds its basic shape in the letter 'O'. That said, of course, there are an enormous number of different variations of this script which vary from the very plain and easy to read to the very fancy and more difficult to decipher. Try to get to grips with the way your ancestor wrote particular letters. You could even create an alphabet sheet upon which you record how he or she wrote each capital and lower-case letter. But remember that a letter might be written differently if it occurs at the beginning, middle or end of a word, or if it is doubled. Remember also that 'n' and 'u' can be easily confused, as can 'h' and 'k.' In older documents spelling might not be standardized. A useful look at some common variations in the depiction of certain letters of the alphabet can be found at www.amberskyline.com/treasuremaps /oldhand.htm. It might be useful to compare letters or combinations of letters in a known word with those in an unknown word.

Identifying writers by their handwriting was a common preoccupation of members of the public and specialists in detective work in the late nineteenth century. Differences between individual hands were investigated, for example, in criminal cases in which notes or letters had been left. This happened in the 1871 case of Christiana Edmunds, from Brighton, dubbed the 'Chocolate Cream Poisoner' in the press, who was accused of dispersing anonymous parcels containing poisoned chocolates and sweets to a number of respectable citizens including Emily Beard, the wife of a doctor with whom she was in love (Kaye Jones, *The Case of the Chocolate Cream Poisoner: The Poisonous Passion of Christiana Edmunds*, Pen and Sword, 2016). Graphology expert Frederick Netherclift appeared at the Central Criminal Court and was asked to compare one of Edmunds' love letters to Dr Beard with the address labels of the poisoned parcels. He described to the court how rather than looking at the general style of the handwriting he picked out twelve or fourteen of its peculiarities and considered that if most of these were replicated in both pieces of writing he would have 'good grounds for believing them to be the same handwriting'. By these criteria, Edmunds was found guilty of murder by the Central Criminal Court in January 1872 and sentenced to death.

A Few Other Basic Tips
- If your ancestor has left any personal writings at all, it is likely that there will be more than one example and possibly that they are in more than one genre (kind). Look through all the writings by one ancestor made at approximately the same time. Reading one piece may help elucidate another.

29

This letter sent from Westbury to Melksham, Wiltshire, in 1837 predates the Penny Post by three years and, in any case, is directed to be delivered by hand (perhaps by a servant?), 'this evening'. The content of the letter includes matters that are to happen the following morning, so a quick delivery must have been assumed. (Author's collection)

- If possible, make a photocopy or print out a copy that you can mark up and highlight. A high-resolution digital image that you can zoom into and annotate is an even better option.
- Cut a window or slit into a blank piece of paper that is the length and width of one line of text and scroll this down over the text line by line. This will blank out confusing distractions from other lines.
- Use a magnifying glass.
- On first reading, skim through the document. Don't be concerned with understanding the entire piece all at once. If a word seems unfamiliar, try reading the document out loud. Its meaning might then become obvious.
- On your second copy of an old document draw parentheses around any words that you can't decipher. When you look back through these markings at the end of your reading, you might be in a better position to be able to understand them.
- Bear in mind that a lot of variation in old spellings was concentrated on vowel sounds. Try substituting the vowels given for other vowel sounds in puzzling words.

- Make sense of any abbreviations. Our ancestors often used these for speed or to save valuable space. See Burt Vance, *A Dictionary of Abbreviations*, O.U.P., 2011, or www.oxfordreference.com.
- Look out for words in other languages, especially in French or Latin which might sometimes have been used for special purposes. Typing such a word into an internet search engine such as www. google.com might be enough to resolve this.
- Read and reread a document over a period of time. Keep having breaks and come back to it.
- Show the document to someone else without telling them your idea about what it says and get them to have a go at deciphering it.

You might like to go further and get more expert help. Some archives now have their own paleographical tutorials online, see for example, the National Archives: Reading Old Handwriting 1500–1800 (www. nationalarchives.gov.uk/palaeography) which is particularly helpful with interpreting dates, numbers, money, measurements and the names of English counties in the past (admittedly in a period earlier than the one covered by this book, but still potentially relevant). If after all of this, your ancestor's meaning still eludes you, it may be worth calling in the help of an expert in palaeography from an archive. You will need to pay for this service.

Toolkit for Deeper Understanding of the Document in its Historical Context

The chapters of this book provide detailed advice on how to carry out in-depth research into ancestors' personal writings in specific genres – from signatures through to poetry. But it would be useful to have a few tools to hand regardless of the kind of writing you are intending to investigate:

- Obtain a good dictionary, particularly one which reflects the usage of words at the time that your ancestor was probably writing (see: www.oxforddictionaries.com). Use this to look up unusual words or common words used in unusual ways. You might need to supplement this dictionary with a foreign language dictionary or a dictionary of slang (for example, John Ayto and John Simpson, *The Oxford Dictionary of Modern Slang*, O.U.P., 2010 or J. Redding Ware,

The Victorian Dictionary of Slang and Phrase, The Bodleian Library, 2015).

- Use internet timelines such as www.bbc.ao.uk/history/british/launch_tl_british.shtml to find out when particular historic events, inventions, or personages mentioned by your ancestor might have been around.
- If the piece of writing is dated, look up the year of production at www.wikipedia.org to see what was going on nationally during that year.
- Gain access to the British Newspaper Archive online at www.britishnewspaperarchive.co.uk to potentially find digital copies of newspapers that can tell you about events going on locally at the time your ancestor was writing.
- Have ongoing access to the internet. You can use this to look up all manner of references that might mystify you on first encounter, from references to the Bible and mythology, to the names of famous politicians, national disasters, fashionable books, historic euphemisms and numerous other matters.
- Make sure you have a copy of the family tree alongside you. Your ancestor is more than likely to have referred to family members living or dead who might either already be upon it, or who might find their place upon it as you undertake your analysis.
- Take out a subscription to one of the three main commercial UK genealogy sites (www.thegenealogist.co.uk; www.ancestry.co.uk and www.findmypast.co.uk). Any of these will be helpful in giving access to censuses, certificates, school records and military records and many more aspects of your ancestors' histories.

PERSONALITY IN WRITING: GRAPHOLOGY

You might find facetious the suggestion that the characteristics of an ancestor's handwriting could have any bearing at all on what that person was like. Nowadays graphology has been relegated to the position of a pseudoscience, a bit of whimsy for which you might pay money at a fairground. But before you dismiss it entirely, bear in mind that many of our ancestors themselves thought that a person's handwriting signalled character and indeed that character could be improved upon by improving handwriting.

AN OLD LETTER.

'*An Old Letter*'. *Letters were tangible and enduring evidence of a relationship which were often treasured for years and read over time and time again by our ancestors for entertainment or solace. (*The Girl's Own Paper, *Vol. VI, No. 254, 8 November 1884)*

Some went so far as to note that their own script changed depending on the state of mind that they were in. Consider this paragraph, for example, from the *Commonplace Book* of Manchester businessman Thomas Rylands (1829–64):

> . . . when a fair clean hot pressed sheet is spread before me, no matter what the subject of my theme, if calm, all that is comely in my mind assumes the lead, and I produce a page spotless and satisfactory as the first in any first class copybook, but let a thought that irritates . . . my mind, and then bright calm [succeeds] firstly to small irregularities of form, and then, as grows the feeling, greater ones, until the labouring pen dashes along the widening line heedless alike of form and comeliness and almost of intelligence (Thomas Rylands, *Commonplace Book*, Cheshire Record Office D4298, 4 November 1843).

To put graphological techniques to best use, you will need an extended piece of writing by your ancestor which, as far as you can ascertain, was not produced under pressure (but bear in mind that the circumstances in which a piece was produced might have their own effects – a page from a school copybook will be different from that in an original letter, for example). A signature is really not enough to go on, though it can be handy in tandem with a longer piece of writing. According to some graphologists, a signature might tell you about your ancestor's public persona and an extended piece of writing about his or her private persona.

Most handwriting experts are agreed that handwriting cannot reveal age, gender, race or religion, though it can reveal some cultural features such as an ancestor's nationality and education. One of the most appealing ideas of graphology is that handwriting expresses a need of some sort or another, whether it is a desire for emotional comfort, money, personal satisfaction or career progression. According to some graphologists, handwriting symbolizes how you behave in your environment. When beginning to think about your ancestor's handwriting, consider first the way that space is used in the page as a whole, the general layout of text, the pressure, form, speed, continuity and direction of the writing as it moves across the page. And then look at individual strokes the size of the letters, how 't's are crossed or 'I's are dotted, for example. There is a little more on graphology at the end of Chapter 1. If you interested in pursuing this avenue, get hold of a comprehensive beginner guide to graphology such as Sheila R. Lowe, *The Complete Idiot's Guide to Handwriting Analysis*, Alpha Books, 1999.

If Thomas Rylands were looking over your shoulder as you read a piece of your ancestor's personal writing he might have said exactly what he wrote in his commonplace book. 'It seems to me that on the surface of a letter, as on the heave-bound ocean sheets, may be traced the writer's meteorology of mind' (Thomas Rylands, *Commonplace Book*, pp. 35–6). In other words, if you know how to analyse it, handwriting might be an additional and very illuminating key to your ancestor's personality, character and hence his very self.

NOTE ON EXAMPLES USED IN THIS BOOK
As an aid to family historians who are interested in finding out more about the areas covered by this book, there are frequent examples included herein to personal manuscripts available to view – either in part or in their entirety – online.

QUESTIONS TO ASK YOURSELF OF ALL YOUR ANCESTOR'S PERSONAL WRITING
1. Have you collected together as much extant writing by your ancestor as you can? If not, where might you find more examples?
2. Why do you think he or she chose these particular genres (kinds) of writing, rather than others at this time (e.g. why a letter and not a postcard)?
3. For what purpose(s) did your ancestor write (time-management, self-expression, spiritual motives, keeping in touch with distant family, managing businesses, recording his or her past, registering opinion, asserting identity or something else)?
4. Who did your ancestor write for (him or herself only, other family members, friends, lovers, work colleagues, other members of an association, or possible publication)?
5. What education did your ancestor have? What evidence do you have of this? How literate was he or she?
6. What cultural factors might have influenced your ancestor's writing? Draw a brainstorm diagram indicating his or her gender,

social class, religious leanings, political orientation, employment, country of origin, and other languages, as far as you know them.

7. What was going on nationally and locally at the time this writing was undertaken? What resources might you use to find out more about these?

8. Whereabouts in the timeline of events in your ancestor's family did this piece of writing come (i.e. after the death of a parent, after the birth of a child, just before a marriage, and the like)?

9. Which aspects of your ancestor's writings do you think are going to be most worth pursuing (physical aspects of composition, handwriting, graphology, content, stylistic features)?

FURTHER READING
Books

Adler, Michael, *The Writing Machine*, Allen and Unwin, 1973.

Aldis, Marion, and Indler, Pam, *The Happiest Days of Their Lives? Nineteenth-Century Education Through the Eyes of Those Who Were There*, Chaplin Books, 2016.

Barra, D., and Papen, U., eds, *The Anthropology of Writing: Understanding Textually Mediated Worlds*, Continuum-3PL Rpt., 2011.

Bourke, Joanna, *Working-Class Cultures in Britain, 1890-1960: Gender, Class and Ethnicity*, Routledge, 1994.

Creaton, Heather, ed, *Victorian Diaries: The Daily Lives of Victorian Men and Women*, Mitchell Beazley, 2001.

Horn, Pamela, *The Victorian and Edwardian Schoolchild*, Sutton Publishing, 2013.

Jones, Kaye, *The Case of the Chocolate Cream Poisoner: The Poisonous Passion of Christiana Edmunds*, Pen and Sword, 2016.

Lowe, Sheila R., *The Complete Idiot's Guide to Handwriting Analysis*, Alpha Books, 1999.

Lutz, Deborah, *The Brontë Cabinet: Three Lives in Nine Objects*, W. W. Norton and Company, 2015.

Lyons, Martin, *The Writing Culture of Ordinary People in Europe, c. 1860-1920*, C.U.P., 2014.

Peel, Mark, *The New Meritocracy: A History of UK Independent Schools 1979-2014*, Elliott and Thompson, 2015.

Priestley, Joseph, *A Familiar Introduction to the Theory and Practice of Perspective*, J. John and J. Payne, 1770.

Rose, Jonathan, *The Intellectual Life of the British Working Classes*, Yale U.P. 2010.

Vance, Burt, *A Dictionary of Abbreviations*, O.U.P., 2011.

Websites

www.ancestry.co.uk British commercial genealogy site

www.amberskyline.com/treasuremaps/oldhand.htm Online help with understanding your ancestor's handwriting

www.baph.org.uk The British Association of Paper Historians

www.bbc.ao.uk/history/british/launch_tl_british.shtml BBC British History timeline.

www.britishnewspapers.archive.co.uk

www.britishpostcardsonline.co.uk Old postcards to buy online

www.discovery.nationalarchives.gov.uk Archival records in UK archives

www.ebay.co.uk Worldwide selling site

www.findmypast.co.uk) British commercial genealogy site

www.inspiring-ireland.ie Inspiring Ireland project.

www.nationalarchives.gov.uk/palaeography National Archives: Reading Old Handwriting Tutorial 1500–1800

wwww.oldcards.co.uk Old postcards to buy online

www.oldpostardsetc.co.uk Old postcards to buy online

www.postcardworld.co.uk Old postcards to buy online

www.pencilmuseum.co.uk The Cumberland Pencil Museum

http://www.scottishten.org/ A 3D scanning project to document Scotland's five World Heritage sites and five international ones

www.specialcollections.le.ac.uk/cdm/landingpage/collection/p16445c oll4 - digitized collection of historical trade directories online.

www.thegenealogist.co.uk British commercial genealogy site

www.the-saleroom.com UK auction site

www.twl-calm.library.lse.ac.uk The Women's Library at the London School of Economics

www.ukauctioneers.com UK Auctioneers

www.wikipedia.org Online encyclopaedia

www.writinglives.org/uncategorized/archive-of-working-class-writing-online Archive of Working-Class Writing.

www.writinglives.org Writing Lives Project on working-class manuscript autobiographies.

Chapter 1

WHAT'S IN A NAME? LITERACY AND SIGNATURES

The way an ancestor rendered his or her name on the page might turn out to be as crucial to his or her identity as a photograph, a fingerprint or a fragment of DNA. Handwriting expert and writer Kitty Burns says of her father, 'I have a stash of cards and letters written in his quick spiky script that's as much like him as his image in photographs. If they didn't exist, my world would be a poorer one' (Kitty Burns Flowers, *Script and Scribble: The Rise and Fall of Handwriting*, Melville House Publishing, 2009, p. 89).

If you have access to documents which include your nineteenth or early twentieth-century ancestor's signature then you have something precious, individual and potentially significant of your ancestor. However you choose to interpret it (and several different ways are suggested in this chapter), your family signature is an important adjunct to the process of building up a picture of the person who penned it. For that reason it is certainly a good idea to keep photocopies or digital scans of signatures wherever you find them on official or personal documents. If you have an ancestor's signature, you also have proof of his or her literacy. This might be all he or she was ever able to write, and yet to hold a pen, formulate the letters of the alphabet and join them together rather than print them, denotes that he or she had at least some education – probably several years' worth.

You might wish to start a collection of signatures from a raft of different ancestors at different times in their lives, and this can potentially be particularly revelatory. Indeed there is something of a fad for this sort of collection on the internet with blogs, family history scrapbooks and illuminated family trees often displaying those signatures that have been found. Comparisons between the signatures or marks of men and women from different generations within families might alert you to which of them went to school, their progression from manual to white-collar occupations, or their faltering demise into old age. More fancifully, perhaps, you might conclude that the signatures reveal something of the moral character and personalities of people for whom you might not even have a photograph,

For many of us, however, a necessary and preliminary question to the acquisition of our ancestors' signatures is whether or not he or she was actually able to write at all. In the period 1800 to 1950, literacy, and in particular the ability to write one's own name or signature, was a crucial differentiating factor between people of different classes, different places of origin, old and young, and sometimes between men and women in the same family – and not always in the ways you would expect.

Signatures were required for all kinds of official documents from the mid-nineteenth century onwards – far more than they had been needed in previous generations. The actual signature of an ancestor might be seen on various kinds of official records. The 1911 census, for example, is a good source of original signatures if the ancestors in question were the householders (previous censuses were more often filled in by an enumerator than by the householder him or herself). Other official documents that include original signatures are wills, documents relating to court appearances, passport applications, enlistment papers and so on. You should regard your ancestor's signature on such documents as a mark of his or her intent, and usually as an indication that your ancestors were willing, active and sane participants in whatever business they were about. The inequalities between men and women in the nineteenth century mean that you are far more likely to find signatures from your male ancestors than your female ones. This is partly because of a disparity in their literacy levels, which will be examined later in this chapter, and partly because, on marriage, a woman lost her identity in law and became as one with her husband. A wife, whose first name as well as her last was correctly subsumed into her husband's – Mrs Simon Dell, Mrs Horace Merriman, for example – might never have had to sign a document in her lifetime provided she predeceased her husband. It was always the husband who was required to sign any official documents affecting the couple.

You should be aware of one particularly problematical resource for ancestors' signatures – the marriage certificate. What you will receive through the post from the General Register Office is only a copy of that certificate – a blank form that has been filled in by a modern-day registrar with the details entered by the important parties on the actual day. If you order through a local registry office, on the other hand, you might receive either a photocopy with original signatures or a transcribed copy as described above. It's also possible that at the actual time of the marriage, the returns sent by the parish to the registry office were filled in by the vicar and not by the couple themselves. The only place in fact where you can be sure that you are seeing your ancestors' own handwriting – in terms of birth, marriage and death information – are the handwritten registers of the parish themselves.

As this book is about the *personal* writings of our ancestors, most of the official records that they were required to sign are not really within its remit. However, the ability to sign a name, of course, crossed over into many of the documents that are described in this book. These include the backs of photographs, letters to family members, postcards and greetings cards, on original sketches and at the end of original poems. It is not uncommon to find an ancestor's name written time and time over on the flyleaf of a book that he or she owned, and then on indiscriminate pages throughout. Signatures were, in fact, the main template upon which our ancestors practised their handwriting skills, and they might in fact turn up just about anywhere amongst family papers and –as this chapter will show – on a variety of other physical surfaces as well.

ANCESTORS WHO COULD NOT SIGN THEIR NAMES
Whilst our upper- and middle-class ancestors of both sexes might have received a good education at a public or private school or at the hands of a resident governess within their homes and would have had no trouble whatsoever in signing their names, the likelihood that your ancestors from the lower social orders – and especially the women – would have been illiterate and unable to do so, is, in fact, pretty high in the early nineteenth century.

Though recognising that it is not a perfect indicator, the historian R. S. Schofield has called the ability to sign one's name on a document the best available measure of literacy ('The Measurement of Literacy in Pre-Industrial England, in Jack Goody, ed., *Literacy in Traditional*

Societies, C.U.P., 1968, p. 319). Although literacy rates for both men and women rose throughout the eighteenth century, by the 1780s, it is estimated that only 68 per cent of men and 39 per cent of women in England could sign their names. And, contrary to what you might think, the industrialization of the period that followed did not necessarily bring about greater degrees of literacy. Most of the manual jobs in a textile factory, for example, did not require the ability to read or write. Before 1830, it is generally believed that the literacy rates for both men and women fell in many industrializing areas, particularly Lancashire. Indeed, between 1810 and 1820 literacy rates for women in the large manufacturing city of Manchester may have been as low as 19 per cent.

Literacy rates from the mid-nineteenth century onwards have traditionally been measured by historians by counting the numbers of people who could and could not sign their names on one kind of document in particular – marriage registers. After the advent of civil registration in 1837, details of births, marriages and deaths were sent by local registrars to superintendent registrars. They, in turn, sent copies to the Registrar General in London. From 1839, statistical records of vital events including marriages (broken down by registration district), were compiled in the Registrar's Annual Report. The resulting 'marriage tables' calculated, amongst many other interesting statistics, the numbers of people signing the register with a mark. This was usually a cross, occasionally a squiggle or a circle. Some of our ancestors wrote the initial of their first or last name only – an indication that they had at least learned their alphabet as children.

The number of people who did not sign or who signed very imperfectly became a recognized statistic of illiteracy. In general terms, the 1840 Report of the Registrar General, Thomas Lister, found that men were more literate than women, and that literacy rates varied by region, with the highest literacy rates being in London and the lowest in Wales and Bedfordshire (*Second Annual Report of the Registrar General*, p. 6). In 1844, national figures for those unable to sign the marriage register were 37 per cent for men and 48 per cent for women. In the south-east these figures were 31 per cent and 38 per cent and in the north-west 39 per cent and 67 per cent respectively (figures from Schofield, 'The Measurement of Literacy in Pre-Industrial England'). It's worth taking a look at the Annual Reports of the Registrar General for the time at which your ancestor did or did not write his or her signature on a document. You might then be able to compare his or her literacy with that for the region in which he or she was living to see how typical a writer he or she was.

An examination of family signatures, particularly if you chart the signature of one ancestor over time, can throw up some interesting puzzles. Enoch Fletcher, an engineer in a coalmine, and Margaret Coulson, the daughter of a blacksmith, were married at Wigan Parish Church on 1 March 1842. At this time, Enoch was able to sign his name, as were his two brothers, William and Giles Fletcher (the witnesses). Margaret, on the other hand, was not. As they progressed through their married life, both Margaret and Enoch were occasionally called upon to witness other life events, the births of their children, for example and

On their wedding day in 1842 Enoch Fletcher, an engineer in a Wigan coalmine, could sign his name but his bride, Margaret Coulson, the daughter of a blacksmith, could not. (Author's collection)

Margaret Fletcher (née Coulson) seated, with one of her daughters photographed in Wigan probably in the 1860s. Margaret remained illiterate throughout her life. (Author's collection)

the deaths of other family members. Strangely enough, whilst Margaret never learned to sign her name, Enoch's literary abilities appeared to fluctuate over time. Some twenty years later, in 1862, when registering the birth of one of his sons, he appeared unable to sign his name, resorting to a cross which was duly translated by officialdom as 'the mark of Enoch Fletcher'.

Margaret Coulson's cross on the marriage register and subsequent documents should probably be read as a straightforward indication of her illiteracy. Like thousands of other Lancashire women of her class in the early and mid-nineteenth century, Margaret had probably had no schooling beyond perhaps attendance at a Sunday School and most likely made no attempt to improve her literacy as she got older. Even by the time Margaret married for the second time in 1872 (to a 'forgeman' named James Arrowsmith) – she was still unable to sign her name.

As for Enoch, is it really possible that he had forgotten how to write his own name in that period of two decades? There are a number of other possibilities which might at first glance seem facetious but which were offered up by social commentators of the time as serious reasons why fluctuations in an individual's apparent literacy might occur over his or her lifetime. One suggestion is that some literate people might have been flummoxed by the solemnity of the occasion and that they made a mark rather than signing their names because they were nervous. There is also the suggestion that some literate husbands might not have signed their names for fear of embarrassing their brides. A third possibility is that the participants in the ceremony might have been drunk and therefore incapable of formulating a signature! In 1871, an article in *The Times* (using the crosses on marriage registers as its guide) suggested that education in Lancashire was worse than anywhere else in the country. Upon reading this, a Liverpool clergyman, Mr Wilson, wrote a letter to the paper saying that 'it should not be concluded that all the people who signed the marriage registers with a cross did not know how to read'. He said that in his experience of weddings, 'in one case out of five, one of the parties was *under the influence*'.

There is no doubt about the fact that heavy drinking was a characteristic of the mid-nineteenth century working classes, especially in London and the rapidly urbanizing industrial centres of Manchester, Birmingham and Glasgow to which tens of thousands of rural workers had migrated. Like several other foreign visitors to Britain, the Frenchman Hippolyte Taine was appalled by the drunkenness he saw all around him when he came to Britain on three occasions between 1860 and 1870. Taine's book *Notes Sur L'Angleterre* (*Notes on England*) attributes the problem of drunkenness to the cold, wet, British climate and the harshness of the industrial working conditions. 'A man needs to warm himself up a bit, revive his body and spirits, and to forget for a while the sorrowful and harassed life he has to lead' (Edward Hyams, ed, *Taine's Notes on England*, Thames and Hudson, 1957, p. 229).

Large amounts of alcohol were often drunk on important family celebrations such as weddings and christenings. Thus, the times at which our ancestors were likely to be asked to verify their identity were just the times at which some of them might have been least able to do so. It's possible that Enoch – who did indeed die from drink-related causes in 1869 – was in fact too inebriated to write his name (an act which might well have required painstaking care and attention) on the birth of his son in 1862. Examples like this should inspire caution. Next time you notice a cross rather than a signature on a family certificate, think twice before you jump to the conclusion that your forebear was entirely illiterate and don't stop your search for that elusive signature in other documents.

Drink aside, illiteracy itself was very much a concern of Victorian reformers and conservatives. The increasing democracy of the late nineteenth and early twentieth centuries meant that working men (and then, finally, working women) got the Vote. This was achieved by a series of Acts of Parliament starting in 1832, though it was not until the Representation of the People Act of 1928 – nearly 100 years later – that all men and women over the age of 21 were entitled to vote. Those in power worried whether this privilege could ever be properly exercised by those who could not even write their own names much less read. In 1874 a witness at a trial (concerning the Stroud Election Petition) described 'as a working man and a voter' seemed unable to differentiate between the main political parties except by their colour:

> **Mr Baron Bramwell** – Do you know which party governs the country now? **Witness** – The yellows, I suppose, sir (Laughter) . . . **His Lordship** – Do you suppose Mr Disraeli is a 'yellow'? **Witness** – Well I don't know, sir. (Laughter) **His Lordship** – You don't know? **Witness** – I don't know; I'm a man as can't understand. **His Lordship** – What are the other party called? **Witness** – The blues (loud laughter). **His Lordship** – Don't you know any other name? **Witness** – No sir. I don't know . . . **Mr Hawkins** – This is one of the new voters under the Act of 1867. **His Lordship** – Yes, and I was rather curious to see what he knew about it (*Edinburgh Evening News*, 30 April 1874)

It was only after Forster's Education Act of 1870 that attendance at school became a likelihood for all British children up to the age of twelve. Before this, many working-class parents, if they sent their children to school at all, were in most cases more likely to send their sons than their daughters. This explains why – in some mid-nineteenth-century marriage registers – the groom, like Enoch Fletcher, was often able to sign his name and the bride, like Margaret Coulson, was not. But the Act still did not make education compulsory, and nor was all education free. Whilst the parents of a child might genuinely wish him or her to be literate, economic demands continued to be more important than schooling in some communities.

Such a situation caused some strange demographics in the acquisition of literacy at the end of the nineteenth century which might have affected the families of your ancestors. For instance, whilst parents might not have been able to write, their children might well have been literate. Additionally, it might seem bizarre to us knowing that girls were generally disadvantaged in the past, to find that the girls in some families could sign their names whilst their brothers could not, but this is possibly because the boys, with a greater earning potential than their sisters, might have been the first to have been pulled out of school when family finances were low. This letter from A NORFOLK MAN to the Editor of *The Norfolk News* in 1870 makes the position and general frustration clear:

> As a general rule it is a mistake to think that the poor are indifferent to the advantages of education. However illiterate parents may be themselves, they have, in almost every case, expressed a wish that their children might, if possible, be able to read and write . . . It is well known that as soon as a child is able to contribute by its labour ever so little to the common fund of the family, the parents are compelled by the pressure of circumstances, increasing family, etc, to withdraw it from school, in order to avail themselves of its eighteenpence or two shillings a week (*The Norfolk News*, 16 April 1870).

There were also some situations where a wife in a family could write and her older husband could not, simply because she had been able to benefit from the new, more democratic education system, and he, if he were even a few years her senior, had missed out on it. Another configuration was where the older generation of foreign immigrants to the big British cities of Manchester, Birmingham, London and Glasgow might have been literate – and even scholarly – in their own languages, but could not read and write in English, and were too old on arrival in the country to partake of the National Education system.

Towards the end of the century, there were still serious concerns expressed in newspapers about jurymen who were illiterate. In 1895, in Shoreditch, London, two inquests were held on the bodies of persons who had died suddenly from natural causes. As the nineteen working men of the jury were sworn in, it was discovered that only six of them were able to write or sign their name:

> The Coroner's Officer proceeded to fill in the names on the inquisitions, to which the jurymen appended marks. The first man was named Benjamin Gonolay. **The Officer** – How do you spell your surname? **The Juror** – The same as everybody else does; there's only one way of spelling Benjamin. **The Officer** – Yes; but the surname? **The Juror** – Benjamin. I told you once. Are you deaf? **The Officer** – Yes; but the other name? **The Juror** – How do I know? I tell you I can't write. My son knows but he ain't here. There's only one way of spelling Benjamin. **The Officer** – All right; Sit down. **The Juror** – You're very thick-headed! (*The Evening Telegraph*, 27 August 1895).

The division between literate and illiterate could breed deep mistrust and antagonism between the different social classes. At the same inquest another illiterate juror, 'Dick', put his mark on a piece of paper, but then refused to do it a second time saying: 'Not me! I can't write, I know; but you ain't going to swindle me. If I sign again, you'll fetch me here again next week and say I signed for it. Not me! I can't write, but I ain't a fool' (*The Evening Telegraph*, 27 August 1895).

Of course, the fact that these extreme cases of illiteracy made the press suggests that by the end of the nineteenth century, they were becoming remarkable. This was especially the case in England. Illiteracy in Scotland and Wales which had proportionately larger rural populations remained higher. The rise in literacy rates took a while to 'kick in'. It was not until 1914 that over 99 per cent of couples marrying in Britain were able to sign their names according to the Seventy-seventh Annual Report of the Registrar General (1914).

Even then, great shock was publically evinced during the First World War, when it was discovered that many men recruited into the Army, though they might be able to write their names, actually had very poor literacy skills. Strong attempts were made to teach them whilst they remained in the military. But the matter of illiteracy or inadequate literacy persisted. In 1927 when it was discovered that a witness at an inquest in Woking was unable to read the oath, and that several of his relations were also unable to read, officialdom, as ever, vacillated between exasperation and encouragement.

> **The Coroner** – How do you go on if you cannot read? You don't know what is going on in the world except what people tell you. The young man agreed, and the Coroner advised him to take every opportunity of learning. (*Aberdeen Press and Journal, 28 September 1927*)

SIGNATURES

Family historians often become most interested in signatures when they have occasion to compare them between documents, to try to ascertain whether they were made by the same person. This can be more problematic when two people in the family have the same name (which is, of course, often the case). Where a signature is difficult to decipher, the question is whether it can be attributed to any individual writer at all. It can be relatively difficult to check if a signature is made by the same person on two different documents. Sometimes, an ancestor might have changed the way he signed a piece of writing because he had actually changed the way he spelt his name. Other people's signatures changed with age, the onset of illness, with life experiences and even with mood. As we shall see in Chapter 4, Charlotte Brontë changed the way she signed her letters to her friend Ellen Nussey depending on what kind of news she had to impart and how she was feeling on any given day. Other correspondents added characteristic extra descriptions to their signature which changed as they grew older and according to whom they were writing. Mary Gladstone, for example, daughter of the Liberal Prime Minister William Ewart Gladstone, signed letters to her father from 'your little girl' until 1859, when, at twelve years old, she must have considered herself too old to do so any longer.

The way our ancestors signed their names will to some extent depend upon the kind of handwriting they were taught at school. Beyond that, signatures are, according to the qualified graphologists, a matter of personality. (See The British Academy of Graphology (www.graphology.co.uk) and The British Institute of Graphologists (www.britishgraphology.org). There are numerous internet sites that aim to be able to deduce aspects of your ancestors' personality from his or her signature. The crucial features to look out for are the size of the signature, the content (whether all names are written out in full or some are just initials), the degree of legibility, the degree of legibility of a signature in comparison with a whole script written by the same person, whereabouts the signature is placed on a document, the direction and slant of the signature and any embellishments it might include. In many cases it is said not to be advisable to analyse a signature without simultaneously considering a larger body of text written by same person.

By the latter part of the nineteenth century, the great variety of ways of signing a name were causing some consternation, particularly amongst bureaucrats and clerks who were often responsible for deciphering them. Chief amongst the pet hates was 'the flourishing signature', especially those underscored by a swirling line or 'paraph'. But there were other annoying kinds of signature too:

Akin to these signers, are the men who have a fancy for underlining their signatures once or twice or even oftener, no doubt as an instruction to the future printer of their biography to put it in italics or small capitals . . . Then there is the shorthand signature, the one with a trunk and a few odd limbs attached here and there which may mean anything from 'Hobson' to 'Wilson' or from 'Longton' to 'Simpkins'. And there is the signature of the man who thinks that large writing must necessarily be legible, quite irrespective of how the letters are formed. There is the angular signature of the lady of the old school who seems to have for appellation nothing but 'n's' or 'm's' as the case may be; and there is the running hand signature, which conveys no idea to the mind but that of a worm with the cramp (*The Star*, Guernsey, 12 June 1886).

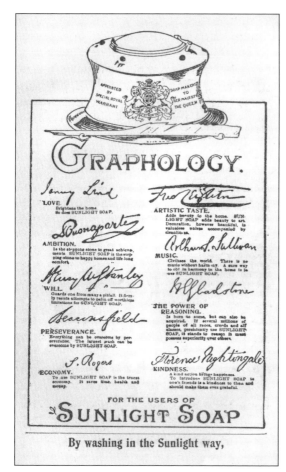

*The Victorians were deeply interested in signatures. The pseudo-science of graphology suggested that people's personality traits could be understood by analysing their handwriting. (*The Sunlight Year Book for 1899, *Lever Brothers Ltd, 1899, p. 170).*

Others go further. If graphology appeals to you, you might want to use it to analyse other aspects of your family history, to question whether, for example, a married couple were potentially suited to each other by analysing their signatures, whether an ancestor was really cut out for the kind of job he found himself in, or whether the way he or she dealt with life experiences is borne out by the characteristics determinable from his or her signature.

Before dismissing these ideas out of hand, bear in mind that our Victorian and early twentieth-century ancestors themselves wrote with the knowledge that 'good handwriting' was commonly thought to tally with 'good character'. In a signature, look out for such matters as whether the first and surnames are of different sizes. Where the surname is larger, does this indicate a certain pride in family name and tradition? Where the first name is larger, does this suggest that the writer is more enamoured of himself than of his family? Graphologist Sheila Lane suggests that a man who writes his signature with a smaller last name than first name might have suffered at the hands of his father, and that a woman doing the same might have suffered at the hands of a dominating husband! If extra-large initials dominate a signature they might be a means by which the writer compensated for a sense of low self-esteem; surnames and first names that slant in opposite directions might suggest an inner conflict or emotional turmoil, illegible surnames might indicate problems between the writer and the wider world, whilst an illegible first name could be taken as a sign of an insecure ego (Sheila Lane, *The Complete Idiot's Guide to Handwriting Analysis*, Alpha Books, 1999, pp. 251–66).

One common problem for family historians is where an ancestor's signature differs entirely in style from the rest of the text (for example, a letter) that he or she has apparently written. Modern-day graphologists would say that a signature that is similar in style to the text it accompanies confirms that the writer has such qualities as straightforwardness, honesty and dependability. Where a signature is illegible and the text is clear, however, the reverse might be the case. This distinction between clear text and virtually illegible signatures is one that bothered nineteenth-century commentators too. The same journalist quoted above called these inconsistent writing habits 'grossly selfish and conceited . . . the cause of much torment and bad language'.

> There is the signature that differs greatly from the body of the letter, as though the writer wished it to be understood that he had two egos. Why a man should wish it to be thought that he has two egos, is not quite clear; other people usually think his one ego quite enough; but so it is. It may be that one signs in approval of what the other has written, to assure it, perhaps that both 'Philip sober' and 'Philip drunk' are of one mind about the matter. This seems to be probable, from the fact that the letter is usually fairly legible and the signature only to be guessed at,

clearly indicating the cooperation of the two Philips (*The Star*, Guernsey, 12 June 1886).

A final bugbear of the late Victorian period worth mentioning was the new trend for hyphenated surnames and other names. The same correspondent despaired about the future:

> What new developments the signature is next to take is difficult to forecast. People not to be outdone by each other may come to hyphen on, not only their Christian names, but their native places, and such signatures as John-Vere-Mortimer-Noakes-of-Slumley, may come to be actualities (Ibid.).

Look out for the ways in which an ancestor's signatures might differ between his or her official and personal documents. On letters, greetings cards and original artwork and poetry, for example, you might find names crossed through (self-hatred?), encircled (requiring protection?), or underlined (defiant?). Whatever you make of these graphological explanations, bear in mind that signatures on official documents (in the past as now) were required to be legible, consistent and quickly written – part of the apparatus of an industrializing and increasingly bureaucratic world. Those on more personal documents on the other hand were commonly more artistic and idiosyncratic.

NAMES IN OTHER PLACES
Our Victorian and early twentieth-century ancestors did not stop at practising their signatures on bits of paper. You may come across their signatures (together with other personal information including dates and even short meaningful phrases) in a variety of other places. Not burdened with the same guilt about graffiti that we feel now – and with fewer avenues to express their individuality, and in particular, their writing persona – men, women and children in the past frequently etched graffiti into all manner of natural objects including rocks and trees, as well as into manmade objects such as walls, desks, doorposts, lintels, church pews, beds and windowsills (to name just the most obvious). Setting out in search of this might be a long shot, but it is possible that you have evidence of an ancestor's signature within your home or environs, even if it is not written conventionally onto paper.

Four names inscribed on the Hitching Stone near Cowling, North Yorkshire. The stone, a geological oddity marking a boundary between Lancashire and Yorkshire, was a favourite destination of Victorian day-trippers. (Wikimedia Commons)

A hundred and fifty years ago, areas of natural rocky beauty were covered in graffiti (mainly names and dates) from Victorian and Edwardian daytrippers let loose from the cities and keen to carve evidence of their visits into the sandstone. Good examples can be found on the hillside path between Dunsdale Hollow and Frodsham Hill (Cheshire) and at Ash Fell (near to Ravenstonedale, Cumbria), for example. At Dwarfie Stane, a chambered tomb on the island of Hoy, Orkney in 1850, Major William H. Mounsey (1808–77), a former British spy in Persia (and known eccentric) wrote his name backwards in Latin together with an inscription in Persian which read, 'I have sat two nights and so learnt patience'.

Our ancestors who travelled abroad also sometimes carved their names on ancient monuments as a means of advertising the extent of their journeys (an indirect indicator of their wealth) or even their physical powers of endurance. A good case in point, and one of great interest to his descendants, is that of the Scotsman John Gordon (1776–1858). Some aspects of Gordon's life can be deduced from military records, political records and records of land ownership. Born in 1776, he was the son of Charles Gordon of Braid and Cluny, Aberdeenshire and Johanna (née Trotter). John Gordon was successively appointed Second Lieutenant in the Royal Aberdeenshire Light Infantry (1800), Lieutenant in the 7th Company of the 55th Aberdeenshire Militia (1804); Major (1808); Lieutenant-Colonel (1820) and an Honorary Colonel (1836). In addition to his military career, he also was M.P. for Weymouth and Melcombe Regis from 1826 until July 1830. He inherited vast lands in Scotland and the West Indies and was at one point the richest commoner in Scotland. Gordon never married but had four children out of wedlock. He died at his home, 4 St. Andrew Square, Edinburgh, in 1858, aged eighty-two.

These are the public details of Gordon's career, but how much more thrilling are the facts about his life that can be gleaned from the signatures he left on his prodigious travels abroad. In 1804, Gordon

Nineteenth-century tourists took every opportunity to leave their mark, as witnessed by copious graffiti on these medieval marble effigies at St Mary's Priory Church, Abergavenny, Wales. **(Wikimedia Commons)**

made a tour through Europe, the Near East and Egypt, returning home by way of Gibraltar. He kept no diary or other written record of the journey, but his progress up the Nile can be charted by way of the inscriptions that he left on many of the famous Egyptian monuments. He left his name (in various variations, sometimes with just an initial for his first name, sometimes with the date, sometimes enclosed in a rectangle) at the Dendara temple, the Temple at Edfu, the Tomb of Paheri, the Temple of Esna, Gebel el-Silsila, the Temple at Karnak, the Temple at Luxor, the Temple of Medinet Habu, the mortuary Temple of Ramesses II, the Temple of Sethos I and in the Valley of the Kings. It is probable also that he left his name on the pyramids but that thousands of other signatures later obliterated it. From these repeated offerings, we get a picture of a man ambitious to leave his mark, physically robust – many of the inscriptions would have required him to scramble over ruins and climb walls – and confident, even arrogant, in his sense of the British entitlement to make some claim over exotic foreign treasures.

There are more recent and more poignant examples of ancestral name carvings. British soldiers in Northern France in the First World War, for example, scratched their names, the date and their country of origin on the bark of trees (smooth barks – beeches, birches and aspens – were the easiest to carve and created a more permanent memorial). Indeed, there are so many examples of these wartime 'arborglyphs' that they have become the subject of academic study which might be enlightening for some family historians. Academic Chantelle Summerfield of Bristol University has recently catalogued carvings made by First World War soldiers including initials, names, dates, place names and occasionally entire messages (www.bristol. academia.edu/ chantel summerfield/papers). She notes that soldiers recorded far more personal information in their graffiti when in France as they approached the terrors of battle than when in the grounds of the institutions in Britain where they previously were stationed.

Comparing the tree-graffiti with military records, censuses and information about Commonwealth War Graves, Summerfield has been able to piece together the wartime histories of some soldiers who would otherwise have been virtually lost to history. One carving in Northern France which read 'Frank Fearing – Hudson Massachusetts, 1945', followed by a love heart and the name 'Helen' was made by an American GI during the Second World War. From this, fairly full information, Summerfield was able to trace Frank back to America (he had unfortunately already died), but she was able to meet the elderly Helen Fearing (whom Frank had married secretly before going abroad) and was able to show her a photograph of the tree upon which Frank had written.

Our ancestors personalized indoor architecture as well as the natural world. Nineteenth-century tradesmen, for example, often scratched, painted and wrote their names onto the walls and roofs of the buildings that they constructed, painted or repaired. Some of these names have now come to light as a result of restoration work. Dove Cottage, home of the poet Wordsworth from 1799 to 1808 bears an inscription on the reverse of a window shutter by late nineteenth-century paperhanger, W. Martin, a local man who decorated the room just before the cottage opened to the public in 1891. He wrote: 'Our heads will happen cold when this is found' – a line of such poetic cadence that it was eagerly taken up by a twentieth-century writer, Tony Harrison, his poem 'Remains', as an illustration of a rare voice from the lower classes, as it were speaking to us from the grave.

Less poetic examples abound, some of which have provided great excitement for the descendants. In 2013, as repair work was being carried out on the roof of the Oxford Museum of Natural History, a message was found (painted 49 feet up in the rafters) which read, 'This roof was painted by G. Thicke and J. Randall, April 1864'. Two other forgotten workmen 'Robert Robson' and 'John Milbanke' were briefly brought back to life by their signatures written in pencil on the timbers of a bookcase in the Monks' Dormitory in Durham Cathedral (during the cathedral's Open Treasure renovation in 2014). Together with a couple of newspapers dated 1880, found underneath the bookcase, this information was enough to identify Milbanke as a Durham builder and Robson as a carpenter and builder who employed twenty-one people and who was twice made Mayor of Durham. Robson's great-great grandson was contacted and the connection made.

QUESTIONS TO ASK OF YOUR ANCESTOR'S MARK, NAME OR SIGNATURE

1. From which documents do you think you might be able to obtain your ancestors' signatures or personal marks? Think of as many places as possible.

2. In each case, what do you think was the purpose of the signature at that point (to confirm or prove identity, to stake belonging, to claim something, to signal intent)?

3. Does your ancestor's signature differ between official and personal documents?

4. What particular factors might have influenced the way your ancestor wrote his or her name (gender, age at the time the document was produced, education, country of origin, first language, type of employment)?

5. How does your ancestor's ability to sign his name compare with that of other members of his or her household in the past (compare with people of different ages and different genders), with that of previous and subsequent generations, and (particularly in respect of the 1911 census) with that of his or her neighbours of similar (and dissimilar occupations? Why is this, do you think?

6. Did your ancestor's signature change over time (because of age, illness, access to education, experience of trauma)?

7. What form did your ancestor's signature take, (initials only, a combination of initials and surname, fully-written-out names)? Why do you think this was the case?

8. Do you possess any books or other inherited objects that might include an ancestor's name and signature? Might your ancestor have left any other written marks of his identity on furniture, trees, windows or walls?

9. Does your ancestor's signature differ greatly from his or her script otherwise? Why do you think this might have been the case?

10. Does your ancestor's signature have any distinctive qualities that might be worth analysing using the techniques of graphology?

FURTHER READING
Books

Flowers, Kitty Burns, *Script and Scribble: The Rise and Fall of Handwriting*, Melville House Publishing, 2009.

Hallay, Amanda, *The Popular History of Graffiti: From the Ancient World to the Present*, Skyhorse Publishing, 2013.

Higgs, Edward, *Life, Death and Statistics: Civil Registration, Censuses and the Work of the General Register Office, 1837-1952*, Hatfield, 2004.

Lowe, Sheila, *The Complete Idiot's Guide to Handwriting Analysis*, Alpha Books, 1999.

Schofield, Roger, 'The Measure of Literacy in Pre-Industrial England', in Goody, J., ed., *Literacy in Traditional Societies*, C.U.P., 1968, pp. 311–35.

Stephens, W. B. *Education, Literacy and Society, 1830-70: The Geography of Diversity in Provincial England*, Manchester U. P., 1987.

Vincent, David, *Literacy and Popular Culture: England, 1750-1914*, C.U.P., 1993.

Websites

www.bristol.academia.edu/chantelsummerfield/papers More on arborglyphs.

www.egypt-sudan-grafitti.be/An_early.htm More on the graffiti of General John Gordon.

Chapter 2

'GIVEN TO CORRESPONDENCE': LETTERS AND LETTER-BOOKS

Letters are probably the most widely available source of personal writing from the past. For family historians, the rewards of studying letters between family members can be huge. Letters written by our ancestors can be an exciting resource because they often contain a fullness of information and an indication of a writer's personality rarely obtained from official documents or from other kinds of personal writing. You should bear in mind too that since a letter between family members was rarely written with a wider public audience in mind, it is quite likely that such a source will give a truer account of a family history matter than any other source – although the bias of the writer must always be taken into account.

When you come across a letter written by and/or to a family member, first be glad that it survives at all and ask yourself why that is the case. Many people in the past burnt the letters that they had been sent, or used the paper for some other domestic purpose as a matter of course. If a letter has been preserved it is likely that it has particular resonance or import for your family history. Letters written by soldiers in the First World War, for example, were sometimes kept as a relic if the soldier had been killed. Where letters – particularly whole bundles – have survived, you can imagine that the family where they were received was probably a fairly stable one. These ancestors probably did not change address much over the years and the business of preserving correspondence was important to them, perhaps built into their daily routine. Always, however, be aware when confronted by piles of saved correspondence (or even by individual letters) that certain items or parts of items might have been removed at the discretion of the receiver for some reason or another.

Handwritten letter sent 15 December 1837 from Henry Pinninger in Westbury, Wiltshire, to Mr Broome Pinninger (perhaps his brother) in Melksham, about 9 miles away. The content deals with the distribution of money left in a trust under the will of their Aunt Spackman. (Author's collection)

Secondly, it is advisable to read the letter out loud. Sometimes the true import of a communication and the possible permutations in tone (occurring sometimes with every sentence or paragraph change) become apparent only when the words are spoken. Your ancestral letter might generally fall into a particular category, a letter of condolence, a love letter, letter of recommendation, of thanks, of congratulation, of consolation, commiseration or rejection of love. Each of these had their own special characteristics in the past. But letters sent between members of a family rarely actually served one purpose only. Missives announcing a death for example, might also bring news of an

The letter, though written to a family member, has many formal features including the fact the recipient, 'Broome', is addressed in the third person, ('he') throughout. This is possibly because the matter under discussion is the formal redistribution of monies under a will, and, therefore, a high degree of exactitude was required. (Author's collection).

inheritance. When analysing a personal family letter from the past, try to work out early on what the primary, secondary and other reasons for sending it might have been.

You are far more likely to find letters written by your ancestors after 1840 than before. At this point indeed, the number of letters sent nationwide increased exponentially. This is not only because of improvements in education and literacy (which have been discussed in the Introduction and Chapter 1) but more particularly because, for the first time in history the post became affordable to virtually everybody in the population. Prior to 1840 – crucially – the cost of a letter was borne by its recipient and depended upon the number of sheets included in the envelope and the number of miles covered for it to reach its destination. The postal costs of the early nineteenth century were very inconsistent and depended to a large extent on guesswork by postal workers who would hold letters up the light (a process known as 'candling') to estimate how many sheets a letter contained.

Letters in envelopes were charged doubly – a fact which meant that many people simply folded their letters over and sealed them with a wax seal to save money. Other correspondents made sure that they placed more than one letter in an envelope or had their letters hand-delivered by friends who were visiting the parts of the country to which the letters were addressed. Letters were also smuggled in folded-up newspapers which passed through the mail free at this time. Some localities developed their own system for charging a penny for letters sent and received within their own radius. The costs of the pre-1840 postal service were prohibitively expensive – as much as a day's wages amongst some sections of the population – and the postal system was also slow and unreliable. Imagine with what frustration a letter might have been welcomed by an ancestor with little money during this period. Would paying the postage be worth the expense? Or would it be wiser to turn the postal carrier away from the door unpaid with the letter in his hand unopened?

With these issues in mind and a burgeoning economy eager for quicker and cheaper methods of communication at her back, Queen Victoria appointed a Select Committee on Postage soon after her coronation in 1837 and charged it to examine the condition of the post with a view towards postal rate reduction. In the same year, the postal reformer Rowland Hill published *Post Office Reform: Its Importance and Practicability*. Both moves led to a new uniformity in the postal system and a massive reduction in postal costs. On 17 August 1839, Queen Victoria gave royal assent to the Postage Duties Bill and, in May 1840, Uniform Penny Postage (using the very popular adhesive postage stamp) began.

Our ancestors could now send a letter anywhere in England for one penny provided it weighed less than half an ounce. Any letters which weighed more than that bore a Twopenny Blue Stamp. The most important change – of course – was that the sender now paid the postage. An unpaid letter now cost the recipient two pence. The new system also removed the privilege for Members of the Parliament and the Queen to send mail freely. The business of sending a letter had suddenly come within the reach of the pockets of just about everyone in society and our ancestors embraced the change warmly. No longer

INTERIOR OF THE GENERAL POST OFFICE AT THE TIME OF THE
INTRODUCTION OF PENNY POSTAGE.

Interior of the General Post Office – Inland Letter Office – in 1845, five years after the introduction of Penny Postage. This was Britain's first purpose-built mail facility. It was constructed between 1825 and 1829 in the area of St Martin's-le-Grand in London. (Sir Herbert Maxwell, Sixty Years A Queen: The Story of Her Majesty's Reign*, Eyre and Spottiswoode, 1897, p. 23)*

dreading the arrival of the letter carrier, they welcomed anything and everything that came in the post and eagerly reciprocated. Letters became a daily – even, as we shall see, an hourly – excitement, a method of connecting with others and especially with distant family. As one commentator has put it, from 1840 onwards, 'Letters were knit into the fabric of the lives of ordinary citizens and famous Victorians' (Catherine Golden, *Posting It: The Victorian Revolution in Letter-Writing*, University of Florida Press, 2009, p. 19). The Penny Post was extended throughout the British Empire from Christmas Day 1898, and to Australia and New

Zealand in 1905. The Penny Post rate did not end in Britain until 1918.

SOCIAL NETWORKS
After 1840, because of the Penny Post, distances did not seem so great, moving away from home no longer meant a loss of communication between family members, emigration no longer seemed as permanent a separation as death, and families retained strong and multiple connections even if far apart geographically. It is surprising indeed just how far and how quickly news travelled in the Victorian period. Letter-writing became the essential means of holding together ordinary families who had been separated for reasons of work and emigration, enabling them to continue to manage their collective affairs. If you are lucky enough to come across an entire stash of letters written to or by an ancestor you might be able to draw up some idea of the kind of familial and social networks to which he or she belonged. Through letter-writing, individuals were able to work from a distance to retain their identities within the family group and could offer a physical expression of the love that they felt for their families despite their

Letters became a vital method of communication at times when families were dispersed across the country and across the world as a result of social and economic forces. An early twentieth-century painting by Belgian artist J. A. Heyermans (1837–1922) entitled 'For the Great Prize Competition from Dear Jim'. (Author's collection).

absence, and their desire perhaps to eventually return.

You should also remember that your family letters were not necessarily written from one family member to one other person. Often they were joint efforts by several members of an extended family in one place, writing to several other members of the family living in another place. Imagine all the hands (or brains!) that might have had an input into your letter, all the eyes that might have read it and all the ears that might have had its contents read out to them. Different paragraphs of a single letter might even have had different audiences with some less personal bits being read out to friends and acquaintances as interesting news from another part of the country or even another country. Sometimes letter-writers wrote personal information at the tops and bottoms of letters with the understanding that the main recipient would read and remove these before the letter was passed around to a wider audience. Alternatively, separate sheets within the letter might carry information meant for different readers.

Bear in mind that letter-writing was one kind of personal writing at which many of our middle-class female ancestors shone. Letters were considered to be a natural choice of genre for women since they could be written at odd moments in and around the domestic business of the house. In terms of content too, letters often concerned private family issues, such as engagements, marriages, childbirth and death, The tone of personal letters, as will be discussed more fully below, was often sentimental (the offering of consolation, love and empathy), all of which were considered to come more easily than to women than to men. Finally, because letters packed with domestic news were not primarily about the ego of the writer – at least not in theory – this kind of writing was considered ideal for women (conventionally the helpmeets rather than the captains of the family). Having said this, at the lower levels of society women were less likely to write letters than men, often relying on husbands, sons and nephews to be their scribes.

THE PHYSICALITY OF LETTERS
For family historians, a letter written by an ancestor can feel like the discovery of an ancestor him or herself. Indeed letters in the past were considered to be very much an indicator of the social standing, character and personality of the person who sent them. As one commentator puts it: 'the palpable whole of the folded, enveloped, addressed and sealed

letter being sent out into the world said something about the letter-writing self' (Lutz, *The Brontë Cabinet*, p. 137).

Letters were also the embodiment of a significant relationship between a sender and a receiver. Holding a letter received or written by a family member or prospective spouse (at a long distance) our ancestors must have almost been able to imagine the touch and warmth of their skin. If the saliva of a loved one had graced a letter by sealing the envelope or licking the back of a stamp, the communication might seem all the more intimate and physical. By kissing it, you could actually fancy that you were kissing the absent person – quite something in a world long before telephones and video links in which all other sensory communication with the other participant was lost once they had moved away. This physicality of the letter, however, had its negative side: newspapers warned about not sending letters in times of illness (particularly when epidemics such as cholera were on the rampage) for fear that the contagion might spread between families. As late as the 1880s and beyond, the public worried about diseases being spread by the lickable surfaces on envelopes and stamps. Paper, sealing wax and any of the enclosures potentially carried by letter were also sometimes considered to carry risks of infection.

One newspaper recounted with horror the following, surely extreme, story. A person who habitually took large quantities of morphia hypodermically had licked the adhesive seal on an envelope. The receiver opened the letter and then resealed it, also by licking the adhesive. The result was that the receiver was violently sick. *The Tamworth Herald* of 30 May 1885 commented that, 'If this could happen, obviously, there must be grave peril of the transmission of disease by such means.' And the press returned to the folly of licking postage stamps again and again over the years with the *Portsmouth Evening News* suggesting somewhat dramatically on 23 August 1907 that 'it is impossible to insure the perfect health of the persons who handle [letters] [i.e. postal workers]. An employee with an incurable disease might spread his ill health throughout a whole country.'

Stationery

Our ancestors often exercised a great deal of choice over the way they presented their letters, and it is therefore worth paying quite a lot of attention to the way your family letter looks. Postal reformer Rowland

Hill devised prepaid, pre-printed stationery that became known as 'Mulreadies' but this never really caught on. But our ancestors could always express themselves with other features of their written communication, from the colour of the paper they chose to use, to the use of ornamentation including ribbons and (by the end of the nineteenth century) monogrammed letterheads, to the perfume that might have been sprayed across the pages. Letters of condolence, for example, were often sent in black-edged envelopes and black-edged stationery was often used by people suffering a bereavement for up to a year after the death. Before 1840, keeping one's letter confined to one sheet was considered polite since additional sheets and envelopes raised the cost to the recipient. Most personal letters of the early nineteenth century, therefore, consisted of one page folded and sealed so that the address could be written directly on the letter. The return address was often either not included, or written on the inside after the signature to save paper. A rarer method of saving paper involved turning the page upside down and writing between the lines, otherwise known as cross writing.

Note also how your family letter has been sealed. Did it have a separate envelope? Was it sealed with wax wafers and dried gum? Or coloured wax pressed into place with a ring or handheld seal? Black wax often signalled mourning, red often graced letters between two male correspondents or between a man and woman, and any colour wax might be used between two women. Enclosures such as locks of hair, pressed flowers, seeds, drawing and photographs, might still be included in your family letter, or alluded to within the content of it.

Stamps
Up to the 1950s, British commemorative stamps were few and far between; most of the stamps available were definitive issues in which the portrait of the reigning monarch was the dominant element. For more on the history of stamps see James A. Mackay, *British Stamps*, Longman, 1965. From the start, postage stamps had adhesive backs but still required licking or wetting. It is theoretically possible – though expensive – to have the back of a stamp or envelope tested for DNA. To work, the stamp or envelope would have to have been carefully preserved and removed from sources of contamination. The DNA would

then need to be checked against that of a living descendant of the putative stamp licker!

Layout

Our ancestors will have taken great care in the actual writing of their letters. You should consider the way they are laid out, whether or not lines were first ruled in pencil and then rubbed out, the room left for a margin, the consistency and elegance of the handwriting and the number of blots and crossings out. In the Victorian period, as Deborah Lutz puts it, 'caring about one's personal appearance and caring how letters looked went hand-in-hand' (Lutz, *The Brontë Cabinet*, p. 126). There really is something to be said for seeing a letter as a kind of mirror of your ancestor.

Postcodes

In the early days of postal reform, postcodes were not added to addresses but slowly appeared, first for London and then for some of the main provincial towns over the course of the 1850s and 1860s. Even then, they were not as long or complex as they are today (in fact, postcodes as we know them were first rolled out across the country as late as 1974). For more on the development of the postcode see http://www.postalheritage.org.uk/explore/history/postcode/.

DELIVERY

The new affordability of letters was matched by greater ease and speed in their delivery. Delivery time depended very much upon the methods used by the postal service to convey the mail at any given time, whether railway lines existed between places, for example. It was indeed, mainly the advent of the railways that had made the cheap rate of postage possible in the first place. The first railway lines opened in the 1830s and expanded speedily. Trains eventually carried specially-built mail cars, which replaced the earlier horse-drawn mail coaches.

The developing postal system was itself a source of wonder (and occasional frustration) for our ancestors and provided them with plenty of opening content for their letters. They might comment, for example, on how quickly they had received a previous letter. You should look carefully at the date upon which a letter was sent and, if you still have the envelope, compare it with the date of posting. It is worth thinking a little about the time taken for the letter to have reached its destination. If it simply went from one end of a city to the other, it might have arrived within a few hours. Look out for letters that not only give the date but also the time of day, 'Friday afternoon', 'Tuesday 6pm' etc. At some points in the Victorian period, in London, people could expect post to be delivered up to twelve times a day which meant that letters could go back and forth with almost the regularity of today's emails. Towns in the provinces also quickly developed regular postal services with up to six deliveries a day for mail to people living locally. Letters sent between towns could, of course, take much longer to reach their destination.

The postal service and ongoing technological changes continued to affect our ancestors' relationship with their post and to change their perceptions of time, space and community well into the twentieth century. At the turn of the twentieth century, for example, a 'cycle post' – by which mail was delivered by bicycle – was announced in Grantham, Cambridgeshire. It was thought worthy of a mention in a Scottish newspaper which commented approvingly (and with wonder) that 'a mounted postman leaves the Grantham post-office daily at 12.30' to deliver post to the surrounding villages. 'The bicycle is specially constructed for postal purposes and is enamelled in pillar box red' (*Falkirk Herald*, 27 September 1899). In the 1940s, with many male postal workers enrolled in the armed services, local post offices called for women to offer their part-time services in sorting and delivering mail.

During the First World War, the physical business of shifting letters and indeed parcels from England to Northern France was a massive undertaking. A purpose-built sorting department was built at Regent's Park. By the end of the War it had dealt with two billion letters (twelve million a week) and 114 million parcels. Letters written by soldiers were subject to censorship and sometimes took the form of field postcards. Others were sent in so-called 'honour' envelopes (which soldiers signed as a declaration that they contained only private and family matters), or were self-censored. For more on the postal service in the First World War see, http://www.bbc.co.uk/guides/zqtmyrd. It's difficult to over-emphasise the importance of letters to soldiers in the First World Wars. Those they received were 'fetishised, treasured and infinitely re-read' (Lyons, *The Writing Culture of Ordinary People in Europe*, p. 37).

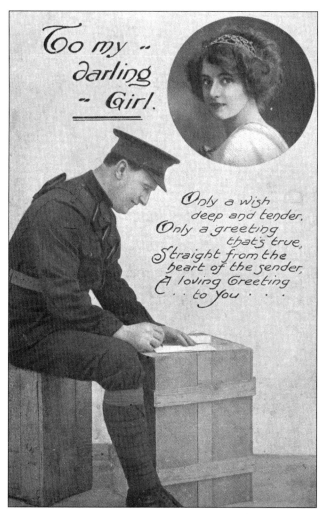

The First World War created a huge appetite for personal writing in the form of letters to and from the Western Front. (Author's collection)

They were a reminder of the past and provided hope for the future, they guaranteed sanity in the worst of times and preserved a sense of identity.

CONTENT
Openers

Since a letter is very often dated, you can immediately find out a great deal more about the context in which it was written. The huge number of digitized newspapers available to view for a small fee at www.british newspapersarchive.co.uk include many national and local papers which can tell you what was going on in the country and in the immediate locality at the time the letter was written. Your ancestors might comment on the weather on the day that they were writing their letter and you can check this against the weather forecasts given in the local papers.

It was almost a matter of ritual for a writer to apologize for something or other when they opened their letter and perhaps to offer an excuse. Perhaps your ancestor's letter states that he or she is sorry for writing too often or not often enough, perhaps he or she senses that the letter is not meaty or long enough to warrant the postage as we have said (paid by the recipient until 1840). Nearly every letter writer apologized at some time or another for being too tardy about replying to a previous letter, blaming everything from illness to the postal system. In a society where, without a letter, no one had any definite proof that the other person was still alive, this was no small apology!

Those ancestors less familiar with the skills of writing might also apologize for their spelling or punctuation Some might claim that they cannot find the right words to express themselves. Many writers begin their letters with an apology for poor penmanship, for forthcoming blots and mistakes, or even for weakness in style or inadequacies in expressing themselves. Bear in mind that this was a familiar and expected trope of letter-writing and does not necessarily mean that your ancestor really was a poor writer. Many of these openers show that there was a kind of common unspoken agreement (what Martin Lyons in *The Writing Culture of Ordinary People in Europe* has referred to as an 'epistolary pact') between sender and receiver. Both parties were aware of unspoken rules about their interchange, how regular it was to be, how formal it was to be, whether or not enclosures were to be sent. Often opening remarks will show that one or other parties has broken this pact in some way.

Another common ingredient at the start of a letter was where the writer described himself sitting at his writing table or desk, or at his bedside, asking the correspondent to picture him as he wrote. These moments are special amongst family letters since they almost stand in for a photograph of your ancestor as he went about the business of writing.

Facts, Opinions and Gaps

Beyond this, most of the content of your family letters will be factual information of one kind or another, family matters, local news, and even, though less commonly, national news. There might be a mixture of different kinds of factual information – familial, business, religious, political or intellectual – and it is worth making a note of what these different areas are and how and when they are introduced into the letter. What is the key news and what are the secondary items? How does the writer indicate their relative importance? Facts of various sorts can be checked against other sources – censuses and certificates, newspaper reports and history books.

Additionally and crucially, the letter was also an important way for ordinary people to convey ideas and personal opinions. It gave a voice (and more importantly the notion of a permanent record) to the ideas of people who would not otherwise have one. It is important, therefore, to note down which words and lines in the letter are indicative of the mind of your ancestor – his or her sensibility, intelligence or emotional life – at work. This is personal writing at its very best and most illuminating.

Also bear in mind what is left out as much as what is covered. In wartime, letters were either self-censored or censored by the authorities, but people have always been selective about what they put in their letters. What you may be reading might only be one view or part of a story that has been altered because of concerns about privacy or the need for secrecy. And, of course, it may be heavily biased towards one view of a situation or another.

STYLE

The overall layout of a letter is something that you can have an opinion on immediately. Has it been formally laid out with the address and date included, or has the writer merely launched into what he or she want to say? Does the writing adequately fill the pages or has the writer had to cram some words in or resort to cross-writing to finish off what he or she wanted to say? These aspects of letter-writing give invaluable clues about the quality of the relationship between writer and sender, as Martin Lyons has observed, for example, 'The amount of blank space at the head of a letter is usually in direct proportion to the reverence attached to the addressee' (Lyons, *The Writing Culture of Ordinary People in Europe*, p. 57.)

The salutation in letters will also tell you something about the degree of intimacy between the sender and the receiver as will the way the letter is signed off. Sometimes senders of letters varied their signatures according to their circumstances or mood. So when Charlotte Brontë signed off a letter to her friend Ellen Nussey, she sometimes wrote, 'Charlotte Scrawl,' 'Charivari' or 'Your affectionate Coz (cousin)', sometimes she wrote a row of 'CBs' descending in size, sometimes used the pseudonym 'Charles Thunder' (since Brontë was the Greek word for thunder), and sometimes the name 'Caliban', a character from Shakespeare (Lutz, *The Brontë Cabinet*, p. 125).

Don't assume that the style of an ancestor's letter is all his or her own. Middle-class writers might have taken ideas on how to craft their letters from letters sent to them by others or by the many examples of letters to be found in epistolary novels of the period, educational textbooks or even in newspapers. Some writers, and especially those who were acting as scribes for others, had a short list of conventional phrases which they would put into action time and time again.

Additionally, letter writers bought and borrowed advice books which suggested do's and don'ts of correspondence and also gave sample phrases that might be used in different kinds of letter. Books with useful titles such as the *British Companion to the Writing-Desk; or, How to Address, Begin, and End Letters to Titled and Official Personages* R. Hardwicke, 1861, and Rev. T. Cooke, *The Universal Letter Writer; or New Art of Polite Correspondence*, Milner and Company, c. 1850, and the American *A New Letter-Writer, for the Use of Gentlemen*, Porter & Coates, 1868 and *Webster's Ready-Made Love Letters*, De Witt, 1873, increasingly found their way onto shelves in the homes of the aspirant bourgeoisie who knew only too well that their penmanship would be read as a mark of their good character, breeding and education. But working-class ancestors too might have read pamphlets about how best to construct a letter. The Society for the Diffusion of Useful Knowledge (1826–48), was just one educational organization that promoted self-education (and especially letter-writing) amongst the poor, before schooling became universally compulsory.

Some examples from a female and male letter-writer taken from the *Ladies and Gentlemen's Model Letter-Writer* (Routledge, n.d., c. 1870) http://www.victorianlondon.org/publications/ladiesandgents.htm) show the variety of different purposes for which a letter might be written. The level of specificity is impressive; there are, for example, model letters on such pragmatic daily matters as 'accompanying a basket of fruit to an invalid' or 'requesting a loan of some books'. Others letters suggest how to deal with suspected social slights, for example, 'from a lady to another in a friendly style complaining of not hearing from her'. But then there are other far more worthy examples, 'asking a relative to attend a funeral' or, 'from a lady to her friend, announcing the serious illness of a child'. The model letters for men in the guide tend, of course, to cover far less personal matters more indicative of a man's public role in the world: 'Applying for a Clerkship' or 'A Sugar Refiner applying for a situation'. There are, however, other more personal examples too, 'Urging a son to relinquish the Naval profession' and 'A letter from a Father to a Son at School on the necessity of attention to his Studies'.

Letter-writing guides had to care for every permutation of pairs of correspondents. Different language was required, for example, by women if a wife was writing to her husband, or a mother to her son, or a city dweller to a female friend in the country or to a male relative in the town. Of course, even with such richness, letter-writing guides could not hope to cover every subject or social circumstances. Writers were encouraged to dip into these books of model letters and to combine bits from them to make up the kind of letter they required.

Useful Ways of Thinking about the Style of an Old Letter
1. Sentiment versus restraint
Whilst some letter types were classed as personal, there was always the possibility, as there is with any communication sent out into the world, that the contents might become public, even when a correspondent assured you that they had burned your letter. 'Personal' for most of our ancestors did not mean a total unburdening of the soul. Emotion, even in a love letter, was always balanced by caution. The Victorians wanted to appear to write from the heart but were also always inclined to hold

back, to express sentiment but with restraint. Letter-writing guides, therefore, advised people to write with absolute feeling but also to be wary about saying too much, saying the wrong things, or saying the right things but in too emotional a way. One good way, therefore, of thinking about your ancestor's letter is to consider whether a balance of the two impulses of sentiment and restraint has been achieved.

One American letter-writing manual popular in Britain, Henry J. Wehman's *The Mystery of Love, Courtship and Marriage Explained* (first published in 1890 but later reprinted many times), which is digitized in its entirety on the internet (www://archive.org/details/ TheMystery OfLoveCourtshipAndMarriageExplained), makes this point very clearly. It advises young men, for example, not to 'put too many adjectives in their letters and not to repeat endearing terms too frequently. One dose of adulation is quite sufficient to be given at any time.' And yet the lover is also advised not to be cold because women 'love to be loved, and how are they to know the fact that they are loved unless they are told?' The book goes on to provide the following example of a suitable letter from a young man wishing to declare his love:

> Tuesday Afternoon.
> Dear Miss Thorne:
> I hope you will forgive me for presuming to write to you without permission, for I assure you it is with reluctance I take up my pen, But I feel that I must reveal to you my feelings and my hopes. Trusting that my attentions have, in a measure, prepared you for a demonstration of some kind as regards the future, I now throw myself at your feet, and ask your love! If I know my own heart, it has an unalterable affection for you. Can you, and will you respond to it? I will be with you this evening, when I hope to be greeted with loving smiles of approval. Adieu till then.
> (www:://susannaives.com/wordpress/2012/02/the-mystery-of-love-courtship-and-marriage-explained-victorian-love-letters/)

In this example, sentiment is expressed in such phrases as, 'I must reveal to you my feelings and my hopes'; 'I now throw myself at your feet, and ask for your love'; 'If I know my own heart'. But the letter is also couched in restraint, 'I hope you will forgive me for presuming to write to you without permission'; 'with reluctance I take up my pen'; ' . . . my attentions have, in a measure, . . . prepared you for. . .'; 'hope' and 'approval.' The idea is of course that this letter will set this lady's pulses racing but will not offend her in any way.

2. Bucking conventions
Another useful way of thinking about a family letter is to see it as a set of conventions which would have been familiar to many writers at the time and then think about whether or not your ancestor modified those conventions to his or her own purposes.

Here is how one academic, Phillis Weliver, has described the conventions of a Victorian birthday letter for example

> The formula is essentially this: After (1) an extra special salutation ('dearest'), (2) the writer expresses her wish for 'many happy returns of your birthday', followed by (3) other kinds of good wishes (blessings, health, longevity, heavenly rewards), and (4) offers to help (to achieve peace, happiness, comfort). The writer might next discuss (5) gifts, or the lack thereof, (6) offer some news, and (7) say 'God bless you'. Finally (8), an especially affectionate sign off, followed by (9) either the first name alone or the full name (www.phyllisweliver.com).

If you have a Victorian birthday letter which significantly differs from this format, it will be of especial interest since it indicates perhaps an ancestor with his or her own agenda or special set of circumstances.

LETTER-BOOKS
You might be lucky enough to find in family papers a 'letter-book' into which an ancestor copied out his or her letters just before posting them so that they might be kept for posterity. When a letter of several pages was copied, it could extend the whole letter-writing business to up to a few hours duration. You should treat letter-books with a certain amount of caution as evidence of a real correspondence, however. The copied letter might not be exactly the same as the letter that was sent. It might be a sanitised or improved version, or it might be quite different from the one actually sent. In other cases – and quite fascinatingly – different letters to different people on the same topic might have been included

in a letter book, showing how a letter writer might have shaped his or her account of an event according to whom he or she was writing.

Many of those who kept letter-books did so for business purposes of one sort or another. With no photocopying facilities, the skills of a clerk who could copy letters quickly was very much in demand. Thomas Rumney, a clerk in South Sea House, must have enjoyed writing very much indeed since when his business copying of the day was done, he settled down to make copies of the personal letters he had written to his relatives. These letters, written between 1796 and 1798, covered such matters as matchmaking, finance, military matters and speculation. They were found to be of sufficient antiquarian interest that they were published over a century later (Thomas Rumney, *From the Old South-Sea House – Being Thomas Rumney's Letter Book, 1769-1798*, John Murray, 1914).

Perhaps one of the strangest cases of letter conservation in the form of a letter-book was that of William Harvey, a 'shabby-looking' billiard-maker who was charged in September 1895 with endeavouring to obtain charitable contributions by false pretences at Croydon Petty Sessions. When his house was searched, it was discovered that Harvey 'appear[ed] to have carried on an extensive system of begging letterwriting, and he did it in a thoroughly methodical manner, keeping a letter-book and a diary giving a daily account of all his transactions. These shewed [*sic*] that he had written no fewer than 900 letters and received 570 replies many enclosing sums of money' (*Whitstable Times and Herne Bay Herald*, 21 September 1895). Some of the noblemen who were tricked by Harvey were the Duke of Wellington, Baron Rothschild, Lord Barnard, Lord Ampthill and the well-known bookmaker Mr H. Fry.

Letter-books were valuable and treasured possessions of our ancestors. When they went missing, their loss sometimes made the press! At his bankruptcy hearing in 1887, ship's chandler and sailmaker, T. P. Dobbin, commented that he did not have many letter-books and that one usually lasted him two years. Nevertheless, his case was not helped by the fact that most of his old letter-books, with details of his past business dealings, 'had been used by captains of ships frequenting the office for cigarette papers' (*Liverpool Mercury*, 29 January 1887). In the same year, the Bishop of Gloucester and Bristol 'sustained a very inconvenient loss' when a packet containing 'his current letter-book, some memoranda . . . and 30 or 40 manuscript pages of a forthcoming theological work' were lost whilst he was purchasing a ticket for Clifton down station on the return journey from a visit to London (*Gloucestershire Echo*, 7 February 1887).

Letter-books enabled people to keep a tally of the people to whom they had written, the dates at which they had written and what they had actually said. Some people (the writer Lewis Carroll [1832–98] is one example), who did not go to the lengths of copying out their letters, nevertheless recorded in 'A Register of Letters' or maybe just a plain notebook, to whom they had written when, with some indication of the purpose of the letter and whether or not they had received a reply. Alternatively, letter books were kept into which letters received were pasted. One such belonging to the writer Sir Walter Scott, and containing some 6,000 letters from correspondents was sold for a huge price at auction in 1930. The discovery of a letter-book with copies of letters sent alongside evidence of letters received might give you a fantastic insight into both sides of a long correspondence, something that is rarely achieved by historians or genealogists.

QUESTIONS TO ASK OF YOUR ANCESTOR'S LETTER

1. Who wrote the letter and who was probably party to it being written? Who received it and who was party to receiving it? Who paid the postage?
2. What was the likely gap in time between the writing of and the receipt of this letter? Is there anything in the content of the letter that relates to that fact?
3. What was the first purpose of this letter (e.g. condolence) and what the attendant purposes (e.g. arranging a visit)? Why was a letter sent and not a telegram, postcard or greetings card, do you think?
4. What can you learn from the physicality of the letter (the type of paper, its sheer length or brevity, the existence of an envelope, the way it was sealed, the stamp, and the overall cost of it all)?
5. What can you say about the addresses given (are they still extant, do they reflect differences in social class between sender and recipient)? You can check addresses at www.royalmail.com and by using historical maps online (www.oldmapsonline.org) or in local libraries.

6. Has this letter been written to a formula do you think? Or does it include originality on the part of the writer?
7. When was the letter dated? What more can you find out about what was going on at this date (historically, locally, at a family level)?
8. What family detail in the letter might be chased up (names, significant events or places mentioned)?
9. What can you learn from the apparatus of the letter about the social position, education and intent of the writer (the way it opens, the way it closes, how it is signed, the addition of a postscript)
10. Is this letter a first draft, one revision of many or a fair copy, do you think? Might it have been copied out into a letter-book or otherwise recorded for posterity?

FURTHER READING
Books
Campbell-Smith, Duncan, *Masters of the Post: The Authorised History of the Royal Mail*, Penguin, 2012.

Golden, Catherine J., *Posting It: The Victorian Revolution in Letter Writing*, University of Florida Press, 2009.

Hemeon, Joseph Clarence, *The History of the British Post Office*, Bibliobazaar, 2009.

Mackay, James A., *British Stamps*, Longman, 1965.

Poster. Carol, and Mitchell, Linda C., eds, *Letter-Writing Manuals and Instruction from Antiquity to the Present: Historical and Bibliographic Studies*, Studies in Rhetoric/Communication, University of South Carolina Press, 2007.

Wehman, Henry J., *The Mystery of Love, Courtship and Marriage Explained*, Wehman Bros., 1890.

Websites
www.bbc.co.uk/guides/zqtmyrd – More on the postal service in the First World War.

www.britishnewspaperarchive.co.uk – British Newspaper Archive.

www.phyllisweliver.com/new.blog.1/2014/9/27birthday-letter-formula – How to write a Victorian birthday letter.

www.postalheritage.org.uk/collections/stamps/postalstationery/ The British Postal Museum and Archive.

www.royalmail.com – Website of Royal Mail.

www.royalmailheritage.com/accessible.html#t_1500F – a visual tour through the history of the British Postal Service.

www.victorianlondon.org/publications/ladiesandgents.htm – *The Ladies' and Gentlemen's Model Letter-Writer.*

www.victorianweb.org/victorian/technology/letters/works.html – some good examples of individual letters sent in the Victorian period and analysed

Chapter 3

'EIGHT WORDS OR FEWER': TELEGRAMS

Even a hundred and fifty years ago, there was a technological alternative to sending a written message in the mail – the telegram. It is hard to overestimate the importance of the advent of telegraphic communication to our ancestors. As one commentator has stated, 'the telegraph, the first of the electrical communication machines, [was] as significant a break with the past as printing before it. In an historical sense, the computer is no more than an instantaneous telegraph with a prodigious memory, and all the communications inventions in between have simply been elaborations of the telegraph's original work' (Carolyn Marvin, *When Old Technologies Were New*, O.U.P., 1988, p. 3).

Embodied in short, simple messages sent as pulses over electric wire, the telegraph system was eventually to become nothing less than a subculture of personal writing with its own customs and vocabulary. From the 1840s onwards, our ordinary ancestors, who understood probably nothing about the business of transmission by electricity, nevertheless threw themselves into the business of communicating by wire with gusto. Like all the other available methods of communication, the telegram presented its own problems and sources of concern. Nevertheless, its novelty and convenience was widely embraced by our ancestors. For family historians, the telegram presents a different set of considerations from the kinds of pen-and-paper communication that we have so far come across and these need to be fully recognized if you are to get the most out of the handful of words which make up the average telegram from the past.

DEVELOPMENT
An optical telegraphic system which depended on the sender being able

to see the recipient had been developed in France as early as 1791. Frenchman Claude Chappe used synchronized clocks and a large wooden panel painted white on one side and black on the other. By showing one face or the other of the wooden panel in co-ordination with the moving hands of the clock, Chappe could encode a message into numbers which could be read by someone far away watching the panel through a telescope. A later model for telegraphic communication involved a moveable pair of arms on a moveable bar which could be put into any one of ninety-eight different positions, with each position corresponding to a letter, a number or a coded word or phrase. The French government saw the potential of Chappe's 'optical semaphore telegraph' for communicating military and political information. Chappe originally called his system the 'tachygraphe', from the Greek words for 'fast writer', but later renamed it 'télégraphe' – 'far writer' – instead.

Optical telegraph systems were expensive to maintain and difficult to operate. A particular problem was that they didn't work well after dark. The search was soon on to find an alternative, with electricity and magnets being the favoured means of transmission. Two separate systems, one devised by Samuel F. B. Morse (America) and the other by William Fothergill Cooke (Britain) developed independently on either side of the Atlantic. Morse (with inventor Alfred Vail) developed a system which used a code of long and short bursts of electricity that caused a stylus to emboss or draw dots and dashes on a strip of paper. Cooke, on the other hand (working with Professor Charles Wheatstone), built a system that used electromagnetic needles to point at letters on a printed grid. Cooke and Wheatstone's system became the first commercial telegraph system in the world but both systems were adopted at different times and in different places in Britain. The very idea that a message might be sent from A to B without need for intervention by a human or animal carrier must have been wonderful if not magical to our ancestors. 'MAGNETIC Electricity for telegraphic purposes has nearly superseded pigeons', commented writer and translator Thomasina Ross in *Household Words* (3 August 1850, p. 454), reminding us of just how revolutionary the change had been.

Whether or not our ancestors of the Victorian period or early twentieth century ever sent or received a telegram themselves, the fact that it was now possible to send messages so quickly over long distances would have shaped their world view considerably. The first electric telegraph was demonstrated in London in 1837, and the first telegraph service to be set up in the UK opened in 1845. Much news from around the world appeared in newspapers because it had been sent by telegram. Our ancestors must have been amazed to get information within hours of an event having taken place rather than the weeks and months which had characterized its transmission by letter in the past. If the world itself was shrinking because of telegraphic communication, it was relatively easy to see how the extended family could be brought into line in the same way.

In the early days, Victorian newspapers were both buzzing with excitement and yet perplexed at the idea of electricity replacing pen and paper. Having reminded the readership how extraordinary so-called 'ever-pointed pencils' had been considered in the 1820s, a journalist in *Household Words* fantasised about the seemingly infinite possibilities of telegraphic communication:

> And now, what have we not arrived at? We are so saucy as to look beyond our improved pencils; beyond pen and ink; beyond our present need of a cumbrous apparatus to carry about with us;—ink that will spill and spot; leads that will break and use up; pens, paper, syllables, letters, pot-hooks, dots and crossings, and all the process of writing. Perhaps the Electric Telegraph has spoiled us: enabling us to imagine some process by which thoughts may record themselves; some brief and complete method of making 'mems' without the complicated process of writing down hundreds of letters, and scores of syllables, to preserve one single idea. All this, however, is as romantic now as ever-pointed pencils seemed to be at first; and instead of dreaming of what is not yet achieved, let us look at the reality before our eyes (*Household Words*, 31 January 1852).

And our ancestors did indeed take up the telegram with great alacrity; it soon ran alongside other forms of communication, offering its own unique condensed writing experience. The word 'telegram' was coined in 1852, when it first appeared in the *Albany Evening Journal* of 6 April. E. P. Smith, of Rochester, New York, wrote the following letter to the newspaper: 'A friend desires us to give notice that he will ask leave . . .

*The London-Slough Telegraph Line – Britain's first true telegraph service –
opened for messages on 16 May 1843. (Sir Herbert Maxwell,* Sixty Years A
Queen: The Story of Her Majesty's Reign, *Eyre and Spottiswoode, 1897, p. 15)*

to introduce a new word. . . . It is telegram instead of telegraphic
dispatch, or telegraphic communication.' Within a few years the new
term had become standard on both sides of the Atlantic.

In the 1850s and 1860s a number of small, private and regionalized
telegraph companies operated in Britain using offices in railway stations.

Early telegraph instrument, from Paddington Station. The original caption states that a murderer, named Tawell, was apprehended by means of this instrument on 1 January 1844 after he was spotted, in the garb of a Quaker with a brown greatcoat on, boarding a train from Slough to London. (Sir Herbert Maxwell, Sixty Years A Queen: The Story of Her Majesty's Reign, *Eyre and Spottiswoode, 1897, p. 15)*

In 1870, however, the telegraph system was nationalized by the GPO – a move which brought complaints as well as congratulations. Here a journalist complains about the lack of printed detail about timings on telegrams in the new system:

> The Post Office authorities have such a passion for revenue that they appear determined to economize wherever it is possible . . . I am surprised that the public make no effort to procure reform in one particular, the non-statement at the time at which a telegram is received and sent out. Under the management of companies both times were stated but now there is merely a stamp notifying the date. Thus there is no means of proving any delays which may take place, which suits the Post Office very well, but not the public (*The Wrexham Advertiser*, 16 April 1870).

By the late nineteenth century, the towns and villages in which our ancestors lived would have been visibly altered by the addition of telegraph wires, whilst, amazingly, undersea telegraph cables were capable of sending communications across the Atlantic and to all the countries that made up the British Empire and beyond by the end of the century. Before she embarked on her Diamond Jubilee procession on 22 June 1897, indeed, Queen Victoria stopped at the telegraph room in Buckingham Palace, pressed a button, and within minutes the Central Telegraph Office relayed her message to every country of the Empire. 'Thank my beloved people,' it read, 'may God bless them.'

If you have a telegram amongst family papers, bear in mind the actual mechanics – and effort – of sending and receiving it. In the early days, our ancestors will have sent telegrams by appearing in person at a telegraph office and writing their message onto a blank form, which was then, more often than not, rendered into Morse code by a telegraph operator and sent down the line. At the other end, an operator in a telegraph office close to the receiver's address would transcribe the coded message by hand onto blank forms. The form would then be delivered to the receiver's address by a telegraph boy. From the 1890s onwards, it might have reached its final destination by bicycle. After the arrival of the telephone (first invented in 1875 but not in any way widely available until the 1920s and 1930s), wealthier ancestors who had their own instrument at home might have sent telegrams by calling a

" GHOSTLY, SILENT MESSAGES."

*At the end of Queen Victoria's reign a book celebrating her Diamond Jubilee
commented proudly, 'The number of telegraphic messages transmitted from the
various London offices in the year 1895–6 was 27,025,193, and the total for
the United Kingdom 78,839,610. As many as six messages – three in each
direction – are now transmitted along a single wire at the same time.' (Sir
Herbert Maxwell,* Sixty Years A Queen: The Story of Her Majesty's Reign, *Eyre
and Spottiswoode, 1897, p. 15)*

telegraph office and dictating a message to an operator: the cost of the
service was added to the customer's phone bill. It was only after the
Second World War, however, that a large number of people had access
to their own telephones.

Further developments increased the speed and efficiency of the
service. Donald Murray's teleprinter (first invented in 1903) eventually
became known as the teletypewriter. This extraordinary breakthrough
meant that operators no longer needed to know Morse code. Messages

were typed on an ordinary keyboard which then converted the letters into electronic impulses which were sent down the wire. The incoming electric signal could then automatically be decoded and typed onto a strip of ticker tape, which was then glued to a blank form for delivery.

Whilst the idea of the telegram had been around for many decades, our ordinary ancestors really only began to make use of it in the twentieth century, especially around the time of the First World War. The possibilities of telegraphing changed according to historical – especially political – circumstances. And it's important to find out just what could and could not be sent to which places, at the time your ancestor's telegram was transmitted. In 1912, for example, such communications across the world received a boost when the Postmaster General reduced the cost of telegrams to the British Colonies:

Telegrams to Colonies at Half Rates
The Postmaster General announces that on and from today plain language telegrams for Australia, Canada, India, Newfoundland, New Zealand, South Africa, and other British overseas Dominions and the United States will be accepted at half the ordinary rates on condition that they may, if necessary, be deferred for more than 24 hours in favour of full-rate traffic.

The new tariff, which it is hoped to extend shortly to other European countries, has been arranged for the benefit of senders of private telegrams in plain language of an urgent character in respect of which existing rates press heavily (*The Courier*, 1 January 1912).

From this point onwards, communication by telegram really took off: eighty-two million telegrams were sent in 1913. But with the start of the First World War, restrictions were put in place to stop them being sent to Germany or Austria:

TELEGRAMS FOR ABROAD: NONE ACCEPTED FOR GERMANY OR AUSTRIA
The Postmaster-General states no telegrams of any kind are accepted for places in Germany and Austria-Hungary. Ordinary telegrams for other places abroad and radio-telegrams, however, addressed, can only be accepted at senders' risk, and if written

in plain English or French. In the case of telegrams for Switzerland or Turkey, French only is allowed.

All telegrams are subject to censorship, and must bear the sender's name at the end as part of the paid text, otherwise they are liable to be stopped until the name is notified by paid telegrams.

Registered abbreviated addresses will not be accepted either as the addresses of telegrams or as names of senders. Ordinary telegrams in code and cypher or without text are prohibited (*Birmingham Mail*, 14 August 1914).

The heyday of the telegram was in the 1920s and 1930s: in 1936, for example, the GPO sold 50,000 Valentine's Day telegrams and over 50 million telegrams were sent in Britain in 1939. Telegrams were eventually brought down from their position of prominence amongst written communications as more people acquired telephones from the 1930s onwards. Historical conditions continued to affect the system. In 1943, all personal telegraphic communication was stopped because of the Second World War. Telegrams were, however, reintroduced in 1951 but in fact never regained their popularity. Nevertheless telegrams continued to be widely used alongside other forms of personal communication right up until the computer age.

SOME SPECIAL CONSIDERATIONS
When confronted with a telegram amongst family papers, it is all too easy to dismiss the few words without much attention. But it's worth reminding yourself just how different telegraphic communication was from any other sort of personal writing and asking if any of its special characteristics might help you better to read between the lines.

Distance and Time
The telegram had the combined ability to cover distance quickly and to eat up time. In the 1840s, it had taken ten weeks for a message to reach India from Britain, and for a reply to be sent back. By 1870, the same message and reply could be sent within just four minutes. Our ancestors sometimes refer, directly or obliquely, to the wonder of this phenomenon in their telegrams.

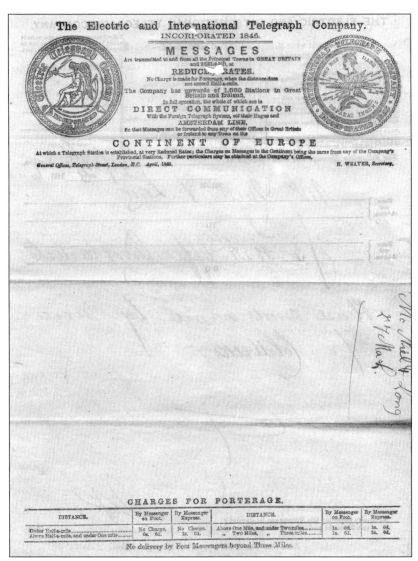

This telegram (delivered by the Electric and International Telegraph Company) is from the days when private telegram companies proliferated. The companies were taken over by the GPO in 1870. The bottom of the telegram gives the charge rates for delivery of the telegram by foot messengers. Under half a mile was free, above half a mile and under one mile 6d, above one mile and under two miles 1s, and above two miles but under three miles 1s 6d. There was no foot messenger service beyond three miles. Messages could also be delivered by Messenger Express, which presumably meant horse and carriage. (Author's collection)

The following Message has been received at _____ Carlisle _____ Station,

27 3 1866

FROM

Name and Address } Mr Neill V Long

TO

Name and Address } J Irwing 3 Post Office Court Carlisle

D Q

Please send name by wire

for Coldbecks

No inquiry respecting this Message can be attended } to without the production of this paper. }

Clerk.

Please enter Time of Delivery, and sign Messenger's Ticket.

Inside, the telegram reveals that it was sent by Neill V. Long to J. Irwing, 3 Post Office Court Carlisle and received at Carlisle Station, 27 March 1866. The message reads, 'Please send name by wire for Coldbecks'. (Author's collection)

Brevity

Most telegraph companies charged by the word, so customers had good reason to be as brief as possible. Telegrams were almost always short, to the point, and momentous with a brisk, snappy prose style that was unmatched by any other form of communication. Pronouns (such as 'she', 'he', 'we' 'them' and 'us') and articles ('the' and 'a') were often omitted, something which ironically could sometimes make a straightforward message look ambiguous.

Impropriety

The older generations in our ancestors' families were sometimes wary of the use of telegrams by younger members. Those delivered over the phone could easily be sent without the knowledge, and certainly without the supervision, of other family members. The telegram became associated with ideas of surreptitiousness, dishonour and even criminality. There seemed to be a lack of propriety about relationships which were being conducted secretly and quickly over great distances. Rather than the traditional slow business of courtship, monitored by interested family members and other people in the community, an intimacy, it was feared, could now be established in minutes from which there was no going back. As Carolyn Marvin has put it, 'traditional courtship protected traditional young women from inappropriate advances by placing insurmountable obstacles in the path of all but the most devoted swains. Electrical communication threatened to shortcut the useful insulation of these customary barriers' (Marvin, *When Old Technologies Were New*, p. 71).

Sadly it was the women who received or sent telegrams who were, at times, vilified in the press for being loose or racy. Unscrupulous men meanwhile made hay from the system, using its flexibility and anonymity to get what they wanted from unsuspecting females and then disappear. The case of Cyril Skipt (alias Grierson, aged 29) from Colchester who duped a Blackpool woman and her mother out of quite a lot of money in 1926 and then sent a mendacious telegram supposedly from the firm he worked for to say that he had been killed in an accident, was widely reported in the papers in 1926 (*The Lancashire Daily Post*, 3 April 1926).

Openness

Paradoxically, telegrams – though considered an aid to secrecy – were also distrusted as a means of communication because their contents were open to the view of people other than the sender and the recipient. Since the message had to be dictated to a telegraph operator and then decoded by another operator, it was highly likely that other sets of eyes

– albeit impersonal ones – would be cast over the communication. There were stories in the press about dishonest or gossipy telegraph operators who divulged the contents of telegrams to local communities. There was also always the possibility that a message might be tapped. No doubt these considerations sometimes had an effect on the degree of openness with which our ancestors wrote. Bear in mind that some telegrams might have ended up very much more public than the writer at first intended, with the contents being printed as news in newspapers, or being pasted up in in shop windows around the country as was the case with copies of telegrams announcing the sinking of the *Titanic* in 1912.

Civilizing Influence

Telegrams sent to and from abroad may appear amongst family papers and might bring to mind certain ideas about the typical values of the British Empire, which might no longer be as palatable today as they were in the past. Ancestors who sent messages to the colonies were not interested in establishing proper two-way relationships with the indigenous people of those places, but only with confirming a relationship with people like themselves at the other end of the line. Likewise, those overseas officials and residents writing back from the colonies were hardly likely to convey news that showed them immersing themselves in the culture in which they found themselves. They were far more concerned with establishing a link with other 'civilized' types around the world, in a kind of elite club in which the English language and British values were singularly espoused. As Carolyn Marvin puts it: 'many writers assumed that messages which made sense at home, and the assumptions on which they were based – especially acceptable and proper procedures of hospitality, courtesy and reciprocity – would make sense all over the world. If they did not, the flaw would be always with the Other, whose inferiority could be demonstrated if proof were needed' (Marvin, *When Old Technologies Were New*, p. 195).

Politeness

Whilst conventional terms of politeness such as proper greetings, titles and enquiries after health and well-being were often avoided in telegrams as a means of cutting costs, there was quite a body of opinion in favour of retaining some polite forms. Some commentators were adamant that, whatever the cost, a telegram should say 'please' and 'thank you' and should be correctly addressed and signed off. In telegrams sent abroad, these issues of politeness were a crucial aspect of the kind of 'civilizing' influence believed to be transmitted by British communications to undeveloped nations.

MESSAGES

As far as the family historian is concerned, telegrams immediately present a boon since the first line might give evidence of the date, time, and location of the sender when the message was left at the telegraph office and then the time when it was actually sent; the same information might also appear for the receiver. Bear in mind that telegrams were sometimes sent to the person who would read out the news to others, rather than the person for whose attention the message was primarily intended. Wedding telegrams, for example, are often addressed to the Best Man or Maid of Honour rather than the bride and groom.

A portion of a telegraphic operating room at the GPO, London. This was in a new building added to the main GPO in St Martin's-le-Grand in 1870. (Sir Herbert Maxwell, Sixty Years A Queen: The Story of Her Majesty's Reign, *Eyre and Spottiswoode, 1897, p. 15)*

As we have said, telegrams were priced (in part) by the word, so senders tended to be succinct. Hyphens, speech marks and the like were generally omitted as each counted as a word and had to be paid for, and individual words were usually not more than eight letters long (though this limit could vary). Fortunately for family historians, the messages in telegrams tend to be very clear and unambiguous, written in capital letters, with numbers spelt out in full, for example. After the First World War, the word 'STOP' instead of an actual full stop was commonly used for clarity. Telegrams are unlikely to include mistakes of spelling or grammar, since these were rigorously checked by the operators at both ends. Whilst these features make for perspicuity, they, of course, detract from the personal qualities of the communication. You must always bear in mind that a telegram has been corrected and possibly edited by a telegraph operator and that you are, therefore, necessarily, seeing the words of your ancestor through something of a filter.

CODED OR CIPHERED TELEGRAMS

If your telegram includes what appears to be cryptic wording, it might be difficult to decipher. As a first port of call, consider that some of the words might be in a foreign language: Latin, Italian and French were commonly used in an attempt to keep messages secret from prying telegraph operators. But some telegrams will boast much odder words written, not in other languages, but in a code ('cablese') of some kind. There was no universal telegram code, but rather, numerous different codes were developed over the course of the nineteenth and early twentieth centuries. Regular telegram users could purchase code books which enabled them to convey a great deal of information in an abbreviated form, rather like the acronyms used in text messaging today. A couple of examples, taken from *The Adams Cable Codex*, Forgotten Books, 2016, show how necessary these codebooks might be in helping you to decode your old family telegram: EMOTION = 'think you had better wait until . . .' and NALLARY = 'it is not absolutely necessary, but it would be an advantage'. Of course, both the sender and receiver would need a copy of the same code book, but its use would save money and give a bit of confidentiality to the message. The first telegram codes were just lists of words translated into numbers ('A1645', for example, meant 'alone' in one such code), but messages consisting entirely of numbers were prone to errors in transmission and, therefore, subsequent codes used Latin or nonsense words to replace entire phrases of English. The Phillips Code of 1879 was a shorthand code devised by Walter R. Phillips to enable the rapid transmission of press reports by telegraph. In this code, extremely common words were replaced by single letters (e.g. C = see and A = letter) whilst less frequently used words used longer abbreviations. Take a look at this at www.radions.net/philcode.htm.

Various other code books have been transcribed and are available to view in their entirety online, or can be purchased fairly cheaply over the internet. Their titles and dates are indicative of the kind of people who might have made use of them and when, (e.g. George Ager's *Shipping Telegram Code*, 1877, and *General and Social Telegram Code*, 1887; William H. Hawke's *The Inland and Foreign Telegram Code*, 1888; and W. M. Saunders' *The Motor Trade Telegram Code*, Society of Motor Manufacturers and Tradesmen, 1920). As a start towards deciphering your coded telegram, it might be helpful to purchase a code book from an online bookstore such as www.abe.com or www.amazon.co.uk.

In 1885, a codebook was issued by a Mr Labouchere. It was satirised in *The Edinburgh Evening News* of 17 October.

> By making use of the abbreviations he suggests you can certainly get a good deal into a sixpenny telegram. Thus 'Jones, agony antidote borage archangel' if sent by a husband in the City to his wife, means our old friend Jones is coming out with me to dinner. As he is a bit of an epicure, do your best in the time, and let us have a good glass of wine. He will probably stay the night. [The paper suggests that the wife might make a very good one word response (not included in Mr Labouchere's code book) which would encompass the following message]: 'What on earth made you invite the man today? For goodness sake, don't bring him here. Chops only. You know there is no decent wine in the house. Mother has the spare bedroom tonight.'

Then, the paper goes on, 'without referring to Mr Labouchere's code, the husband would see things clearly, and take Jones round to his club!'

It's worth checking through other family papers to see if any clues are given to the kind of code that might have been used in family telegrams, or for clues to the way a cipher might have worked. Some codes appertained to particular industries and whilst we are discussing personal telegrams only here, it is worth considering that an ancestor might have made use of a code with which he or she was familiar in a work setting in a personal message. In 1897, *The General Commercial and Mining Telegram Code*, published by C. Algernon Moreing and Frederick G. McCutcheon (W. Clowes and Sons, 1897), was produced as a labour-saving and pocket-sparing handbook: 'It comprises little short of a quarter of a million words and phrases, selected and arranged upon an analytical and grammatical method, and preceded by a complete index to the most important words in the language, together with groups of words expressing ideas closely related, to suggest and facilitate the compilation of sentences' (*The Daily News*, Tuesday 14 September 1897).

By the time of the Second World War, so many telegram codes were in operation that the Postmaster-General felt compelled to specify which might be used in messages abroad (*Bentley's Second Phrase Code*; *Bentley's Complete Phrase Code*; *ABC Code* (6th Edition), and *Peterson's International Code* (3rd Edition): *Press and Journal*, 29 December 1939). One code only was allowed in any one telegram and 'decodes of all Code messages' had to be submitted to a censor before sending. Some countries did not accept telegrams in code at all at this time.

Of course, the code used by your ancestor in a telegram might defy all rational explanation and might be based on an agreement known only to the sender and recipient. Such was the case in an affair reported in *The Lancashire Post* of 9 January 1920 about the trial of two thieves who had used telegrams to communicate with each other. Servant Agnes Higgins (aged 25) pleaded guilty to a charge of stealing jewellery and clothing from two homes where she had worked. Higgins sent her accomplice Thomas Nash (aged 33) a telegram after one of the robberies which 'bore only the signs "G8". She explained to the court that this was a pre-arranged method of making an appointment. "G" meant "The Griffin Hotel, Manchester" and the figure represented "eight o'clock"'. Nash, however, was having none of it, telling the court that he denied having asked the girl to commit any robbery and that the coded telegram referred not to a meeting but to a betting transaction! He was found guilty and sentenced to six months with hard labour with the Recorder describing his offence as 'outrageous'. Agnes Higgins suffered the same penalty.

Look out also for telegrams amongst family papers which appear to include very conventional phrases or clichés. It's just possible that these too were coded messages. In 1931, a case came to court in which William George Shepherd (25), a sailor, and George Allison (36), a trades-union organizer were accused of incitement to mutiny aboard ship in Portsmouth. In an agreed code between the two transmitted by telegram, they had agreed that the following message: 'Mother ill. Come at Once. Walter' would indicate that the money would be found and that the plot should go ahead. The message 'Bottle of Fizz', on the other hand, would indicate that the matter was off (*Edinburgh Evening News*, 26 November 1931).

In their working lives, our ancestors might have used telegrams for a wide variety of business purposes including wiring money, for advertising, conveying stock prices, investigating crime, passing on news bulletins and military uses. What we are concerned with here, however, are telegrams that were sent for personal or greetings purposes. In the early days, they were more often sent to bring news of calamity than of joy, but as time progressed they were favoured as a method of conducting romances, announcing or congratulating the birth of a baby, passing on news of exams passed, qualifications gained or a new job obtained, and – popularly – congratulating couples on their nuptials.

The fashion for sending telegram messages for a wedding – or a Silver, Ruby, Diamond or Golden Wedding anniversary – was most popular between the 1920s and the 1970s. Indeed, newspapers in the 1930s, reported that it had become twice as common at that time to send a telegram of congratulation as it had to send a telegram importing bad news. Before the advent of fast modern aids to travel such as a localized rail network, cars and aeroplanes, relatives who lived at a distance were often unable to make wedding celebrations in person and had to communicate their good wishes in other ways. At the wedding, it was customary for telegrams – often judiciously edited if they were thought to be risqué in any way – to be read out by the Best Man after the other speeches were finished.

Because they cost more than a straightforward letter, greetings card or postcard, the sending of telegrams, especially those sent as congratulations rather than as an absolute necessity, indicates a certain degree of affluence on the part of the writer and, by association, on the part of the reader. The more telegrams at a wedding and the more different places they had been sent from, the higher the perceived sense of the bridal couple's social position. It's worth checking local newspaper accounts of family weddings to see if telegrams are mentioned. The following example shows how a useful snippet of information may be gleaned in such a way. On the Golden Wedding celebrations of Mr and Mrs William Blackwood, of 4 Roselea Terrace, Church Street, Ladybank, the *Dundee Courier* of 15 December 1942, commented: 'Telegrams of congratulation were received from friends in Ladybank, Culross, Newburgh and Liverpool, where Mrs Blackwood's sister resides.'

But telegrams at weddings did not always bring messages of congratulation, and newspapers, of course, revelled in those occasions where a telegram in one way or another broke up the happy proceedings. A particularly heart-breaking case reported in the *Framlington Weekly News* of 15 December 1934 told the story of Ivy May Holton, aged 22, of Stretham who had returned from the hairdressers on the morning of her wedding to find a telegram from her fiancée, Richard James Baldock, an invoice Clerk, aged 23, simply stating, 'WEDDING CANCELLED, COMING UP, BALDOCK'. Whether or not Baldock ever in fact 'came up' to explain himself is unclear but the wedding did not go ahead, Such an experience was the interwar equivalent of being 'dumped by text' and its repercussions were dramatic as the newspaper continued: 'You can imagine the state of mind of a young woman receiving such as message within an hour of her wedding. The shock was terrible. She became hysterical and, as a result, was ill for three weeks . . . at one time there was a serious risk that her mind would become unhinged by the shock.'

In another intriguing case, *The Dundee Courier* reported on 8 January 1923, that a London wedding between Mr Howard Elliott Booker, an American citizen and director of several London dance clubs, and Miss Ivy Featherstone, had been delayed because Miss Featherstone's brother had received a telegram alleging that the groom was already married to a named woman. The groom begged to be allowed to visit the American consulate. This he did and it was proved that the woman mentioned in the telegram was in fact not married to him but was the wife of an American army officer. The marriage to Miss Featherstone went ahead with the bride asserting that she had never for one moment doubted her prospective husband!

QUESTIONS TO ASK OF YOUR ANCESTOR'S TELEGRAM

1. Are your family telegrams mentioned in any other public or private sources (e.g. newspaper accounts of an event, diary)?
2. Why do you think that on, this particular family occasion, a telegram was sent rather than a card or letter?
3. How unusual would it have been at this time for your ancestors to have been sending a telegram rather than another kind of communication (think about the history of telegraphy at this time, your family's income and geographical location)?
4. At the date mentioned on this telegram what would have been the logistics of getting this communication from sender to receiver, and how long might it have taken?
5. What other details can you glean from the top line of the telegram (for example, the time that the message was left at the telegraph office, the time that it was actually sent, the cost, the name of the sender and of the receiver, any useful addresses)?
6. What efforts have been made in terms of the language of this telegram to keep the message as brief as possible?
7. Why exactly were these particular words in this particular order used, do you think?
8. Might your telegram be written in code? Are there any indications – or do you have clues from any other sources – as to what kind of code this might have been?
9. Are there any other special considerations that need to be taken into account with this telegram, (e.g. propriety, or the lack of it, the possible public nature of the telegram, issues of politeness, transmission of British values)?
10. What emotional or practical outcomes might there have been for the ancestor who received this telegram?

FURTHER READING
Books

A.E. Adams and Co., *The Adams Cable Codex*, Forgotten Books, 2016.

Kieve. J. L., *Electric Telegraph: A Social and Economic History*, David and Charles, 1973.

Lister, Raymond, *Private Telegraph Companies of Great Britain and Their Stamps*, The Golden Head Press, 1961.

Marvin, Carol, *When Old Technologies Were New: Thinking about Electric Communication in the Late Nineteenth Century*, O.U.P., 1988.

Standage, Tom, *The Victorian Internet: The Remarkable Story of the Telegraph and the Nineteenth Century's On-line Pioneers*, Phoenix Reprint, 1999.

Standage, Tom, *Writing on the Wall: The Intriguing History of Social Media, from Ancient Rome to the Present Day*, Bloomsbury, 2014.

Websites

www.distantwriting.c.uk Distant Writing: A History of the Telegraph Companies in Britain between 1838 and 1868 by Steven Roberts.

www.history.com/topics/inventions/telegraph The history of Morse Code and the telegraph system.

www.radions.net/philcode.htm Phillips Telegraphic Code.

www.telegraph-office.com/pages/telegram Ross, Nelson, E., *How to Write Telegrams Properly: A Small Booklet*, 1928.

Chapter 4

'PERSONALISED PICTURES': GREETINGS CARDS AND POSTCARDS

Amongst the grey blandness of a pile of family papers, the brightly-coloured corner of a greetings card or picture postcard might cause you to smile. Here is a connection with your ancestors which is not first and foremost about the written word but also about visual, tactile and sometimes – since cards could be perfumed – olfactory clues to their identity. Greetings cards and postcards recreate – if only in a fleeting way – something of the look and feel of our ancestors' lives. Such personal correspondence was once displayed upon their mantelpieces, tucked into the corner of their mirrors or picture frames or used to mark the pages of their books. All in all, greetings cards and postcards from the past are a showy demonstration of the relationship between sender and receiver, regardless of the messages within or behind them.

In keeping with this feeling that greetings cards and postcards are primarily physical (rather than 'writerly') heirlooms, books about their history have tended to focus most on the pictorial and/or craft elements of both kinds of communication. They have looked mainly at developments in art and artists, technological changes in terms of the new kinds of paper, colouring agents, and photographic techniques used, and the history of postage. Sometimes such books barely include any reference to (or even images of) what is written inside or on the back of such missives. Old greetings cards and postcards advertised on the internet surprisingly very often don't mention the message at all. And yet, properly to appreciate what you have in a family greetings or postcard, you need to really understand what these new genres offered to our ancestors in terms of the writing experience that they had never had before. Greetings cards from the 1850s and postcards (widely) from the 1890s, provided a very different vehicle of personal communication; they did not replace the letter of course, and they did not threaten the telegram, but they offered a useful alternative with their own rules of engagement, and their own expectations of writing skill.

The greetings cards and postcards which have remained preserved amongst family papers probably appealed to our ancestors for a particular reason or struck a chord in some way. That chord might have been connected to the physical look of the card. It's worth remembering too that the presence of photographs, sketches, watercolours, or craftwork (with lace, silk, satin, feathers or flowers) turned correspondence in the past into an act of gift-giving. These missives, indeed, often stood in the place of a gift – a reminder of the time, dexterity and affection which had been accorded the recipient by the sender. These were physical objects which had been made, or at least chosen and paid for, with a particular recipient in mind. They were probably displayed, no doubt passed around, indubitably admired or commented on by others, and then carefully preserved, perhaps in a scrapbook or album where they might have been ordered, pasted and attributed. However, your ancestor might also have saved a greetings card or postcard for the message rather its physical appearance, or for the clever combination of the two (which was often a feature of correspondence by card). In fact, the wording that our ancestors chose to dash off on these missives can be a source of great interest and fascination. The great advantage of greetings cards and postcards as far as our late nineteenth-century and early twentieth-century ancestors were concerned was that writing them required a far lower degree of literacy, less effort, less time and even less physical writing space than its old equivalent – the letter. This was all good news in the society of Victorian and early twentieth century Britain which was class-riven, exhausted, pushed for time and, here and there, disastrously overcrowded.

GREETINGS CARDS

Whereas in the early nineteenth century letters expressing birthday greetings, condolences or other sentimental messages had required a certain skill with language (or at least the purchase of a good letter-writing guidebook), our ancestors from the mid-nineteenth century onwards often chose to make contact much more quickly (and impressively!) on important family occasions by sending card.

There are a number of reasons why greetings cards became more popular from the mid-nineteenth century onwards. Partly the increase was simply down to the speed, accessibility and low cost of the Penny Post after 1840 (as described in Chapter 2). Previously, cards (as opposed to letters) were more commonly sent locally, where they could be delivered by hand, than nationally. Secondly, greetings cards started to be mass-produced from the 1850s onwards, although many continued to be made by hand. In the 1860s, companies like Marcus Ward & Co, Goodall and Charles Bennett employed well-known artists such as Kate Greenaway (1846–1901) and Walter Crane (1845–1915) to design cards for them.

Thirdly, with the popularity of the mother of the nation, Queen Victoria, the patriotism induced by the expanding British Empire and a general flourishing of culture in an economically vibrant country, family occasions were celebrated more fervently and with a greater degree of luxury than ever before. Cards flew across Victorian and early twentieth-century Britain for an ever-increasing number of purposes, marking Christmas, Easter and anniversaries, expressing congratulations and condolences. In the higher reaches of society, birthday parties for children were held with fancy ices and moulded cakes. These were usually quite structured affairs with games being followed by dancing, tea and perhaps a magic lantern show. To have a mantelpiece brimming with highly decorated birthday cards was a sign of social success. At the same time, the Victorian period was an era in which romantic love was beginning to supersede other reasons for getting married – something which led to romantic cards and valentines gaining in popularity. There was a particular upsurge in the number of valentines cards sent in the mid-nineteenth century. In 1841, one year after Uniform Penny Postage was introduced, for example, 400,000 valentines were posted throughout England. By 1871, three times that number passed through the General Post Office in London alone (Debra N. Mancoff, *The Arthurian Revival in Victorian Art,* Garland Publishing, 1995).

Design of Cards

The design of cards can, of course, be an invaluable aid to analysing cards when they have not been dated by hand or when they have become separated from date-stamped envelopes. Artwork on greetings cards followed the artistic movements of the day, including for example, Impressionism (1870s and 1880s), Art Nouveau (1880–1910) and Art Deco (1920s–1940s) to name but a few. Likewise images and the printed messaging on cards reflected the public preoccupations of the moment, women's suffrage, the two World Wars, coronations and changes in women's fashion. It also followed more subtle changes in public taste. There was, for instance, an improved appetite for humorous greetings cards in the 1940s and 1950s after the austerity and seriousness of the Second World War. There were also significant technical developments in the making of greetings cards that can help date them (e.g. the colour lithography of 1930). Such developments can be researched through various useful and well-illustrated books including Michelle Higgs, *Christmas Cards: From the 1840s to the 1940s*, Osprey Publishing, 1999.

Sometimes collections of greetings cards received by our ancestors (and occasionally stuck into albums or scrapbooks for posterity) have been donated to local archives or small museums. You can check for the location of these through the Discovery part of the National Archives website www.discovery.nationalarchives.gov.uk). If your local repository holds some of these, it might be worth taking a look (for comparison purposes with your own cards if nothing else). The kinds of greetings cards that tend to have been preserved often celebrate key birthdays such as 21st, 70th, 80th or 90th. Occasionally greetings cards form part of a bundle of other sorts of records all related to the same event. The Royal Society, for example, holds a set of cards, telegrams and letters sent for the 86th birthday of Sir Henry Hallett Dale, FRS (1875–1968) in 1961. Other cards have been kept because they are unusual in some way. Such is the case with a card held in Devon Archives and Local Studies Service, South West Heritage Trust and sent by the pupils at Tiverton Girl's Middle School to their teacher Miss Pinkerton in 1902. If you have a particularly interesting selection of greetings cards, you may want to compare them with one of the well-known collections of greetings cards held in UK libraries. A large collection of greetings cards which can be viewed by appointment only is the Laura Seddon Collection held at Manchester Metropolitan University which includes 32,000 Victorian and Edwardian greetings cards. Another useful point of contact would be the British Ephemera Society (www.ephemera-society.org.uk) dedicated, in the words of its founder Maurice Rickards, to 'the minor transient documents of everyday life'.

Messages in Greetings Cards

Many Victorian and later greetings cards can prove disappointing in terms of original writing. A sender might have considered that a printed message on a card might suffice and all that was really required was a signature. Indeed the presence of a signature, or at least a name, was considered vitally important on a greetings card (unless, of course, it was a valentine's card which usually remained anonymous). But usually signatures were accompanied at the very least by marks of affection in keeping with the growing national mood of sentimentality. Whilst affection could not readily be shown publically between lovers, married couples or even parents and children in the Victorian or even in the Edwardian period (amorous touching in photographs was completely out of bounds, for example) it could be demonstrated in words of greetings and farewell such as 'darling', 'dearest' and 'affectionately'. An undated card held in Nottinghamshire Archives has, in addition to the printed word, MOTHER, a handwritten message which reads, 'to the loveliest mother-in-law that ever lived'! These words, of course, when written in greetings cards, might be widely read by family members, friends and neighbours, and they were thus chosen with care.

Whilst messages in greetings cards were usually short and followed a well-accepted format, it was important that they were conveyed in the cursive handwriting of the person actually sending the message, printed or (later) typed names were definitely frowned upon. In 1895, the actress Mary Anne Keeley posted a birthday message in the press on the occasion of her own 90th birthday in which she wished her 'sisters of the stage . . .as long and as happy a life' as she had had. It was accompanied by a facsimile of her signature as a sign of its authenticity and the honesty of her sentiments (*The Evening Telegraph*, 21 November 1895).

Our ancestors sometimes augmented the sparse messages that had written in cards with non-verbal devices. One method of conveying wordless messages in a greetings card was to spray the card with perfume. Certain pictures (printed on the cards themselves) were chosen with specific ends in mind: a church, for example, might suggest the good intentions of the sender in respect of marriage. Much has been written about the Victorian 'language of flowers' (floriography) in which individual flowers had sentimental meaning and could be grouped together in different combinations to increase that meaning. Thus, a red rose might mean 'love' and bluebells 'constancy'. A birthday card sent by Mary Gladstone (1847–1927) to her father (later Prime Minister) W. E. Gladstone (1809–98) (probably in 1859) includes a hand-painted watercolour of two flowers, the purple or yellow pansy (Heart's-ease) which signified 'think of me' and a red poppy symbolizing 'consolation'. Since Mary's father travelled extensively, the flowers were meant to convey in a kind of shorthand the heartfelt sentiments of reassurance that his daughter had expressed in words in other longer communications. From this, we can see that the correspondence between the Gladstone father and daughter is a good example of an exchange of personal writing better interpreted in its entirety, than piece by piece.

There were always correspondents who went the extra mile even on a greetings card. Some, for instance, copied well-known verses onto cards or wrote their own. A box in the Sandwell Community History and Archives Service contains manuscript and typescript rhymes for a large number of birthday cards by one James Round of Smethwick (undated). See Chapter 11 in this book on poetry for help in determining whether verses are from published material or original to the sender.

When reading an ancestor's valentine card, think about the issue of propriety. Although the following news item is not meant to be taken entirely seriously, there was an implicit indecency in women sending Valentine's cards to men in the late Victorian period. 'Any lady sending a gentleman a valentine will be held *ipso facto* to have tendered that gentleman an offer of marriage, and be bound by the consequences', (*The Comic Press, The Aberdeen Journal* 13 February 1880).

The wording in your ancestor's valentine, more than in any other type of missive, may illustrate a degree of fun and play. Cards were obviously sometimes pre-printed with such wording, but writers often adopted the same spirit within their cards. Look out for poems that are acrostics (where a message is spelt out by the first letters of each line), or in which riddles or puzzles appear (poems with verses in the wrong order, or with words missed out or substituted by a picture – rebuses). Valentine's cards might also include ornamental lettering and other attempts at ornate calligraphy. The need for anonymity was often paramount. Recipients who were desperate to find out who had sent them a card might even turn to the press for assistance as in the following case of two would-be lovers who each had used quotations from the Bible as a means of romantic communication: 'The lady who sent a Valentine to a gentleman in Grantham this week, containing merely the reference, Genesis 2, 18, is referred to 1 Corinthians vii, 27' (*Grantham Journal*, 27 February 1869). In this piece of personal writing, the Bible had been ingeniously used as commonly understood code through which a message could be kept private. Genesis 2:18 states, 'Then the Lord God said "It is not good that the man should be alone: I will make a helper for him"'. The response in Corinthians no doubt disappointed the lady correspondent, 'Are you bound to a wife? Do not seek to be free. Are you free from a wife? Do not seek a wife.'

The rise of gaily-decorated, sentimental greeting cards inevitably caused something of a stir of dissension in a society dominated by somewhat serious middle-class letter-writers. And the popularity of Valentines fluctuated with the ups and downs of history. Valentine's cards, in particular, met with a fair bit of censure in the press in the late Victorian period:

> . . . these 'missives' circulate for the most part, in the lower middle-class of society and the class below it; and the element of burlesque and buffoonery predominates in them. A valentine nowadays is apt to be something offensive and rude – it is an anonymous insult. So one must conclude from the things displayed by thousands in certain shop windows in February. They may safely be described as the choicest productions of quite graceless humour, of the clumsiest fun, of vulgarity, unmixed and pure. St Valentine, it would seem, is supposed to be given a licence to be impertinent. But his name is taken in vain. The sooner such a fashion becomes wholly extinct the better ('Antiquary', reproduced in *Shields Daily Gazette and Shipping Telegraph*, 13 February 1882).

The sending of valentines became far less popular in the bleak early decades of the twentieth century, but it was set for a revival just before the Second World War as this newspaper item shows:

I wonder how many people will receive a Valentine when the postman calls tomorrow?

Doubtless, a good many more than were receiving these missives a few years ago; for the old custom of exchanging St Valentine's Day Greetings is only in process of reviving after having long fallen into almost complete abeyance.

You may have seen for yourselves in the shops, the brave show at a 'comeback' these amorous greetings cards are making. The number of people of all classes I saw purchasing valentines in one city shop at the weekend, moreover suggests that the revival is being attended with a considerable degree of success.

I doubt, however, if we are yet within reach of repeating the old days of the valentine, when St Valentine's Day was looked forward to as early as Christmas for what the post might bring in the way of greeting and loving cards (*The Evening Telegraph*, 13 February 1939).

POSTCARDS

If greeting cards had been a cheap, convenient and non-intimidating way of communicating, a blessing to some and an abuse to others, then postcards, which were open to the world and could be read at a glance, took things a stage further. The postcard had originated in Vienna in 1869 where one of its proponents, Dr Emmanuel Hermann, had been 'forcibly struck by the fact that a large number of letters were sent, the importance of whose contents was in no proportion to the waste of trouble and polite sentences involved and which might as well have been forwarded without covers [i.e. envelopes]. One third of all the letters, he reckoned, contained merely simple information which might easily have been posted open at a lower rate of postage' ('The History of the Postcard', *Liverpool Mercury*, 2 November 1899).

Postcards were a late runner in Victorian Britain. There had been a number of antecedents in the shape of pictorial trade cards, decorative hand-drawn and printed envelopes, visiting cards and cartes-de-visite photographs, but postcards proper were first introduced in Britain in 1870. They were significantly cheaper to send than a letter or a card, saving the need to buy writing paper and envelopes as well as incurring less postage. It would be wrong to think that only working-class people used them. In fact, all sorts of people thrilled to their convenience. Businessmen realised the potential of such cards for advertising their products and privately-printed publicity cards were among the first to bear pictures. The Liberal Prime Minster Gladstone was a fan of postcards, using them in the 1880s to respond to queries sent by members of the public and later being a staunch advocate of the so-called 'stout' card (printed on thin card or 'stout' paper) and of the practice of being allowed to write one's signature on the front of the card.

As far as the family historian is concerned, there are a number of different ways of dating a postcard. The card itself underwent several different manifestations in size and format including the development of reply postcards in 1882, 'stout' cards in 1874, 'court-cards' from 1894–1902 (sized 4.75in x 3.5in), and the increase in the size of postcards to 5.5in x 3.5in in 1899 (though the smaller-sized cards could still be purchased and sent). It was not until as late as 1894 that commercially-produced picture postcards were widely available and that adhesive stamps could be bought and added to the cards before posting. The space upon which to write a message on a postcard was originally pretty tiny since the whole of the front of the card bore the address of the recipient and the back was shared between the message and a picture. Since the picture often dominated, there was sometimes little room to write anything at all. From 1902, however, postcards as we know them appeared with the front of the card covered by a picture whilst the back, divided in two for the purpose, had space both for the address and a message. Further information about the dating of postcards from their shape, size and postal features is given in Martin Willoughby's *A History of Postcards*, Bracken Books, 1994.

We must read our ancestors' postcards against the background of how postcards were considered at the time in which they were written. In general, the new method of communication was greeted with great positivity, joy and playfulness. It is difficult to overestimate just how much the postcard revolutionized the business of communication and, in particular, the matter of personal writing under discussion here. The so-called 'Golden Age' of the postcard was the two decades between 1890 and 1910s. Indeed, during the Edwardian period and the First World War, the postcard was the standard way of transmitting short messages. During this time as Martin Willoughby has commented the sending of postcards was, 'on the verge of being an international addiction' (*A History of Postcards*,

I wonder why a fellow feels so lonesome when there's a new baby in the house!

The message on this postcard posted in Birmingham to an address in Northampton in 1913 shows just how useful postcards could be in making arrangements to meet at short notice: 'My Dear Doris I shall be very pleased for you to come on Monday write and let me know the time you will be here and I will meet you I wish Bob [?] was coming with you Love to all from Maud'. [The original lack of punctuation has been retained]. (Author's collection)

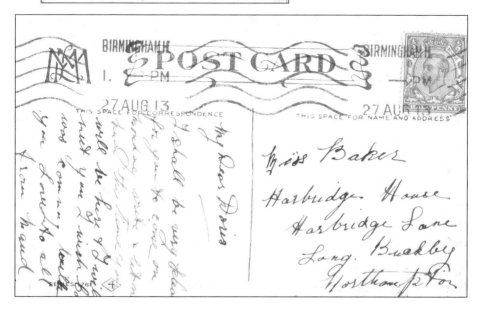

p. 7). Postmen complained about the sheer number of cards they had to carry, post offices had to take on extra staff, particularly during holiday periods to deal with increased throughput of mail. Anyone and everyone started to send postcards.

One of the chief reasons for the popularity of postcards, as we have said, was just how cheap they were to send – approximately half of what it cost to send a letter in the early period. Until 1918, a stamp for a postcard cost only ½d, for example. And although the price of sending a postcard went up to as high as 1½d in the early 1920s, by 1922, it was back down again to 1d. This meant that our ancestors of just about every income bracket could share in the novelty of this new kind of correspondence. And working-class people who had found letter-writing a daunting incursion into a world of literacy that had previously excluded them, importantly entered into the postcard bonanza at exactly the same time as the upper and middle classes. It was an amazingly freeing moment for writers all round.

A second vitally important ingredient in the success of the postcard was the dizzying lack of any rules for writing that accompanied its appearance and the fact that people didn't have to write much. *The Liverpool Mercury* of 2 November 1899 voiced the opinions of many when it reported that: 'The postcard with its entire freedom from all ceremony or formality is [. . .] an obvious boon to thousands, if not millions of correspondents in these days.' Not only did people who had never written before start to write, but these new correspondents sometimes sent many postcards a week and even on occasion, several a day! The sheer number of acts of writing taking place across the country multiplied exponentially. *The Liverpool Mercury* in 1899 commented further on the fabulous number of cards being sent.

The postmaster general states that the number of postcards used in the year is at the present time at the rate of 382,200,000, which means that if the whole population were given to postcard writing the average number of cards used by each person would be 9.5. So rapid indeed has been the growth of correspondence by postcard that the number now used annually is more than double the number used twelve years ago ('The History of the Postcard', *Liverpool Mercury*, 2 November 1899).

A third bonus of the postcard was its ability to cut straight to the point, something that was absolutely necessary in a practical society where time equalled money. Postcards were sent to organize appointments between friends or with tradespeople, to give ongoing information about medical situations to relatives at a distance, to alert recipients to times of arrival, to order food for the next day, and other equally banal but very necessary matters.

> Without postcards our daily correspondence would become a much more troublesome and cumbersome affair than it now is, there are innumerable occasions on which a postcard is quite sufficient for the few lines that require to be written. It would be impossible to attempt to define or enumerate such occasions, and it must be left to the judgment and good taste of the writer to describe when a regular letter should be substituted for a postcard (*Dundee Courier*, 29 October 1898).

Images

A vast array of possible views, scenes or themes appeared as pictures on postcards in the early years of the twentieth century and they will have been chosen by senders with the recipients very much in mind. As a postcard sent by Cecil from Altrincham in June 1903 to Dora Wain demonstrates: 'Your most sedate postcard came to hand all safely yesterday. I must tell you I like your selection very well.'

Early images included holiday views, ships, railway engines, animals, military leaders, royalty, comical scenes and portraits of famous people, especially actresses. Given the immense variety of cards available, it is important to remember that the card itself often became the reason for the communication, not merely the vehicle for it. Postcards might tell you something about the hobbies, interests, sense of humour, artistic aspirations or the like of the sender and /or the recipient.

Occasionally, an unusual but illuminating set of postcards turns up in the archives. One example is that of postcards sent to Mrs Caroline (Carrie) Gandy (née Gamble) on her successive birthdays in the 1920s from her friends Margaret and Carol. The varied addresses over the years (which are all seaside hotels) suggest that Caroline liked to be away to celebrate her special day. In 1926, a card from Margaret to Caroline at the Cliffe Hydro Hotel, Ilfracombe, dated 22 September, shows a photo view of a landscape with flowers, with embossed borders. On 21 September 1929, the postcard (a colour photograph of pansies and lilies of the valley and an embossed border), is addressed to the Imperial Hydro, North Shore, Blackpool. In 1933 (2 September) Margaret writes her birthday message to Caroline at the Queen's Hotel, Eastbourne. It is a photograph of a thatched cottage. In 1935, Carol writes to Caroline at the Savoy Hotel, North Shore, Blackpool. Again the card is a colour photo of pansies dated this time 2 September. Several facts and ideas can be gleaned from these cards: the likely date of Caroline's birthday, her location at the time of her birthday each year, the possible location of her friends, her holidaying tastes, her wider tastes, and the quality of her relationship with her friends.

Messages

Postcards with scenes upon them avoided the need for much description, indeed the picture was supposed to stand in for the words. As Margaret Meadows commented in *The Girl's Realm* of 1900, 'A little card will suggest what we can't put into words. The picture postcard meets the needs of those slow of expression or too hurried to write' (quoted in Asa Briggs, *Victorian Things*, Penguin Books, 1990, p. 362). There were even postcards that totally obviated the need to write anything at all. Some, for instance, had pre-printed clocks upon them upon which you could mark the time of an appointment. Additionally, lists of printed phrases were issued to people at Post Offices which could simply be copied out onto postcards (a bit like the predictive texts of today).

Unlike greetings cards which celebrated a specific event in more or less conventional ways, your ancestor's postcard could be about anything. There was no need for adherence to Victorian letter-writing formality anymore. Writers made different use of the space available to them by writing upside down or from side to side, filling the space with a sentence or a question, or writing densely in wobbling unruled lines. As long as the receiver understood the thrust of the message, conventions of spelling, orthography and etiquette could be cast aside.

The content of messages on postcards varied enormously, but there were some common tropes. Look for examples of the writers thrilling to the convenience and portability of the genre itself. They wrote about their delight in the fact that the hard little pieces of card could be balanced on the knee, that they didn't require a desk or a writing board or that they could even be written outside despite the vagaries of bad weather. 'I am writing this outdoors while Peter swims!': Postcard from Bill in Scarborough to Jack in Liverpool, 1910 (Author's own collection). Very often, our ancestors' postcards, like their letters, begin with an apology for a lack of communication and comment on the general pattern of the exchange of postcards between the two recipients.

Postcard communication also gave people the opportunity to rethink how they dealt with their social networks. In a world largely without telephones, it was nothing short of miraculous for ordinary people living at a distance to be able to meet each other at a day or half a day's notice. In towns where there could be up to about ten deliveries of mail a day, postcards were used in much the same way as a text or email is now. Even between towns and villages at a distance, by the time the postcard came on the scene, delivery of a message could be within two or three hours of its being posted. Postcards (like the much later mobile phone) allowed people to micro-coordinate their activities; they might write, for example, that they were 'just doing the washing', but would be 'around in the evening'. With postal collections frequent and sorting offices continuing to work even during public holidays, the idea of holding a conversation by postcard was a very real one. Some messages on postcards demonstrate considerable verbal ingenuity. They are clever and concise, sometimes coded and cryptic to confuse postmen and readers other than the recipient who might come across them. Other handwritten messages connect up with the printed message on the card itself. A postcard sent from Blackpool in 1904 comments 'Dear Sister, I hope you have not been like this', referring to a drawing of a crying girl on its front (@eviipc).

Postcards from the Edwardian period and around the time of the First World War, more than any other form of personal written communication of the same period, might include slang expressions. Ex-military men especially those who had served in India bandied about such terms as: 'Blimey' – from 'Gorblimey' or 'God Blind Me!, 'clobber' (uniform or clothing), and 'cushy' (from the Hindi 'Khush' meaning 'pleasant') . An Edwardian correspondent might describe an exciting experience as 'wizard' or mention 'getting the hump', being 'off his chump', or 'shaping himself' (preparing). The First World War brought a new vocabulary which – due the mingling of different classes of men in the military – crossed more social levels. Thus, your ancestral correspondents might have written about Britain as 'Blighty' – a word which derived from the Urdu word 'vilayati' meaning foreign. This term had been around in Britain since the late nineteenth century, but did not become popular until the war period. These years also gave rise to a whole range of new popular slang words. Look out for an ancestor who describes him or herself as 'being in a flap', 'mucking about', 'mucking in', 'making wads' of money or 'wangling' something, for example. For more on the slang of the First World War, see Julian Walker and Peter Doyle, *Trench Talk – A Guide to First World War Slang*, The History Press, 2012, or an online dictionary of slang such as www.peevish.co.uk.

If you are lucky your family postcard will provide multiple details for analysis. In a card sent from 'Pat' in Pontypool to 'Ethel' in Neath in 1919, Pat gives the demands of her new baby as an excuse for not having written sooner. The picture on the card shows a woman in her First World War employment as an army driver, with another picture juxtaposed of a woman pushing a pram filled with babies. The pre-printed caption reads 'Plenty women are still carrying on: The only difference with some is – they used to drive the Army, now they're pushing one.' The message on the reverse of the card reads, 'My Dear Ethel. Don't collapse, I am still in the land of the living. Thanks very much for p.c. [postcard] of so long ago. I am a fine one to write aren't I? no time see, someone insists on taking up all my spare time. too bad say. I am having a spiffing time, love from Pat.' [Original spelling and punctuation retained]

This card provides a great deal of historical interest. The picture has been selected because it connects with the sender's and perhaps also the recipient's own experiences. Perhaps new mother Pat had an important job in the First World War. It is now 1919, she has started a family and feels the contrast sharply. The picture then works in tandem with the message which alludes to a newborn. The handwriting is well developed and the message well-constructed, but the punctuation is erratic. The use of the word 'spiffing' (meaning 'great') is typical for the times – a legacy of the World War, but it is used slightly ironically. This is possibly the kind of slang normally used by men, but this woman knows that she has crossed the gender divide in her life by working as an army driver before becoming a mother. She no doubt feels completely entitled to use the word 'spiffing'

Just as greetings cards before them had been greeted with hostility by a deeply conservative Victorian press, so too were postcards. Objections to the pretty picture messages flying through the post were of several different kinds. Some critics thought that the rise of the postcard – if not checked – foretold the end of letter-writing skills in the population at large. Correct grammar and spelling would disappear, as in the following example from 'Minnie' to 'Bell Gudgeon' in Kendal, Westmoreland, in September 1913, 'I arrived home safe + sound yesterday. Work has gone down bad today' (@eviipc). Postcards, some said, were also destructive of style and did not allow for the play of the emotions, they should be confined, it was declared to the use of such lowly and 'semi-literate' people as tradesmen.

> [There] were those who still regarded letter-writing as a fine art. This old school of letter writers naturally looked upon the innovation as the death-blow to the carefully written epistles of the past. That the postcard may have had some such effect is not perhaps to be altogether disputed, but in an eminently utilitarian age like the present the fact that postcards have become a most useful and indeed indispensable adjunct of social and commercial intercourse must far outweigh any disadvantage which the old-world letter writer ascribes to its use ('The History of the Postcard', *Liverpool Mercury*, Thursday 2 November 1899).

Then there were those who thought that the nature of postcards would give rise to abuses: they seemed too open, too immediate, too brash and impolite; certainly cards without envelopes seemed to lend themselves to the transmission of shocking news in one way or another. Whilst postcard-lovers were quick to dispute these arguments, there was some truth in the fact that postcards seemed to bring out the worst in people. The brevity and openness of postcards, the lack of space for signatures, writers' addresses and extraneous formalities, spoke to the moment and made them seem eminently apt as vehicles for hoaxes and tomfoolery.

Accusations, poisonous remarks, slander and messages of revenge also all presented themselves as suitable content for the succinctness of the postcard. Of course, a poison-pen letter might equally have done the trick, but in the case of a letter the insult was privately received. If you defamed someone in a postcard, you made that defamation visible

This postcard was posted in Stamford, Lincolnshire in 1906. The front shows a sketch of local hero, Daniel Lambert (1770–1809), weight 52 stone, 11lbs who was once Britain's largest man. The message with the characteristic apologetic (and then humorous tone) reads as follows 'Dear sister and Brother I ham sending this card hope you will like it I should [] been over if my tire hanted given way I dont think my close would fit this man yors RG' [Original spelling and lack of punctuation has been retained]. (Author's collection)

Valentines Series 40603

DANIEL LAMBERT (weight, 52 st. 11 lbs.), Stamford

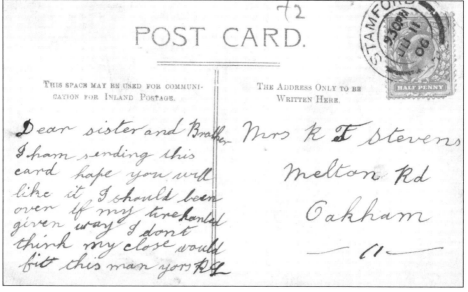

not only to the person who received it but also all those who saw it on its journey from sender to recipient. What better way to pass round malicious gossip about someone's bad morals?

> The main argument against the postcard was that it would afford an opening for the ill-directed efforts of those who indulge in public libel and defamation of character acted for the purposes of venting their spite and malice. The argument was, of course, not without reasons, for the moral assassin is unhappily one of the evils of the age ('The History of the Postcard', *Liverpool Mercury*, Thursday 2 November 1899).

As well as malice, postcards seemed custom-made to convey dramatic news. Newspapers at the end of the nineteenth century are spattered with accounts of suicides in which the perpetrator sent a postcard or postcards announcing his or her own imminent death. Bear in mind too when analysing the message on a postcard that it might have crossed a threshold for cheekiness, particularly if it is written upon a card which is unsigned. Postcards, even if they did not seek to wound, were very much a repository for dramatic exclamations, astounding facts and impertinent questions, much as text messages are today.

Finally there were those who simply thought that sending a postcard rather than a letter was discourteous since it implied that the recipient was not worth the cost of a one-penny stamp. The general notion that a postcard was in some way too vulgar a kind of communication for certain kinds of message was expressed by a Scottish journalist in 1898:

> I know one lady who holds that postcards should never under any circumstances be employed, declaring that it shows a lack of respect to the receiver, and indicates that the latter is not worth the expenditure of a penny stamp. This is an absurdly exaggerated notion of course, but it is worth remembering that sometimes a postcard does savour little of disrespect . . . When any private matter is to be communicated, any important business or delicate subject, a postcard is utterly out of place. One never knows who may read the contents of a postcard, or what annoyance may be caused by such open correspondence. Finally, it should be borne

119

in mind that terms of affection and endearment must find no place in the necessary abrupt wording of a postcard, and lovers, however, humble their circumstances, should strive to attain to the dignity of a closed envelope and a penny stamp (*Dundee Courier*, 29 October 1898).

If you are wondering whether your ancestor ever answered the postcard that has been preserved amongst your family papers, bear in mind that many people believed that a message sent by humble postcard simply did not merit a reply.

QUESTIONS TO ASK OF YOUR ANCESTOR'S GREETINGS CARDS AND POSTCARDS

1. Why has this particular greetings card or postcard been preserved, do you think?
2. Why did your ancestor choose to send a greetings card or postcard rather than a letter on this occasion do you think?
3. What can you learn from the materiality of the card or postcard (its size, format, whether the back of the postcard is divided or not, the stamp, whether it is handmade or mass-produced, whether it includes craftwork, a sketch or photograph?
4. What can you learn from the picture on the greetings card or postcard (likely date, geographical location, tastes, interests, sense of humour of sender and /or recipient)? How far does the picture 'speak' the message?
5. Does the written message acknowledge the pictorial message, or interact with it in any way?
6. What sentimental effect is this card/postcard meant to provoke?
7. What details about family might be followed up in other records (addresses, references to family members or family events)?
8. How formulaic is the message? Does it have any content or feature that is extra to the main import of the message?
9. Does anything in the vocabulary, grammar, spelling or punctuation of the message indicate that the sender had less than an average degree of literacy?
10. Does anything in the vocabulary, spelling and punctuation of the message indicate that the sender is playing with these systems for special effects ?

FURTHER READING
Books
Bradford, Emma, ed., *Roses are Red: Love and Scorn in Victorian Valentines*, Albion Press, 1986.

Briggs, Asa, *Victorian Things*, Penguin Books, 1990.

Dickens, Charles and Wills, W. H., 'Valentine's Day at the Post Office', *Household Words: A Weekly Journal* (30 March 1850), pp. 7–12.

Gillen, Julia, and Hall, Nigel, 'The Edwardian Postcard: A Revolutionary Moment in Rapid Multimodal communication', Paper presented at the British Educational Research Association Annual Conference, Manchester, 2–5 September 2009.

Higgs, Michelle, *Christmas Cards: From the 1840s to the 1940s*, Osprey Publishing, 1999.

Holt, Tonie, and Holt, Valmai, *Till the Boys Come Home: The Picture Postcards of the First World War*, Pen & Sword Military, 2014.

Mancoff, Debra N., *The Arthurian Revival in Victorian Art*, Garland Publishing, 1995.

Walker, Julian and Doyle, Peter, *Trench Talk – Words of the First World War*, The History Press, 2012.

Websites
www.discovery.nationalarchives.gov.uk – Nationwide archival holdings at the National Archives.

www.ephemera-society.org.uk – British Ephemera Society.

www.peevish.co.uk – Online dictionary of UK slang.

Twitter account @eVIIpc Breathing new life into the Edwardian postcard by retweeting messages from between 1901 and 1910

Chapter 5

MARSHALLING MEMORIES: DIARIES

Family historians can often ignore diaries as sources of information about their ancestors. This is perhaps because there is a general view that unless a diary is either crammed full of detail that can be followed up in other sources, or deeply subjective so that it gives an indication of the emotional life of an ancestor, it will be of little research value. In fact many diaries found amongst family papers display neither of these attributes. Many simply consist of a sparsity of facts repeated over and over again. But even where this is the case, a diary can in fact yield a great deal more about an ancestor and his times that you might at first suppose.

If not found amongst family papers, ancestors' diaries might possibly be found in an archive. You can search for these, as for any material possibly relating to your ancestors, at the Discovery section of the National Archives website, www.discovery.national archives.gov.uk. One or two regional archives also have special collections of diaries. Wigan Archives and Record Office in Lancashire, for example, is well-known for its collection of approximately 360 diaries many of which were collected and deposited by just one man, Edward Hall, in the early years of the twentieth century. They include travel journals, letter-books, memoirs, notebooks, honeymoon journals, musical diaries, scrapbooks and logs of voyages. The writers are from diverse backgrounds including nurses, colliery apprentices, merchants, reverends, schoolboys, soldiers, authors, architects and singers, and the diaries date from the eighteenth to the mid-twentieth centuries. They can be searched online either via the National Archives (as above) or through the Wigan archives website www.archives.wigan.gov.uk.

A number of projects to collect together manuscript diaries, catalogue them and make the catalogues available online might also prove useful to you in potentially retrieving the diary of an ancestor. These include: The Great Diary Project (www.thegreatdiaryproject. co.uk) which was set up in 2012 to provide a permanent home for unwanted diaries of any date or kind (and now includes over 2,000 diaries available for inspection by appointment at the Bishopsgate Institute's Reading Room, London); the Mass Observation Archive (www.massobsorg.co.uk) including diaries generated by the original Mass Observation social research organization (1937–early 1950s), and some newer material (at the University of Sussex); and a large collection of personal war diaries written by British and Commonwealth servicemen since 1914 and held by the Imperial War Museum (www. iwm.org.uk).

A few – by no means comprehensive – lists of unpublished manuscript diaries have been produced by scholars over the years. These include John Stuart Batts, *British Manuscript Diaries of the Nineteenth Century: An Annotated Listing*, Rowman and Littlefield, 1976, Heather Creaton, ed., *Checklist of Unpublished Diaries by Londoners and Visitors*, London Record Society Publications, 2003, and William Matthews, *British Diaries: An Annotated Bibliography of British Diaries Written Between 1442 and 1942*, California U.P., 1992.

THE DEVELOPMENT OF DIARIES

Unless your ancestors were famous or aristocratic, you are unlikely to find a personal diary more than 150 years old. Most of the diaries that turn up in family papers are from the nineteenth and early twentieth centuries. It is worth considering, however, that people actually began using the diary form as long ago as the sixteenth century – a time when they started to move away from recording only public events and to recording private ones as well. There was sometimes a religious impetus for this: from the late sixteenth century, Puritans were urging the faithful to keep track of their own spiritual progression and develop a personal relationship with God rather than one mediated by the priests of the Catholic Church.

By the seventeenth century, the practice of keeping 'regular entry records' of one sort or another was becoming more widespread. There are a number of extant travel diaries from this period as well as daily records of military campaigns or of the activities of embassies or professions. Such 'diaries' often contain a mixture of information that was useful to the writer rather than simply a personal record. For example, the manuscript diary for the year 1687 of the MP John Wyndham of Norrington (held in the Somerset County Archive) includes notes on the misbehaviour of soldiers, press gangs, robberies, his estate and dates of Assizes, as well as the personal memoranda that we expect from later diaries.

The philosophical movement known as the Enlightenment (of the seventeenth and eighteenth centuries) brought a new emphasis on human reason and a greater recognition that men could shape and control their own experiences, that they could learn from the past in order to plan for the future. Observation of the world around and organization of one's own thoughts about it became highly valued mental skills. Additionally, in the late eighteenth and early nineteenth centuries, there was a new emphasis on individuality and interiority in published poetry and novels. The diary, with its personal anecdotes and self-realisations, was one popular written medium, in which ordinary people with some education might emulate the sentiments of these other kinds of writing in respect of their own lives.

At the start of the nineteenth century – our period of interest – the idea of diary-writing took a greater hold of the public imagination due to the publishing of some key seventeenth-century manuscript diaries including those by John Evelyn (1620–1706) and Samuel Pepys (1633–1703). Evelyn's diary (William Bray, ed., *Memoirs Illustrative of the Life and Writings of John Evelyn Comprising His Diary from 1604-1705/6 and a Selection of his Private Letters*) was published in 1818; Pepys' diary (Lord Braybrooke, ed., *The Diary of Samuel Pepys Esquire*), was published in 1825. The following century witnessed a huge increase in the number of diaries (written particularly by public figures such as politicians and writers) that were commercially published. Starting with Letts Diaries in 1812, many more companies saw the potential to make money by printing notebooks of a variety of kinds that were largely blank, though divided by date in some way or another. Other people simply appropriated totally blank notebooks for the same purpose adding their own dates.

In the Victorian period, the middle and upper-class women in our families were increasingly likely to keep a record of their daily doings (and more). Like needlework, diary-writing was a consuming task which could conveniently and quietly occupy clean hands on a regular basis. Victorian women's diaries often include detail of the tasks that they undertook on an everyday basis, tasks which were not necessarily challenging on an intellectual level, and therefore did not produce prose of a great literary quality. The regular keeping of diary entries, however, might have helped to reinforce amongst such women (domestically subjugated as they were to their husbands) a sense of self and agency that they might have found difficult to express in any other way.

Very few diaries were written by our working-class ancestors before the Education Act of 1870 made elementary schooling more or less compulsory. It was only in the twentieth century, with the rapid increase in popular literacy, that diary-writing became common to all social classes. Major world events, such as the First and Second World Wars, encouraged many more people to put pen to paper to record their experiences. In the twentieth century, diaries became more secular and were more of a means of psychological self-scrutiny than they had previously been, recording more frequently emotional well-being and self-discovery.

SOME IMPORTANT CONSIDERATIONS

Diaries are one of the most useful kinds of personal writing for telling us something about the way the writer saw him or herself. As academic Anne-Marie Millim says 'by writing a diary, the writer has decided to elevate the trivial to the significant and thus affirm the importance of his or her existence' (Anne-Marie Millim, *The Victorian Diary: Authorship and Emotional Labour*, Ashgate 2013). All diarists, even the most humble, must somewhere along the line be convinced that their own experiences are somehow remarkable. If you have found a family diary, you are somewhat closer to knowing your ancestor than you might be through any other source that we have so far investigated.

When first approaching a diary kept by a family member, remember that he or she must have had a certain amount of spare time, a certain access to materials and writing space, and a certain degree of self-awareness to commit to keeping a daily journal or diary in the first place. To state the obvious: a weaver sharing a cottage with a wife and a dozen children is far less likely to have been able to keep a diary than a gentleman farmer with a retinue of servants!

JULY   7th Month   1916   1916   31 Days   JULY

2 Sun—2nd after Trinity. Ramadân begins

3 Mon

4 Tues

5 Wed—Dividends due

6 Th

7 Fri

8 Sat—☽ First Quarter, 11.55 a.m.

Mem

Pages from one of four manuscript diaries kept by Miss D. M. Field, during the First World War. She was a Voluntary Aid Detachment (VAD) Nurse in France and Italy. (Wikimedia Commons. Original held by the Imperial War Museum)

One great advantage of the diary as a source of family history is that, since your ancestor probably wrote it on the day that the recorded events took place or soon after (and then most probably did not alter the account after that), and since it most likely was written for his or her own consumption and not that of anyone else, it might be a truer version of what actually happened than that in other kinds of written account. Where our ancestors wrote of the same experiences some time after the event and for the eyes of others, as in letters, autobiographies or memoirs, he or she might have forgotten certain aspects of what happened in the past, and might also have had more time to reframe or recraft his or her material. Indeed, there is likely to be a spontaneity and emotional candour about a diary that your ancestor could not render in a letter, card or any other written medium. Another bonus of the diary form is that since the entries are very often habitual and frequent, an accidental bias at one point in the account might be rectified as time goes on. A good diary will give a record of all the different states of mind that someone has passed through over a long period of time, allowing a reasonably balanced picture of your ancestor's character or personality to shine through.

Diaries tend to be predicated on being removed from the public world rather than being part of it. A few diarists did write specifically to record the historic events they were living through (locally or nationally), but on the whole, historical events appear in diaries simply where they impinge upon the writer's private life to any real degree. The juxtaposition of 'real history' with an ancestor's usual diurnal activities can make for some interesting reading: a Londoner who sees Queen Victoria passing in her carriage, or a twentieth-century schoolboy evacuated to avoid the Blitz, for example.

Remember too that keeping a diary required discipline, and that your ancestor might have embarked upon writing one for that reason alone. Moreover, diary-writing was a regular and quantifiable means of practising handwriting or writing technique, and children in the nineteenth-century were often encouraged to keep a diary for just this reason. What better material to consolidate rules learned in spelling and grammar than the material of your own life? More recent twentieth-century ancestors might have thought about their diaries as a form of catharsis at a time of emotional upheaval; they might even have been recommended to write a diary as a means of therapy – a safe place for calm self-reflection after a traumatic experience.

The keeping of a diary was an ongoing process that allowed a writer to exercise (or at least to believe that he or she was exercising) some control over the environment in which he or she was living. In the rapidly changing world of the nineteenth and early twentieth centuries this sense of control might have been essential for mental well-being. Ask yourself what this discipline meant for your ancestor. Did it extend outwards to domestic matters, monetary affairs, romantic or marital life, work or health, for example? Is your ancestor trying to conquer a vice in his diary, or show that he or she is sufficiently pious (many diarists kept a lively record of their attendances at churches and chapels and their prayers, for example)? Diaries gave the powerless some sense that their efforts were worthwhile.

Don't forget that our ancestors could re-read their own words in a diary on an ongoing basis. This was something that was generally not achieved in letter-writing (unless copies of letters were kept in letter-books). In a diary, therefore, your ancestor could set about the business of improving upon him or herself. A diarist could look at past events and assess how he or she had responded to them and what the effect of this had been. A diary might then act as a tool of instruction, allowing the writer/reader to steer clear of past mistakes. Consider how your ancestor acknowledges this business of improvement? Does he or she make direct reference to previous entries? Does he or she make links between entries?

Progress might have been measured in terms of the way the writer dealt with particular challenges, learnt how to control his or her emotions, worked out how to deal with an awkward servant, or a difficult mother-in-law, or established a routine in which church-visiting became less onerous. But improvement in diaries can be measured in terms of the business of writing too. Consider whether your ancestor's diary is 'better' written at its end than at its beginning for example. Does it include longer or shorter entries with more carefully chosen detail? Are the descriptions honed? Is the grammar and spelling more carefully considered? Has the handwriting improved at all? And how does your diarist acknowledge these changes? Look out for words which signal development, change and growth.

CONTENT

In theory, the content of a diary can cover just about anything. Given the wide range of material that your ancestor might have chosen to include about his daily life, it is interesting to speculate on why he or she chose to focus on certain kinds of information above all the other possibilities. At the end of the day, diaries included what the writer felt needed recording for some reason or another. Another useful way of thinking about the content of some diaries is to ask what *special aspects* of the events recorded our ancestor have chosen to comment on. Since no writer can describe every aspect of every situation in equal detail, it is the *choice* and *selection* of facts which should interest the family historian. Why, for example, does this ancestor write so much about the relationship with his daughter, or why did another concentrate so exclusively on ordinary financial transactions?

You might find that your family diary has been written with one particular theme or obsession to the fore. If this happens to be genealogy, as is the case with the diary of C.H. Lapidge 1827 to 1829 (Edward Hall Collection, Wigan Archives and Local Studies Centre), then you should count yourself very lucky. But other diaries turn on a theme in ways which help give a good impression of the kind of life an ancestor lived. The diary of Miss Ethel Clementi (written between 3 January 1901 and 26 February 1902) in the Edward Hall Collection at Wigan Archives, for example, focuses almost exclusively on the writer's musical life, and is catalogued with this description:

> A beautifully written diary which concentrates on the musical education of the diarist. Miss Clementi describes all the concerts she goes to and the programmes are included in the diary. She goes to large concerts at the major halls in London, Saturday popular concerts, local conservatoires and operas. She also describes her lessons in London with Wibeling in great detail. Halfway through the diary, Miss Clementi goes to Dresden to study under Lauterbach and gives the same amount of attention to this period as she did to her time in London. Illustrated with portraits and concert and opera programmes.

Most ordinary diaries, however, are not so narrowly and perfectly focused. Rather they are a relatively haphazard collection of content which might be grouped under the headings of 'self', 'social relations', 'work' and 'values'. It is, a useful exercise, however, to estimate the proportion of ink spent on various different common topics in your ancestor's diary. You should also make a very thorough investigation of all parts of the diary because occasionally important matters of content are jotted in margins or in pre-printed sections to which they don't necessarily relate directly. Some diarists, for example, wrote about health matters in parts of their diaries that were supposedly meant for other purposes such as accounts. This might not have been as random an act of writing as it at first looks. Poor health was inevitably linked to time off work which might have had severe financial consequences. Inevitably, as now, the different aspects of our ancestors' personal lives were very much intertwined and the way information is spatially presented in diaries can sometimes be an indicator of this.

Family Dynamics

The chief point of interest in a diary for the family historian will, of course, be content that is related to family matters. A good example of a rewarding find in this respect is the diary of Mary Anne Denham (1836–71), started in January 1857, of Wooton Common, Arreton, the Isle of Wight (recently made available on the internet at www.victoriandiary. org.uk). This is a diary which, at first glance, appears to hold little of special interest, recording, as it does, innumerable walks to church, tea with friends and the like, but, in fact, there is a whole concatenation of detail (names, dates and relationships) about kinship – so clear that you can almost sketch out the family tree in your mind's eye as you read.

Mary Anne and her sister Julia, daughters of John Denham, a brick-burner maker, lived in a cottage with their mother Ann and grandmother, also named Ann. Within a few pages Mary Anne gives us such genealogically rich entries as Tuesday 27 January, 'Grandma received a letter from Uncle John'; Thursday 29th 'In the afternoon, Uncle Thomas came to see us. After tea we went as far as Quarr with him'; 15 March 'Mother's birthday'; Sunday 22 March, 'Cousin William and his two little daughters came to dine with grandma . . . the two little girls stayed with us'. Tuesday 24 March, 'Mrs Dennis came for Emma Jane but Alice Eliza stayed with us.' This diary is also useful in the number of local births, deaths and burials that it records: Monday 27th April, Mrs Stephens confined with a son; and Wednesday 29 April, 'I forgot to mention that poor old Mrs Rogers departed this life last Sunday April 26th.' This diary thus proves the point that any diary from the locality in which your ancestors lived might provide genealogical information about them.

In other diaries, the family detail is yet more revelatory and honest, providing feelings as well as bare facts where relationships are discussed. A diary by L. M. Simpson, for example, (July 1878–July 1880) and held in Wigan Archives records a meeting with Lucy, the illegitimate daughter of her late husband. The writer records 'The sight of her upset me . . . she is not at all pretty and not like W.'

Weather

A regular account of the weather in a diary should not be considered mere idle page-filling. The mid eighteenth-century diaries of gentleman, William Bulkeley from Brynddu, Llanfechell, on Anglesey, North Wales covered thousands of pages and a 26-year period from 1734 to 1760. Each day the entry started with an account of the weather and the direction of the wind. This was all very useful practical information for a concerned landowner at a time before regular weather forecasts were given in newspapers. When reread, such detail could be an invaluable guide to planting, harvesting and all manner of activity the following year. Bulkeley's diaries are housed at The University College of Bangor, North Wales, and are transcribed and freely available on the internet at www.bulkeleydiaries.bangor.ac.uk/index.html.

Sustenance

Many diarists record what they have eaten and drunk on special occasions, but to recount the items partaken of at each and every meal, is a little unusual. The actor John Pritt Harley, however, kept a diary at the age of 70 in 1858, in which he recorded in great detail what he had eaten and drunk each day. His entry for 6 January 1858, for example includes the following information:

> Dinner at four, roast mutton, potato, boiled plum pudding, brandy, biscuit, cheese, ale, port and sherry. Tea at six, theatre half past six . . . acted in one piece, home half past ten. Supped at eleven, old roast mutton, biscuit, cheese, ale, Brandy and water and cake with Betsy. Bed at one. (Cited in Creaton, ed., *Victorian Diaries*, p 49)

And this level of detail goes on day after day. Perhaps it is little wonder that on 20 August of that year Harley collapsed on the stage from a paralytic stroke and died a couple of days later. More usually, an ancestor's record of what he or she has eaten or drunk can be linked to his or her economic situation, or health, with improvements in nutrition being tied to better health and better (use of) resources.

Work

Diarists used diaries to keep track of work situations. A full diary account of work in the coal mines is given, for example, in the diary of R. R. Maddison, colliery apprentice, Chester-le-Street, Durham (Wigan Archive). Maddison was an apprentice to Mr Easton, viewer and part owner of Pelton and Ouston collieries. The diary includes a great deal of information about his work, the mines, working conditions and pay. A work diary of a rather more spartan but no less interesting sort is that of another Lancashire miner, Jack Daniels (1900–67), who kept a single little black notebook – and that only three-quarters filled – of the period 1925 to 1967 (author's collection). The diary starts in 1925, when Jack would have been 25. On leaving school, he took up employment as a miner or a 'hewer' working underground at the coalface. Jack used the notebook as a very sporadic diary using the first pages as a record of his employment in different local pits between 1925 and 1927.

Lancashire miner, Jack Daniels (1900–67), sometime diary-writer and inspirational poet. (With thanks to Mr Colin Daniels)

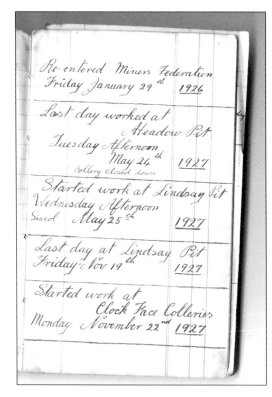

Some diarists made only one entry every few months or years. This one by Lancashire collier Jack Daniels records his employment at different mines around the Wigan area in the 1920s. (With thanks to Mr Colin Daniels)

- Started work at Pearson and Knowles Collieries, August 24th 1925.
- Last day worked at Pearson and Knowles, Friday January 15th 1926.
- Started work at Meadow Pit, Tuesday January 19th 1926.
- Last day worked at Meadow Pit Tuesday afternoon May 24th 1927. Colliery closed down.
- Started work at Lindsay Pit Wednesday afternoon May 25th, 1927.
- Last day at Lindsay Pit Friday Nov 19th 1927.
- Started work at Clock Face Collieries Monday November 22nd 1927.

Money

Our ancestors often recorded a great deal of information about financial transactions of one sort or another in their diaries. This might include an account of wages, the price of school fees, the price of the weekly food budget, or even rises and falls in the prices of stocks and shares. Other diaries will have special pre-printed sections given over to accounts. Again, these entries should not merely be taken at face value. Constant reference to income and outgoings might be evidence of a serious personal struggle against material deprivation on the part of your ancestor.

Health

Some diarists kept an ongoing checklist of health problem, with injuries incurred in the workplace and dental matters appearing with the greatest frequency. Miner Jack Daniels (mentioned above) kept a regular check of his health in his diary, from injuries incurred in the pit to more serious matters.

November 3rd 1934: Accident to leg and back. Night turn; 19th March 1948: My own top and bottom teeth extracted (Friday morning) 20 teeth; Wed 9th 1947: Wigan Infirmary for Medical exam and X-ray; Aug 31st 1953 had X-ray on chest at Wigan Infirmary. Silicosis Pneumoconiosis.

Reviewing such medical information, the diarist, like the family historian at some point in the distant future, might have come to understand how a particular medical condition had developed from a series of more minor conditions. And Jack Daniels also used his diary to record the health matters of other family members:

> Saturday December 16th: Son Raymond admitted into Whelley Sanatorium with diphtheria. Discharged on Friday morning Feb 16th 1940; Monday evening Sept 15th 1941: Son Colin run over by car. Sustained fractured thigh and shock, taken to Royal Albert Edward Infirmary, Wigan. Discharged Sat Oct 25th 1941.

Reading/Cultural Experiences

Diaries very frequently record what the writer has read, watched or listened to. In fact, diaries are more likely to comment on everyday reading habits than autobiographies. Don't assume, however, that such information automatically includes absolutely every cultural experience to which your ancestor was exposed. He or she will probably only have recorded books, plays, music and the like which have had a profound impact on his or her thoughts or actions. Thus, a diarist might comment on a favourite novel but not on the fact that he read *The Times* every morning. Additionally, a writer might not mention the 'low publications' that he or she has read, popular newspapers, comics, magazines, or papers associated with controversial political views such as the Communist-leaning *Morning Star*, for example. Alternatively, he or she might claim to have read highbrow books when in fact those texts were never read.

Twentieth-century diaries might record plays watched, films seen, wireless (radio) programmes listened to, or television programmes watched. Again, some of these records need to be taken with a pinch of salt – they often represent idealised lists of what the writer thought he or she should have experienced. As with all other recorded aspects of their lives, your ancestor might simply be trying to create a 'perfect' view of themselves in their records of cultural engagement.

Relationships and Sex

Romantic associations and even sexual activity might form part of your ancestor's diary account. The following example is so striking that it is included here despite the fact that it comes from a somewhat earlier historical period than is generally covered by this book. Edmund Harrold was born in 1678 and worked for probably his whole life in Manchester as a barber surgeon and wigmaker, selling books to make some extra cash on the side. Between 1712 and 1715 (when he was between 34 and 37 years old) he kept a diary recording aspects of his day-to-day working and domestic life and his problems with alcohol (Craig Horner, ed., *The Diary of Edmund Harrold: Wigmaker of Manchester 1712-1715*, Routledge, 2008). Notably, he recorded the frequency and variety of the marital sex he had. When the diary was first published in 1867 the references to sex were cut out so as not to shock a Victorian audience, but the recent edition (2008) is uncensored. And as the new editor puts it: 'There is no other known published plebeian diary which makes such candid reference to sexual activity.'

Harrold records the number of times he had intercourse with (or, as he puts it 'did' or 'enjoyed') his wife on 'the new corded bed' and 'on the roof bed' and notes the positions they adopted (whether 'old fashion' or 'new fashion'). Harrold did not record the sex for salacious reasons, rather he saw marital intercourse as a religious duty necessary for procreation, and as a sensible means of containing his lust. His activities in the bedchamber produced nine children in all, seven of whom died young.

Pre-printed parts of the diary

Don't forget to look carefully at the pre-printed parts of your ancestor's diary as well as the handwritten daily entries. Diaries that were printed as such – as opposed to ordinary notebooks that simply became diaries – were often customised with information, special sections, tables and (later in the nineteenth century) advertisements, that suggest the kind of person who might have made use of them. Thus a schoolboy diary aimed at the middle-classes of the interwar period might have included French and German verbs, logarithms and information about the metric system, scientific tables, information about careers in the professions, first aid, athletic records, pictures of aeroplane acrobatics and useful foreign phrases. Some pre-printed parts of diaries had blank sections for the writer to personalise with sections for accounts, school timetables, presents received, sporting scores and books read. Whether or not your ancestor made use of these sections, the diary can point to the ways in which society viewed people in the same social category at the time. Interwar schoolboys were supposed to have an interest in international affairs, new technical inventions and team sports, for example.

STYLE

It is impossible to cover all of the many variations in written style that your ancestor's diary might involve. Here, however, are some useful matters to consider.

Audience

Diaries were not always totally private and, when looking at any diary, you should always ask yourself to whom, if to anyone, your ancestor might have given access. Some writers addressed their diaries as persons, as if they were writing a letter to an imaginary friend and in these cases, some of the characteristics we have discussed about letter-writing (see Chapter 2) come into play. Other diaries were genuinely written with another reader in mind. Dorothy Wordsworth (1771–1885), for example, wrote her diary, at least partly, as notes for her brother, the poet William (1770–1850). Other people wrote for their parents, their children or their friends. Some nineteenth-century diarists would share their record with visiting family members and friends by reading it aloud or using it as an aide-memoire when recounting an event from the past. Yet other nineteenth-century diaries were written expressly with publication in mind and are, therefore, far more carefully crafted than purely personal journals would have been.

Apologies

As we have said earlier in this book, non-professional writers frequently apologized for their writing, the condition of their pen, their tardiness in replying to a letter, the uninteresting things that they felt they had to say, but with a diary there is often another layer of apology. Your ancestor might moan that he has not kept his diary as regularly, accurately or as fully as he should. These were general themes, common angsts which should, on the whole, be taken with a pinch of salt, along with the confessions and justifications that accompany them. It is interesting to see how an ancestor deals with the particular discipline of writing a diary. Try to work out at what intervals he or she normally wrote in his or her diary. What reasons does he or she give for writing an entry late? Does he or she ever acknowledge that some of the entries constitute 'catching up'?

Gaps and Euphemisms

Sometimes the gaps in diaries remain unfilled and you should think about why this might have been the case since these lapses might be related to important moments in your family history when the writer was sick, confined with a baby, when he or she had been bereaved, was very ill or was away travelling. Our ancestors, even in personal diaries can also be surprisingly shy about some matters. Pregnancy, for instance, is rarely mentioned and childbirth itself is usually skirted over. Maria Cust was a clergyman's daughter married to a barrister in the Indian Civil service. After her marriage in 1856, she quickly became pregnant, but her diary records only: 'March 18th 1857: Went in the Evening to the Princess Theatre to see Richard 2nd which is splendidly got up, but being the second piece it lasts so late that we could not stay. I was unlucky enough to be so faint as to have to retire into fresh air and, in so doing, lost one of my Florentine bracelets.' Then on 25 March: 'Riding put a stop to, much to my regret, but I suppose it is all for the best.' There is no direct reference to the impending birth until 7 October, when Maria records, 'Symptoms showed themselves which prevented my going down to breakfast.' And then the following day an entry which is – for the times – surprisingly open. 'October 18th Sunday 8.30am: A slight pain caused a note by fly to be dispatched posthaste to Dr Bullar. The pains increased in frequency and severity. Dr B arrived at 11.40 & at 12.20 our little one was brought into the world and cried out loud' (Creaton, ed., *Victorian Diaries*, pp. 41–2).

Short and Long Entries

The length of your ancestor's diary entries might be significant. One word might tell an entire story. The diary of a young professional in the mid twentieth-century recorded just two letters for an entry on 14 February 1961: 'P.M.' (author's collection). The acronym stood for the vitally important piece of information that he had (or was going to) 'propose marriage'. Perhaps the brevity of the entry shows that he was afraid of rejection. In other diaries, entries are characteristically long, giving scope for very well-developed responses to situations which the writer could not possibly put down in other written forms such as a letter. This is one of the real plus points of the diary as a family history resource.

Opposite Impulses

For other aspects of a diarist's style it might be useful to think in terms of opposites. Ask yourself if your ancestor's diary is first and foremost factual or opinionated? Is it rational or emotional? Are the entries made out of habit or when inspiration strikes? Do they conceal your ancestor's true self in some way or reveal it? Does your ancestor seek to efface himself or to assert himself? Is the diary confessional or professional? Commonsensical or neurotic? Is it scientifically precise in its recording of detail, or does it seem quite literary in style, as if your ancestor is imaging him or herself as the chief protagonist in a developing work of fiction?

Code

Our ancestors sometimes wrote their diaries in code to conceal socially unacceptable matters such as love affairs, unplanned pregnancies or financial dealings. In a society where private space was at a premium, especially for women, writing in code was an obvious method of preserving secrecy. A code can be difficult to crack and might perhaps employ substitution of letters, a cipher, so-called 'railfence transposition' or 'pinprick encryption'.

Probably the most notorious case of a diary written in code by a woman was that of Anne Lister (1791–1840) a wealthy and unmarried landowner who inherited Shibden Hall in West Yorkshire from her uncle in 1826 (Anne Lister and Helena Whitbread, *I Know My Own Heart: The Diaries of Anne Lister, 1791-1840*, Virago, 2000). Throughout her life Lister kept diaries which chronicled the details of her everyday life, including her lesbian relationships, her financial concerns, her industrial activities and her work improving Shibden Hall. The diaries contain more than 4,000,000 words and about a sixth of them were written in code – a combination of algebra and Ancient Greek – to conceal details of her homosexual and romantic relationships. The code was eventually deciphered in the 1930s.

The famous children's writer and illustrator Beatrix Potter wrote a coded diary between 1881 and 1897, which involved a substitution of letters. The code was cracked by Leslie Linder, a lifelong collector of

Beatrix Potter artefacts, on Easter Monday 1958, twenty years after Potter's death. Why exactly Potter felt the need to put her diaries into code remains something of a mystery but this decoded extract reveals how deeply personal her entries were: 'Tuesday 17 November, 1890: I remember I used to half believe and wholly play with fairies when I was a child. What heaven can be more real than to retain the spirit-world of childhood, tempered and balanced by knowledge and common-sense, to fear no longer the terror that flieth by night, yet to feel truly and understand a little, a very little of the story of life' (Beatrix Potter and Leslie Linder, *The Journal of Beatrix Potter from 1881-1897*, Kindle edition, 2012).

Of course, the reason your ancestor wrote in code might have been far more dramatic. He or she was perhaps writing in circumstances that prevented open expression (as a prisoner-of-war, for example, or as a victim of some kind of religious or political persecution). In the Second World War, RAF man Ronald Hill was attached to the Far East Command in Kai Tak, Hong Kong. The Japanese attacked on 8 December 1941 and after surrendering, Hill was put into a prisoner-of-war camp. A diary only came to light in 1985, after Hill's death, when his wife Pamela was desperate to learn of the dangerous times that he had never felt able to discuss with her. After several historians had unsuccessfully attempted to decode the diary, it was given to Philip Ashton, a mathematician at Surrey University in 1996. Six months' experimentation later, Ashton remembered reading the full names of the two lovers, Ronald and Pamela, at the bottom of a page in the diary and realised that they were the clue to an incredibly complex cipher. An extract from Hill's diary shows why perhaps he went to such great lengths to keep it secret.

26 December, 1941: Two officers decide to drive me back in a Ford Ten. They don't use any lights and we have several narrow escapes from hitting lamp posts. Suddenly I see we are heading for one of the islands in the middle of the road and shout a warning. Too late and there's a terrific crash and we finish up on our backs. By now I am fed up so, bowing politely, I leave them and walk the two miles to China Command (Andro Linklater, *The Code of Love: A True Story*, Phoenix, 2001).

Typicality

Remember that diaries from the past (coded or otherwise) give a personal point of view but one that will probably closely resemble others written at the same time or place by people of the same social class and gender. What your ancestor chose to write was not simply an outpouring of his or her inner soul but also an expression of what he or she thought was appropriate or satisfying to express within his or her community at that time. Thus, when you are reading a diary you will learn not merely about your ancestor as an individual but also about your ancestor as a member of a particular section of society.

QUESTIONS TO ASK OF YOUR ANCESTOR'S DIARY

1. What can the pre-printed parts of the diary tell you about your ancestor (age, gender, social class, religion, geographical location, interests and hobbies)?
2. Do you get any impression of how the diary was kept (every day, every week retrospectively, haphazardly)?
3. How introspective is the diary? What is the proportion of intimate personal reflection to objective fact?
4. What purposes did the diary fulfil (spiritual, self-help, educational, practical record, source material for other sorts of writing)?
5. What leads have you obtained into the life of your family that can be followed up by further research (names of relatives, places of employment, standard of living)?
6. Does the writer allude to any historical or public happenings? How can you find out more about these?
7. How would you describe the writer's style (brief, wordy, factual, emotional, literary)? Why does the writer write in this way, do you think?
8. How do you account for any gaps in the diary (periods of unemployment, sickness, childbirth, bereavement, absences for other reasons)?
9. Who was the likely audience for this diary do you think?
10. Is all or any part of the diary written in code? Why might this have been? Who might have been able to decipher the code?

FURTHER READING

Books

Blodgett, Harriet, *Centuries of Female Days: Englishwomen's Private Diaries*, Rutgers U.P., 1967.

Creaton, Heather, *Victorian Diaries: The Daily Lives of Victorian Men and Women*, Mitchell Beazley, 2001.

Cullwick, Hannah, *The Diaries of Hannah Cullwick, Victorian Maidservant*, Rutgers U.P., 1984.

Horner, Craig, ed., *The Diary of Edmund Harrold: Wigmaker of Manchester 1712-1715*, Routledge, 2008.

Huff, Cynthia, *British Women's Diaries: A Descriptive Bibliography of Selected Nineteenth-Century Women's Diaries*, AMS Press, 1985.

Lister, Anne, and Whitbread, Helena, *I Know My Own Heart: The Diaries of Anne Lister, 1791-1840*, Virago, 2000.

Linklater, Andro, *The Code of Love: A True Story*, Phoenix, 2001.

Millim, Anne-Marie, *The Victorian Diary: Authorship and Emotional Labour*, Ashgate, 2013.

Potter, Beatrix, and Linder, Leslie, *The Journal of Beatrix Potter from 1881-1897*, Kindle edition, 2012.

Steinitz, Rebecca, *Time, Space and Gender in the Nineteenth-Century British Diary*, Palgrave Macmillan, 2011.

Websites

www.bulkeleydiaries.bangor.ac.uk/index.html – The diaries of William Bulkeley (1734–60).

www.discovery.nationalarchives.gov.uk – National Archives Catalogue.

www.iwm.org.uk – Imperial War Museum which houses a large collection of personal war diaries written by British and Commonwealth servicemen

www.massobsorg.co.uk – Papers of the Mass Observation social research organization (1937- early 1950s), and some newer material (at the University of Sussex)

www.thegreatdiaryproject.co.uk – The Great Diary Project.

Chapter 6

'HUMBLE REMINDERS': APPOINTMENT DIARIES AND BIRTHDAY BOOKS

Our ancestors from the Victorian period onwards were well aware of the rapid modernization going on all around them. Chief amongst the changes was the way in which time was becoming increasingly commodified. Many workers no longer rose at sunrise and laboured until the sun went down but were employed to work in shifts of a set duration at any point of the day or night. The buzz and hum of industrial life, powered by the unremitting punctuality of the developing railway system, created new time-related anxieties for our ancestors: the fear of being left behind, of not completing things, of being unable to anticipate what came next. In the new world, future experience could not be estimated as easily as it had been in previous centuries. It would not necessarily follow the time-honoured cycle of the seasons (the unchanging routine of monthly market days, for example), as it had done for generations. Now, experiences (following constantly unpredictable commercial factors) could be unexpected, bundled closely together one week or spread out over several weeks and months in unguessable patterns.

Into this arena entered a new kind of printed writing tool – the appointment diary (also known as a 'remembrancer,' a 'memoranda book, an 'almanac', 'agenda' or 'calendar'). These pocket or desk-sized notebooks were one of the chief mechanisms by which our ancestors could achieve – or at least feel that they could achieve – a modicum of control over their immediate futures. Unconcerned with the writer's intimate emotional life, these notebooks were more mundane and practical. They contained, on the whole, only factual jottings (entries might amount to no more than a few words or, at most, a few lines) and their primary purpose was to marshal time. An appointment diary allowed people to make sense of the new quivering, fast-flowing river of experience. Like the pocket watch, increasingly worn by more and more of our ancestors in the Victorian period, it became a portable timepiece that gave people the sense – if not the reality – that they were in charge of their own destinies.

Unfortunately, appointment diaries by ordinary people are less likely to be found amongst family papers than other sources. The keepers of appointment diaries themselves often scored out entries after dates had passed, rendering the diary no longer of any interest to a later reader, or destroyed them entirely at the end of a year, believing that they were no longer of any value. Sometimes, appointment diaries are the first items to be thrown out when a descendant is checking through the papers of a deceased relative. On the other hand, where deceased family members have written little else, appointment diaries might have been kept for sentimental reasons. Unfortunately, unless they are pretty well maintained and part of a much larger estate of papers (or unless they are the property of someone famous), the very size of appointment diaries has often ruled them out of preservation in archives.

APPOINTMENT DIARIES AND THEIR KEEPERS
Our ancestors in urban areas who had numerous business and social reasons to organize their time were the most likely buyers and users of appointment diaries. There was a general perception that time continued to stand still in rural areas, but in fact, many farmers and other rural workers kept diaries too. The appointment diary allowed time to be clearly imagined in small slices (mornings, afternoons and evenings, for example). Some diaries, for professionals, even marked in slots of half or even a quarter of an hour. Time was now much more closely allied to the making of money and as such it had to be tracked much more carefully if one was to make a successful path through the world.

The first British publisher to seize upon the possibilities of the new industrial view of time was John Letts who, in 1796, established a stationery business in the arcades of London's Royal Exchange. The first books met the needs of traders and merchants for keeping control of the movement of their stock. The popularity of Letts' diaries for time-management purposes was incredible. As one commentator has put it: 'In 1812, the British publishing company Letts produced only one version of the diary, by 1836, they offered 28 different varieties and by 1862, there were 55' (Rebecca Steinitz, *Time, Space and Gender in the Nineteenth-Century British Diary*, Palgrave Macmillan, 2011, p. 3). Letts' and other companies' appointment diaries became ever more ingenious as the nineteenth century progressed, coming to include a variety of printed information such as poems, signs of the planets and zodiac, lists of eclipses, holidays and feast days, puzzles and charades, and the words to new songs. There were also sections for the writer to fill in, including tables in which household expenses could be recorded. Towards the end of the nineteenth century, the printed 'extras' in diaries started to take a commercial turn and included advertisements for purchasable goods.

Though appointment diaries are mentioned in newspaper reports from early in the nineteenth century, there are far more references around 1869–70 than at any other time, suggesting that this is when many more such books were first produced. It is indeed probable that more diaries of this kind were sold and kept in the nineteenth century than copies of the more introspective and personal diary that were the subject of the previous chapter. References in the press to appointment diaries express pleasure at the ingenuity of their design and an understanding that they might revolutionize the way people led their lives:

> *Letts' Appointment Diary* is a kind of moral disciplinarian. There is a very old saying that 'Punctuality is the hinge of business,' which nobody denied, but somehow the hinge was apt to get dreadfully rusty. Railways wrought a great reform in this respect ... [They have] certainly oiled the wheels of punctuality to a large extent and here comes Mr Letts to supplement the process and help us to maintain the virtue through all our engagements. An excellent compact little book, which will enable us, if duly attended to, to do towards all as we would that all should do towards ourselves, in the economizing of time (*The Northampton Mercury*, Saturday 8 January 1870).

The kind and range of appointment book(s) that turn up in an ancestor's papers might tell you something about his or her class status.

On 10 December 1870, *The Windsor and Eton Express* advertised the stock of diaries, almanacs and pocket books of R. Oxley, Printer and Stationer (presumably so that people might consider buying one for Christmas in time for the New Year) on a sliding scale of elegance and price that was directly related to the class status of the potential buyer. Indeed this list of different types of diary buyer is as good an introduction as any to the class system of Britain in the last three decades of the nineteenth century.

Letts's, Renshaw's and Harwood's

Ladies, are Nos 10, 12, 18, 20, 22, in leather, silk and velvet.

NOBILITY AND GENTRY Nos 8, 9, 10, 12, and 12 enlarged in morocco and russia, spring lock cases or wallets.

CLERGYMEN Nos 9, 10, 12, 12 enlarged, 14, 14 enlarged and the 'Tablet'.

PHYSICIANS AND THE MEDICAL PROFESSION, Nos 1, 28 and 9, 10, 12, Medical and Monthly Editions Nos 14m, 17m, 21m 23m.

LAWYERS AND THE LEGAL PROFESSION Nos, 1, 2, 8, and 9 and Appointment.

LECTURERS AND PROFESSORS AND TEACHERS, The Appointment Diary.

THE ARMY AND NAVY Nos 8, 9, 10, 11, in morocco and russia lock cases.

MERCHANTS, BANKERS, ENGINEERS AND GENTLEMEN IN OFFICIAL CAPACITIES Nos 51, 52, and 53; 1, 2, and 3; 6 and 7, 8, 9, 10, 11, and the Dr. and Cr. Diaries 53b, 55B 3B 4B 5B 7B, 11B.

TRADESMEN Nos 4, 5, 11, 13, 15 &c, the Dr. and Cr. And Rough editions.

FARMERS AND AGRICULTRURALISTS Nos 4, 5, 11, 13, the scribbling diaries and cheap Pocket Series.

WAREHOUSEMEN, MECHANICS, &c Nos 17, 21, 23, the 1s 6d, 1s 9d., and the Scribbling Diaries.

Missing from the list are really only the lowest-paid workers, factory hands, domestic servants, miners and the like. These were people whose time, it was assumed, was managed by others and who had little need for the discipline of an appointment diary.

By the end of the nineteenth century then, appointment diaries were available to suit ancestors in many different sorts of occupation. Some combined a financial function, recording (in one way or another) the small amounts of money going in and out of a household or business together with the relevant dates. As the titles of some of these diaries (chosen randomly from Victorian newspaper advertisements) indicate, it seemed that any activity could be divided into time categories and productive units:

A *Gardener's Daily Register of Wind, Weather, Barometer etc with extra space for a weekly report of vegetables and fruit*;
A *Household Expenses Book*;
A *Washing Book for Ladies, Gentlemen, or Families*;
A *Pupils Progress Book for the Use of Tutors*;
A *Correspondence Register* (to note down letters received and and written);
A *Postal Delivery Book*;
A *Game Register* (to note down animals shot).

The types of appointment mentioned in an appointment diary will give you an idea of the way society operated at certain historical moments. As the nineteenth century moved on into the twentieth, our ancestors will have found that there were more appointments to be kept. Businessmen noted down non-personal appointments such as calls from suppliers and buyers, hirings and firings, meetings, trips overseas and to other companies. Socially-active ancestors marked in lectures or concerts that they wished to attend in the evenings or at weekends, and outings to the theatre or cinema. You are unlikely to find doctors' appointments in old appointment books. Until the 1960s and 1970s, our ancestors will simply have turned up and queued to see the medical profession, or asked them to visit the house, as and when the need arose.

Middle-class women as well as men recorded appointments even if they weren't in paid employment. There were an increasing number of services to be organized in the domestic environment including the visits of tradespeople and dressmakers, the term dates of schools, interviews with prospective domestic servants and nannies, the services of chimney sweeps, piano tuners and gaslight repairers. Bear in mind also that women were often the keepers of the diary for whole families, marking in the birthdays and anniversaries not only of their own brood but also of acquaintances of other family members, and organizing the forthcoming visits of friends and relations.

You should consider also those parts of a well-kept appointment diary which record no engagements at all. With increased and regulated leisure times for many members of communities, our ancestors might eagerly have blanked out the weeks that they were off work on holiday, for example.

WHAT CAN YOU FIND OUT FROM AN APPOINTMENT DIARY?

When analysing an ancestor's appointment diary, it might be useful to have with you a timeline of the year in question, a local newspaper for that year, and a trade directory for the area in question. The timeline will tell you which national and international events were going on at the time, regional and local newspapers will tell you about local events, and the directory might be able to alert you to the names of the businesses or other local people with which your ancestor had appointments. Bear in mind that appointment books might provide useful corroboration of information for evidence that you have acquired about your ancestor from other sources such as letters, fuller diaries, and even registrations of birth, marriage and death records.

Gauging the Public Stature of an Individual

By the first decades of the twentieth century, having a 'full diary' was a mark of social stature and prominence. It was not, of course, quite the same thing as leading a 'full life'. If your ancestor had 'a full diary', however, it suggests that he or she might have exuded an aura of method, purpose and self-control. Take time to work out which appointments in the diary came at the behest of others and which were self-arranged. On 21 Tuesday 1924, *The Daily Mail* recorded the funeral of the late Dr W. H. Coates of South Holderness, Hull. The Doctor was, we are told, the personality of the area, his many friends lined the route of the cortege from the house to the grave, and the funeral itself was attended by some hundreds of people 'of high esteem'. It hardly needed adding that the doctor's appointment diary had been 'a crowded one'.

Tracing Geographical/Chronological Movement

An appointment diary can tell you where your ancestor was at certain times, allowing you to draw up a chronology of his or her movements when no other evidence exists. However, bear in mind the appointment diaries are never 100 per cent accurate and must be used as a guide only. Very often appointments made in the diary will not have been kept, or engagements will have been made that simply didn't find their way into the diary.

Revealing Physical and Mental States

Always be alert to clues that might help you understand an ancestor's state of mind. The twentieth-century writer Virginia Woolf kept appointment diaries between 1930 and 1941 which are now held by the University of Sussex (www.sussex.ac.uk/broadcast/read/17135). They are full of entries that are scored through and replaced with the word, 'Bed'. These, it is believed, indicate the periods when she was suffering from a depressive illness. Woolf's debilitation is known from many other sources but the appointment diaries alert us to the fact that it obviously, at times, prevented her from carrying out her normal everyday life, and they thus make clear the true depth of her depression and its recurrent nature.

Unearthing Secrets

Sometimes the eliptical nature of an appointment diary can point to secret aspects of your ancestor's life. Writer Charles Dickens (1812–70) kept appointment diaries which it is believed he destroyed at the end of every year. One such diary, however, went missing – it was probably stolen – in 1867 whilst he was on a speaking tour of America. The diary turned up again in 1943, and was found to reveal many mysterious entries recording appointments with 'N'. It is now believed that this abbreviation refers to the young actress Ellen (Nelly) Ternan (1839–1914), reputed to be Dickens' lover for many years. When Dickens set her up in a house in 1867, the abbreviation 'N' changed to 'Sl' (for Slough where she was now living). This matter is discussed further in Felix Aylmer, ed., *Dickens Incognito*, Rupert Hart-Davis, 1959.

Revealing an Ancestor's Character and Values

The keeping of a proper appointment diary increasingly became something upon which people judged themselves and by which they were judged by others. On 12 December 1932, an article in *The Citizen* entitled 'My Diary Reminder for 1933', by 'A Practical Woman' gave some suggestions about what a worthy woman reader might enter into her appointment diary in preparation for the year to come. The article suggested that 'one of the last pious rites of the closing year' should be to spend an hour entering important dates for the new year into your appointment diary: 'that hour or less, will save you later endless anxieties, reprimands, misunderstandings and reprisals.' The article recommends the kinds of domestic appointments that ought to be entered in a diary (showing how housewifery could be run along the lines of a small business in some families) and, as such, gives a striking insight into the lives and concerns of a lower-middle class housewife of the interwar period. It is, therefore, worth quoting here virtually in full:

Sentiment First

To take the sentimental side of things first, you will, of course, enter in the family birthdays which it is up to you to observe. But even more touching is it to remember here and there a marriage anniversary.

To recollect the anniversary of a marriage usually goes very well with a couple still devoted. Unexpectedly . . . to send a card or a telephone message on the anniversary of some happy introduction stirs a chord. If you know any such dates, enter 'em all up.

But the diary is for the practical as well as for the sentimental; Somewhere you must have made a note as to the date when the boiler was last cleaned out. If so, make a rough calculation as to the date when it is entitled to expect a repetition of the attention, and enter that in also. If you don't, you'll probably forget all about it, and the boiler may burst.

Remember Sweeps

Sweeps must be called in from time to time, but it seems as if they had only just called. Try to remember when they last paid you a visit, and enter up the date when you should summon another. If you don't, you may forget, and the chimney may catch fire.

The six-monthly visit to the dentist is more often honoured in the breach than in the observance. But it is important, so enter up the respective dates for self and family.

If you happen to be one of the mothers who always manage to be late in ordering the children's spring and winter outfits, you may as well write a reminder as to these under the March and September headings.

I daresay you will think of quite a lot of other and personal matters on your own account . . .

This article shows that by the third decade of the twentieth century, the appointment diary had gone beyond being simply a method of time-management and was now a means by which our ancestors could define themselves in the eyes of others. The 'practical' woman writer of this article states at the beginning that 'I feel that I rather sail under false colours as a woman of courtesy, of nice feeling, and, above all, of a methodical turn.' She sees the positive illusion that she has created of herself by the judicious use of her appointment diary and what is more, she heartily recommends it to others, 'You will, I am sure, agree with me that a well-appointed diary is a real necessity for every woman who wishes to deserve a character for manners and method.'

BIRTHDAY BOOKS

A particularly useful variation on the appointment diary for the family historian is the Birthday Book. These small, intricately designed and often beautifully-illustrated books, bound in leather or red morocco; with gilt edges and ornamental printed endpapers were popular among the middle and upper classes in late Victorian times and were very often kept by the senior women in the family. Such books often included handwritten entries of the birthdays of large numbers of friends and family recorded over a long period of time. They might be passed down through the generations, and in some cases, might still have been in use a century after they were first purchased. Bear in mind that, as Birthday Books were reasonably expensive, they were often themselves given as gifts from one family member to another (usually for a birthday or at Christmas).

It's worth bearing in mind that by the 1880s and 1890s, Birthday Books were available in a wide choice of formats and the particular type

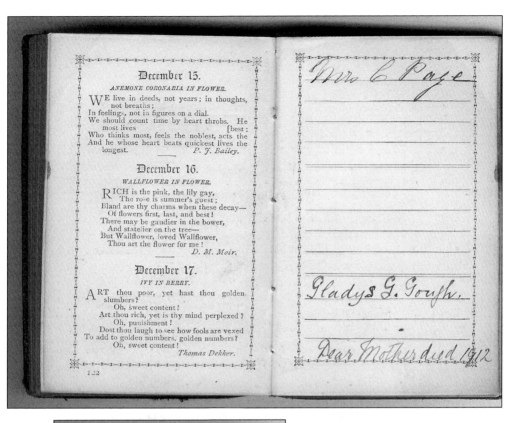

December 15.

ANEMONE CORONARIA IN FLOWER.

WE live in deeds, not years; in thoughts, not breaths;
In feelings, not in figures on a dial.
We should count time by heart throbs. He most lives   [best:
Who thinks most, feels the noblest, acts the
And he whose heart beats quickest lives the longest.
                                        P. J. Bailey.

December 16.

WALLFLOWER IN FLOWER.

RICH is the pink, the lily gay,
    The rose is summer's guest;
Bland are thy charms when these decay—
Of flowers first, last, and best!
There may be gaudier in the bower,
And statelier on the tree—
But Wallflower, loved Wallflower,
Thou art the flower for me!
                                        D. M. Moir.

December 17.

IVY IN BERRY.

ART thou poor, yet hast thou golden slumbers?
    Oh, sweet content!
Art thou rich, yet is thy mind perplexed?
    Oh, punishment!
Dost thou laugh to see how fools are vexed
To add to golden numbers, golden numbers?
    Oh, sweet content!
                                        Thomas Dekker.

122

Mrs C Page

Gladys G. Tough.

Dear Mother died 1912

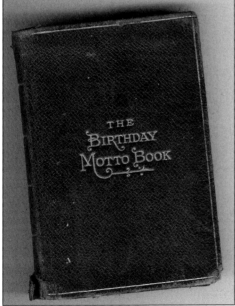

The Birthday Motto Book. *Birthday books were actually used as 'remembrancers' for all sorts of family occasions including births, baptisms, marriages, deaths and burials. (Anon,* The Birthday Motto Book and Calendar of Nature, *Frederick Warne and Co., 1871)*

of book owned by your ancestor may well say something about his (or more likely her) religious interests, literary tastes or other predilections. At the very least, it will tell you something about the times in which he or she lived.

For instance, for devout families, there were a number of Birthday Books on the market with religious themes. A typical one was Jane Borthwick's *The Bible Birthday Book* published in 1885 which gave a 'choice selection of [Biblical] texts for every day in the year'. And other denominations were not neglected: *The Catholic Birthday Book* of 1890 included the name of a saint and a passage from a theological writer for each day. You may also find evidence of the religious persuasion of your ancestors in the names of the publishers of their Birthday Books. For instance, *The Young People's Birthday Text Book (Texts and Verses)* was printed in Norwich by the Wesleyan Methodist Sunday School Union, in 1889. On the other hand, *Ogilvie's Astrological Birthday Book* (1916), might have been a gift for a rather more agnostic kind of ancestor. Rather than scriptural passages, this little book included 'observations of the effect upon character . . . of the aspect of the heavenly bodies at the moment of birth'.

Birthday Books were also chosen as gifts with other aspects of the recipients' character in mind. A large number promoted nineteenth-century novelists and poets and perhaps say less about the individual reading tastes of the owners of the books than about the cultural snobbery of the times. These books included: *The Robert Browning Birthday Book* (1896); *The Byron Birthday Book* (1879); *The Charles Dickens Birthday Book* (1882); and *The Tennyson Birthday Book* (1900) among many others. Scottish publishers celebrated the nation's own literary talent with birthday books entitled, for example, *Auld Acquaintance: A Birthday Book of the wise and tender words of Robbie Burns* (compiled by James B. Begg, a grandnephew of Burns) published by the Edinburgh publisher William P. Nimmo in 1883 and *The Scott Birthday Book*, which contained quotations from the works of Sir Walter Scott (1879).

Other Birthday Books were more light-hearted and eclectic in pre-printed content, *The Birthday Book of Riddles and Guesses* by Mary E. Donald (1918), *The Birthday Book of Wit and Humour*, anonymous, (1879), *Merry Thoughts: A Birthday Book with Selections from Humorous Writers* (1884) and *Happy Thoughts: A Birthday Book Selected and Arranged from Mr Punch's Pages* (1888). A more sober note was struck

The Beaconsfield Birthday Book, *celebrating the life of Tory Prime Minister Lord Beaconsfield (a.k.a. Benjamin Disraeli, 1804–81). This page mentions the birthdays of twins Romulus and Remus, obviously known personally to the writer. At the bottom of the page, in fainter ink, the birthday of the actor Henry Irving (1838–1905) has also been noted. (Anon,* The Beaconsfield Birthday Book, *Longmans, Green and Co., 1884)*

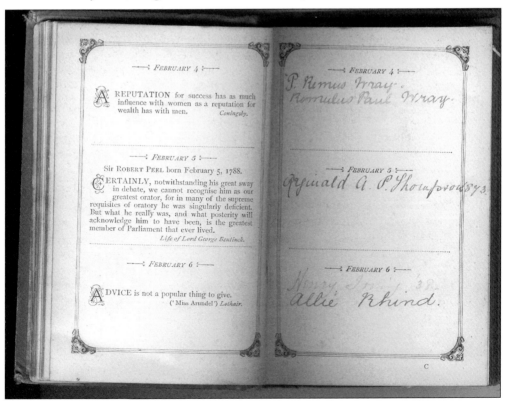

by *The Temperance Daily Text Book and Birthday Record* of 1883 which might have made a good present for an ancestor who had taken the pledge.

The focus of several other Birthday Books was on illustration rather than words. *The Floral Birthday Book* of 1876 included 368 engravings which were printed in colour. Birthday flowers and their emblems were represented 'with appropriate selections from the poets'. One of the most enduringly popular pictorial books was *The Birthday Book for Children* (1880) illustrated by Kate Greenaway with verse by Mrs Sale Barker. Whatever your ancestor's interests, there was probably a Birthday Book out there on the market to satisfy it. Consider, for example, *The Foxhunter's Birthday Book, being chips and shavings of hunting lore, from published and unpublished sources* (1896) and the *Cricketers' Autograph Birthday Book* published in 1906.

In the twentieth century, the titles of Birthday Books often reflected contemporary events. In 1901, shortly after the monarch's death, *The Queen Victoria Birthday Book* 'with numerous portraits' was published, and during the First World War, a nationalistic note was struck by C. E. Thomas's *The Patriots' Birthday Book: Selections from Recent Speeches and Writings* (1915). Between 1908 and 1910, the suffragettes even issued *The Women's Freedom League Birthday Book*, which included a quotation for each day of the year selected by the League's supporters, together with photographs of prominent members on the pages that denoted their own birthdays, for example: Charlotte Despard (15 June); Edith How Martyn (4 August) and Teresa Billington-Greig (15 October).

Entries

Check to see if there is an inscription at the front of the book which might help you establish who owned it. This helps when entries mention the relationship between the owner of the book and the people whose birthdays they have recorded. Detail such as '3rd March, John Andrew McWilliams, great nephew', for example, can be very useful if you are trying to fill in names and dates on the branches of your family tree, and provide a starting point for further research on censuses and certificates.

Birthday books can also contain surprise entries about other family anniversaries and even about events outside the family in the public world. A handwritten entry in a copy of *The Beaconsfield Birthday Book* of 1884 mentions the birthdays of family members Romulus and Remus Wray (evidently twins) and the writer Sir Henry Irving on the same day. Deaths and marriages as well as baptisms and burials were often recorded. Indeed, some birthday books such as *A Book of Memory: The Birthday Book of the Blessed Dead* by Katharine Tynan published in 1906 set out expressly to provide space to record the passing on of relatives rather than other kinds of information. Other entries can be eye-openers that can give your family history research a real boost in other ways. Consider, for example; the excitement you might feel on finding this entry: 'September 30th (1901): George Prior married, 2nd time!'

Remember that various people might have added information to the birthday book. Friends and relatives were often asked to sign their own names in the space allotted to their birthday. This means that when flicking through a book of anniversaries, you may have the extra bonus of seeing – and perhaps analysing – the handwriting of several family members for the first time.

QUESTIONS TO ASK OF YOUR ANCESTOR'S APPOINTMENT DIARY OR BIRTHDAY BOOK

1. Do the format, publishing details and/or pre-printed aspects of the diary or birthday book tell you anything about its owner (age, class, gender, occupational background, religion)?
2. What can you deduce about the public stature of this individual from the appointments recorded?
3. Can the appointment diary or birthday book be used to contradict or corroborate any other written material about a particular ancestor (to be found in other sources such as letters, diaries, employment records, and newspaper reports)?
4. Can the books be compared with other diaries by members of the same family (appointment diaries by a husband and wife might profitably be compared, for example)?
5. What kind of entries does the book include (are the appointments mostly concerned with business, domestic life, or pleasure)?
6. How did your ancestor structure his or her day, week or year (in hourly slots, in fortnightly cycles, with frequent breaks for holidays or none at all)?
7. What do the entries tell you about how far your ancestor moved around geographically? Is his or her business conducted largely

locally, or does it involve frequent and regular trips elsewhere? How might these journeys have been made?

8. Are there any other family history leads which might be followed up such as regularly repeated names or places?

9. How, if at all, did an ancestor indicate that he or she had kept or missed his or her appointments ?

10. What evidence of the mentality of your ancestor emerges from the entries in this appointment diary?

FURTHER READING
Books
Anon, *The Birthday Motto Book and Calendar of Nature*, Frederick Warne and Co., 1871.

Anon, *The Beaconsfield Birthday Book*, Longmans, Green and Co., 1884.

Anon, *The Christian Birthday Souvenir*, London, 1878.

Anon, *The Scott Birthday Book*, London, 1879.

Aylmer, Felix, *Dickens Incognito*, Rupert Hart-Davis, 1959.

Steinitz, Rebecca, *Time, Space and Gender in the Nineteenth-Century British Diary*, Palgrave Macmillan, 2011.

William, D. H., *Lyric Birthday Book: Snatches of Song for Every Day in the Year*, P. Nimmo, 1883.

Websites
www.sussex.ac.uk/broadcast/read/17135 On the appointment diaries of Virginia Woolf.

Chapter 7

TRAVELLERS' TALES: HOLIDAY JOURNALS

Our nineteenth and early twentieth-century ancestors (of all classes) led far less static lives than we may think. Whether your ancestor was a lord, a bank manager or a Lancashire millworker, he or she is likely to have spent some time away from home, either for pleasure or on business of some sort. Amongst your family papers you may find a whole host of documents relating to travel in this country and abroad. These can range from train and coach tickets, to bus passes and passports, from holiday coupons for food and drink, trite messages on the backs of postcards to lengthy first-hand accounts of trips made in letters. And on your shelves and mantelpieces, you may also have more tangible evidence of your ancestors' wanderlust – objects purchased in foreign places, perhaps, such as cuckoo clocks bought in Switzerland or dolls from Germany.

But it is with longer handwritten accounts of trips away from home that this chapter is concerned. And whilst the least literate and poorest members of communities might have been unlikely to undertake such a piece of writing, it is surprising just how popular keeping a detailed record of a holiday or other journey was amongst the middle and upper classes in the Victorian period and early twentieth century. The vogue was begun by Queen Victoria herself, who kept a general diary throughout her long life but began it as a travel diary on her mother's instruction, when at the age of 13, and known as Princess Victoria of Kent, she went to Wales on holiday, 'Wednesday 1st August, 1832, This book, Mamma gave me, that I might write the journal of my journey to Wales in it' (www.queenvictoriasjournals.org/).

Many of our ancestors followed suit. Their travel accounts may be scrapbooks in which sketches and photographs of places visited might have been stuck, holiday diaries which give a day-by-day account of a trip, or lengthier accounts of other societies. These avid observers often spent the idle moments of their time away keeping a rough prose account of the details of their travels which they could use as an aide-memoire when talking about their trip after they returned. Since the public had an insatiable appetite for descriptions of life in other countries, many travel journalists also submitted their accounts to publishers. There will be more about this later in this chapter.

Up until the mid-nineteenth century travelling long distances, particularly abroad, had been an activity which required long planning, a lot of expense and a great deal of time. Travel was a dangerous business which could sap your health and even endanger your life. In the early part of the nineteenth century, the only people who could afford such trips were wealthy landowners, baronets and army officers and their families, but as the century progressed, travel to Europe fell first within the grasp of the professional classes – doctors, lawyers and clergymen – and then to the new commercial classes who included colliery managers, bankers, factory owners, politicians, academics and scientists. Those with private incomes and creative interests such as poetry, novel-writing and landscape painting also travelled extensively. By the early twentieth century, many members of the working classes, too, were enjoying excursions to seaside resorts and places of natural beauty around the country.

By the mid-nineteenth century, there were several factors that made travelling abroad far easier than it had ever previously been. First and foremost, of course, our ancestors were able to get around much more easily because of the railways. As early as 1848, there were 100 million railway journeys made in Britain. By the beginning of the twentieth century, that number had increased to 1,000 million. Alongside this exponential growth in travel, came the rise of seaside resorts and spa towns such as Brighton, Bognor, Margate, Blackpool and Scarborough. Distances seemed to shrink as journey times shortened. By 1855 you could get from London to Brighton or Dover by train in just over two hours. You could even get as far as Plymouth in seven. Additionally, by the late nineteenth-century steam was also making travel abroad quicker and cheaper. Trains took travellers to the ports and, from the early decades of the nineteenth century, steamships carried them on to their destinations. Once in their country of destination, intrepid British travellers made use of whatever local method of travel was most convenient.

From the 1850s, onwards, more and more people also opted for *organized* holidays both within Britain and abroad. This transition has sometimes been described as the moment at which the 'traveller' became a 'tourist' – the active adventurer in other lands, transformed into a passive observer of the customs of other cultures. In practice, of course, both kinds of travel persisted alongside each other as they do today. Ancestors who were of the 'tourist' variety, however, might have benefitted from the business of travel operators like Thomas Cook who organized his first excursion in 1841 – a teetotal one-day trip by rail from Leicester to Loughborough. Over the course of the nineteenth century, Cook extended his range of excursions first to Liverpool and Fleetwood and then on to other seaside towns. The lower classes flocked in their thousands. In 1851, the entrepreneurial Cook even took 165,000 people on a day trip to the Great Exhibition in London. With his middle-class customers in mind, he moved on to organize trips to Paris, Switzerland and Italy. And by 1869, he was more ambitious still, taking holiday makers to Egypt and soon afterwards to America.

Unpublished travel journals from the late eighteenth and early nineteenth centuries may turn up amongst family papers. Many others are stashed away in archives up and down the country. Whilst most were written by members of the middle and upper classes, working-class people too were encouraged to keep a record of trips they had made in holiday diaries. Thomas Cook himself remarked that: 'The value of a diary to the tourist who wishes to remember accurately all that he may have seen is incalculable' (quoted in M. Strong, *Education, Travel and the Civilization of the Victorian Working-Classes*, Springer, 2014, p. 24). He went on to say that travel diaries should exhibit 'system, brevity and exactness'. If you visit the Discovery Section of the National Archives website (www.discovery.nationalarchives.gov.uk) and type the name of a country in which you are interested into the search box, you will probably find listed many first-hand manuscript accounts of journeys made to that place. A holiday diary entitled 'Easter in Belgium', for example, for the week of 24–28 March 1910 by William Benson Thorne, Librarian, is kept in the Tower Hamlets Local Library and Archive. In Birmingham City Archive, there is a holiday journal kept by Elizabeth and George Cadbury (of the chocolate-making dynasty) whilst on holiday in Switzerland in August-September 1893.

Aside from holidays, there were an increasing number of reasons for people to travel as the nineteenth century moved into the twentieth. Ask yourself whether your ancestor was a tourist whose main reason for travelling was 'leisure and pleasure', or a traveller whose reason for travelling might have been more subtle. Missionaries and other religious types, for example, visited the 'back-of-beyond' to try to convert the natives; administrators and soldiers went out to run the new British colonies overseas; and scientists and anthropologists went to explore and document the natural world. Others travellers who wrote went to drier or, at least, fresher climes, at the advice of their doctors for prolonged periods to recover from illnesses such as respiratory diseases or rheumatism. The rich went to hunt game or to practise other sports (for example, fishing, mountaineering and ski-ing). And more and more people travelled for work purposes – to spread ideas, to learn, to share their skills or sell their wares. In the mid-nineteenth century, for example, quite a number of Manchester businessmen visited cities in Norway to spread technological ideas, and, in the early twentieth century, thousands of Lancashire colliers spent repeated periods working in the mines of Washington State, to cite but two examples.

If the trip documented by your ancestor was simply a holiday to the other side of the country or to another country, it may tell you something about the kind of income and expectations your family had. Ask yourself if this seems to have been a one-off trip, or part of a frequent and recurring vacation routine? How high on the agenda were cultural pleasures and sightseeing? Think about the method of travel that your ancestor opted for (or had been forced to take), and the type of accommodation that he or she was staying in. Contemporary travel guides (see below), will give you some typical prices and show you what other options were on offer. If your ancestor describes staying with relatives, you might obtain information about extended family networks. Think also about the length of time that your ancestor was away from home and the time of year at which the holiday took place. Many working-class people were only able to go away at certain designated times of year when factories were closed, for example.

Your ancestors might have travelled only briefly for work or pleasure, but it is possible that significant family events occurred a long way from

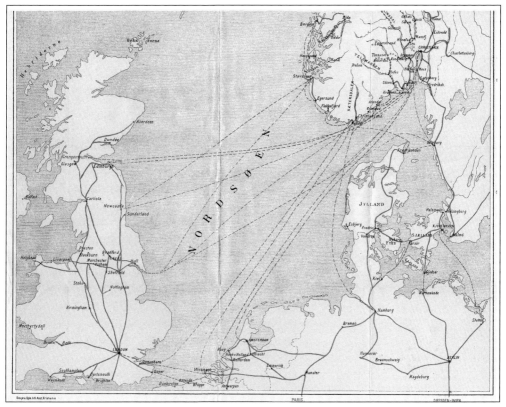

Travel routes to Europe were extensive by the end of the nineteenth century. This map shows all the different possible routes to Norway, a popular holiday destination – and source of many published and unpublished holiday journals – by 1898. (D. M. M. Somerville, Winter Life in Norway: Descriptive of Sports and Pastimes on Ice and Snow, *The Norwegian Winter Tourist Association, 1898, frontispiece)*

home. Future spouses may have met on holidays in other parts of Britain or even further afield. Immigrant ancestors may have made trips back to the countries of their birth. If a family member died whilst abroad, it's possible that that elusive graveyard for which you have been searching in Britain may actually be in Berlin rather than Bradford. If there are children in the family whose birth certificates you cannot locate at the General Register Office, consider the fact that they may have been born in other countries. Or perhaps they were conceived abroad? Look out particularly for children with distinctly foreign-sounding names. On the 1901 census, for instance, there are 170 women with the name Christiania (rather than Christina). This was, of course, the former name for Oslo, capital of Norway, a popular turn-of-the-century holiday destination!

WHERE DID THEY GO?

British people travelled to all areas of the known world in the nineteenth and early twentieth centuries, although some areas were more popular than others and destinations abroad went in and out of vogue according to a number of different factors. To find out just how popular your ancestor's choice of destination was at any particular time in the past – and exactly why it was popular – you will need to do a little research in books (see the bibliography at the end of this chapter as a starting point) and on the internet. Travel to Ireland, for example, was in vogue between 1775 and 1850 but after the Great Famine (1845–52), there was a backlash against visiting the country. Those commentators who did cross the Irish Sea often did so from philanthropic or sociological motives but produced accounts tinged with racial disgust, marking what they saw as the disparity between the beauty of the landscape and the poverty of the inhabitants.

In the early nineteenth century, the middle classes sought to copy elements of the Grand Tour of Europe that had traditionally been part of the education of upper-class youth. They visited the Southern European countries of France and Italy as a matter of priority. Later, however, new destinations in Northern Europe (such as Scandinavia, Germany and Switzerland) as well as some further afield in Greece, Albania and Turkey proved equally attractive destinations. In Italy, British tourists tended to eulogise on the magnificent state of ancient monuments and architecture and, in tandem, complain about how Britain herself had failed to preserve the heritage of her own cities. Travellers to Switzerland, on the other hand, wrote about the attractions of mountains and mountaineering, and those to Scandinavia focused on the natural beauty of fjords, waterfalls and glaciers. In both cases, strong contrasts were often made with the dirt and dangers popularly associated with British industrialization.

Travel outside Europe remained the experience, on the whole, of only the very wealthy or those tasked to control the Empire by the British government. Asia, brimming with wholly different cultures and religions was a place of exotic fascination. But when visiting these places, British visitors stayed in those areas that were already colonies

162

under British protection (for example, in China, British visitors kept to Hong Kong, the Kowlan Pensinsula and the so-called New Territories) rather than wandering off the beaten track. An interest in Africa peaked with the search for the source to the Nile between 1858 and 1875, and the widely reported meeting between Henry Morton Stanley (1841–1904) and David Livingstone (1813–73) in 1871 on the banks of what is now Lake Tangynika. Whilst many African areas were seen as uncivilized wastelands, empty or populated by savages, Egypt presented a rather different prospect. Here there were the remains of a once-great civilization to which Britain might favourably be compared. Egypt was also popular because of the growth of overland and steamship routes to its capital and because, after the end of the Napoleonic Wars (1803–15) it had become a 'de facto' British Protectorate. The country became a more prominent imperial site during the 1880s, when the revolt of the Mahdi in the Sudan brought about the death of General Gordon at the Siege of Khartoum in 1884, and the related fall of Gladstone's Liberal government. Egypt was also, of course, perennially popular with archaeologists and with religious groups seeking places mentioned in the Bible.

CONTENT

Travel journals can tell you a great deal about what the British thought of particular places in the past. This doesn't mean that what they say is necessarily an accurate description of the country in question, but it shows what the writers perceived to be true – which is actually just as interesting. When away from home, your ancestors would have been confronted by a great deal of information that was new and exciting to write about. All their senses – including the intellectual ones – would have been assaulted at once, perhaps to a far greater degree than would be the case today. It is therefore interesting to think about the selection of detail that presented itself as most worthy of being recorded in a travel journal. What did your ancestor consider important? Is he primarily obsessed with his own bodily comfort, the weather, the food or the warmth of the beds in a foreign country, or is the focus more on the strange religious practices of the place or the local attitudes to money, crime or children? Bear in mind particularly that travel writers often observe the new world in which they find themselves through the lens of their own preoccupations. So, an ancestor who comments on the restrictive clothing of the women in the country in which she finds herself, for example, might also have had an interest in women's affairs when back in Britain, and an ancestor who drew detailed pictures of unusual flora and fauna in his travel journal probably had scientific interests when on home territory.

Travel Itself

Since the whole business of travel was so different in the early Victorian period, many journals devote far more time than a similar modern travelogue might do to travel arrangements and the actual business of getting from A to B. Some travellers were heartily impressed by the rapidity with which they could get to their destinations by steamship and train, others lamented the loss of simpler, older methods of transportation. Once at their destination, a traveller had to make use of whatever local methods of travel appertained (rickety horse-drawn carioles in Norway, for example), and again, a great deal of page space was often expended on descriptions of the peculiarities of this in travel journals. As time went on, this focus on methods of travel waned a little and was replaced with more description of the traveller's individual experiences and thoughts.

Scenery

In an age before the invention of the camera, and certainly before the popular adoption of the hand-held camera (something which didn't happen until the start of the twentieth century), travellers were particularly keen to record the *visual* aspects of the places that they had visited. As we have said, this was sometimes done with a sketchpad and pen, and sometimes with a travelling set of watercolour paints or inks, but there was also a propensity for describing scenery in words. The growing dust and dirt of Britain's industrial cities created a fear that the beauties of the country were fast disappearing. Such a sensation meant that unspoilt places such as the Lake District, Scandinavia and Switzerland were in high demand as travel destinations and produced some wonderful scenic descriptions and comparisons in written accounts. In 1858, traveller Frederick Metcalfe, for instance, wrote of the Raven's Gorge in Telemark, Norway, 'What a pity a bit of scenery like this cannot be transferred to England. The Norwegians look on rocks as a perfect nuisance, whilst we sigh for them' (Metcalfe, *The Oxonian in Thelemarken*, p. 55).

Society

Open-eyed and well-educated travellers might have paid particular attention to the ways in which the society of other countries operated. Our ancestors covered an enormous number of topics in their travel journals with comments on everything from the landscape and the people, to the food, hygiene, customs and language of other places. Some described the local political situation, the class system, the role of women in society and the habits of the people (their propensity to crime and drunkenness, for example). Remember that when travellers described other countries, their thoughts often said a great deal about what was going in Britain at the time. For example, when travelling in Catholic countries, writers would often criticise the pomp and ceremony of foreign churches. They were, of course, comparing these with the simple and sober interiors of British Protestant churches.

Unmarried sisters Irene and Morna Tempest Beech from Lancashire took annual holidays together to different countries in Europe in the 1950s and 1960s and kept a record of their exploits. Neither Irene (who worked in the ironmongery department of Bolton Co-op) nor Morna (who was the supervisor of the same shop), had ever kept a diary in the normal way of things, but both felt the urge to record their experiences when they were on the Continent. By the 1950s when Irene and Morna were travelling, foreign holidays were gradually becoming available to people of lower incomes. Air travel had become an additional option to trains, ships and cars, though Irene and Morna always travelled by boat and train. This was long before the package holiday of the 1970s and these ladies booked their accommodation on arrival.

Confined to taking holidays in 'Bolton Holidays Fortnight' during the last week of June and the first week of July each year, Irene and Morna made the most of their time away. By the end of the decade they had produced no fewer than five longish pieces of manuscript writing about their exploits: *Ten Days in Grindelwald, Switzerland* (1951), *Fourteen Days Holiday in Germany and Bavaria* (1955), *Fourteen Days Holiday in Italy* (1956), *Fifteen Days Holiday in Norway* (1960) and *Fourteen Days Holiday in Austria* (undated). On the trip to Italy in the summer of 1956 the sisters assessed the new world around them on a sliding scale of bemusement. Everything they observed was refracted back through their Englishness with the emphasis being on food, clothing and the practical aspects of living:

Sisters Morna and Irene Beech, intrepid mid-twentieth century holidaymakers, who kept handwritten journals of all their holidays to Europe taken in Wigan Wakes Weeks. Here they are standing in the grounds of Hinderhof Castle, Germany on a holiday in 1955. (With thanks to Mrs Lois Wilkinson)

[In Limone] [That night] we chose a nice little inn, but they couldn't speak any English. We tried to make them understand that we didn't want any spaghetti. Italians at nearby tables tried to help. Then one man gave a beaming smile and nodded that he understood what we wanted. He gave the order to the waiter and everyone smiled that the problem had been solved. We felt quite pleased that we had been able to make them understand us, but when the lunch was put before us, to our dismay, we saw that it was spaghetti. We saw the funny side of it, and were quite amused when we first saw one member of the family, then another come into the bar just to have a look at us. (Irene and Morma Beech, *Fourteen Days Holiday in Italy* (1956))

Irene and Morna express surprise at some of the national customs: 'women are not allowed in church with naked arms, nor even short sleeves'. But they reserve their real shock for the toilet facilities that they encounter on a boat trip, 'instead of a toilet, all we could see was a porcelain square in the floor with a hole in the middle, a handle on the wall to steady oneself when using the contraption and a flush above the porcelain. Another custom that we didn't get used to was men and women using the same toilets!'

Irene and Morna Beech wrote for no-one but themselves and other family members. Their handwritten journals lay undiscovered amongst family papers for several decades before an interested relation found them and typed them up. Their accounts show that they were distinct individuals (Irene was outspoken, Morna more conciliatory) but also that they were representative of their times with views that many people similar to them might have held. You might find that the same is true of your ancestors' travel journals.

STYLE

Many of our ancestors wrote holiday journals for their own benefit, to be read through and perhaps pillaged for material for letters on their return. Others will have written with a particular reader in mind, possibly the family circle back home or a wider social group or club. It is possible, however, that he or she was also hoping to reach a wider audience by publishing his or her holiday journal at some point. One such archival holding of a travel journal bound for publication was that of a holiday made by canoe in 1878 by 'E. M.', 'E. A. F.', 'A. G. F.' and 'R. S. F.' on the Yare and Waveney rivers in Norfolk (held in Norwich Archives and relating to the Starling and Freeman families). It appears that this might have been altered (or edited) ready for publication; the title suggests that sketches (which are not present amongst the papers) were to be added.

Travel writing is often described as a hybrid and multidisciplinary genre and it is worth thinking a little about the style or styles of your ancestor's travel journal. One of the questions you will need to think about is the proportion of objective information (fact) to subjective information (opinion). Is the journal similar to a novel or autobiography, or more like a religious treatise or sermon? Does it remind you of a scientific report, a sociological treatise or a geographical textbook? What

Holiday journal of a trip to Norway, written in biro on a lined notepad by Morna and Irene Beech, 1956. (With thanks to Mrs Lois Wilkinson) features lead you to that conclusion (the selection of detail, the layout, or the special kinds of language used)? And why do you think your ancestor adopted this approach?

Another crucial question is to ask how your ancestor presents him or herself in relation to the people in the places visited. Many travel journals perpetuate ideas of cultural superiority, betraying a colonial mindset, which may make difficult reading nowadays. In 1880, Andrew and Agnes Donaldson, their five children and servants made a trip to Rome. Agnes and Andrew alternately kept a diary of the trip, and. Andrew, who was a professional painter exhibiting at the Royal Academy, drew wonderful sketches alongside the entries. The diaries, which remained in manuscript form for over 100 years, have been published recently. Here and there, Andrew's account includes a criticism of the French and Italians amongst whom the Donaldsons are staying. In Paris on 2 November 1880, for instance, he writes, 'I noticed an incident of so-called French politeness – a gentleman crossing the street takes off his hat to a lady and grasps her hand but stands talking to her with his cigar in his mouth the whole time (Creaton, ed., *Victorian Diaries*, p. 82).

All this is part and parcel of the business of 'othering' that goes on in all travel accounts, a method by which the writer makes the country or place visited feel alien. Ask yourself how your ancestor achieves this sense of otherness? Is it by overt criticism (as in Donaldson's case, above), or by more subtle means, the idealisation, exoticisation, or ridicule of the indigenous inhabitants, for example? It is more than likely that your ancestor's account will resonate with a sense of cultural superiority but how exactly does he or she achieve this? And how uncomfortable does it make your read?

Travel journals can also tell us a lot about our ancestors both as individuals and as representatives of the nation – Britain – from which they came. In such accounts, people write about situations in which their tolerance is stretched and their mettle tested, and, therefore, such accounts can potentially tell us more about the personal qualities and indeed the psyche of the ancestor in question than ordinary diary accounts.

USEFUL COMPARISONS

If you want to make a sensible assessment of your ancestor's travel account, it is essential to find out more about the place that he or she visited at the time he or she went there. In addition to the usual internet searches, you should consider looking at contemporary guidebooks to particular destinations and also published travel accounts to the same places at around the same time. If you know that your ancestor travelled with a big travel company such as Thomas Cook, you might also find out more by visiting the relevant archives.

Guidebooks

A number of different companies including Karl Baedeker, Thomas Cook and John Murray published guidebooks to European destinations in the nineteenth and twentieth centuries. These often give other information (shipping timetables, currency converters, lists of useful items to take, brief dictionaries of useful phrases and the like) which can help you gain an idea of the practical details of your ancestor's travels. Old guidebooks often turn up in second-hand book shops and internet book sites such as www.abe.com. Gazetteers, complete with contemporary maps, will also be useful in giving you some general information about countries and cities in the past including descriptions of historical landmarks and population figures

Published Travel Accounts

Published evidence of travel abroad in the nineteenth century is not at all scarce – far from it. Large numbers of people wrote travel journals and got them printed. Even if your ancestor didn't write one of these – and you should always check whether an unpublished manuscript did or did not ever make it into print – it's well worth trying to get hold of a couple of volumes on the country in question at the time they visited it. To find travel journals on a particular country visit www.copac.ac.uk or www.bl.uk. Type the name of the country in which you are interested in the 'title' or 'keyword' section and specify the time parameters between which your ancestor travelled. A quick search of the Copac database for books in English about Spain published in the period 1870 to 1900, for instance, reveals more than 2,600 titles. A search for Italy in the same period reveals over 3,800 titles. Not all of these will be travel journals, of course, but a large proportion will be. The Copac database will tell you the names of libraries up and down the country where these books can be read. Once you have a list of relevant titles, affordable antiquarian copies can also often be bought at www.abe.com. Remember that although the writer may not be your ancestor, his or her account will probably be a good guide to what British people thought and felt about a particular country at the time your ancestor went there.

Archives of Travel Companies

If you have suspicions that your ancestor travelled with Thomas Cook, you can find out more about the kind of trip it might have been by visiting the company archives in Peterborough by prior appointment (Thomas Cook Archives, The Thomas Cook Business Park, Coningsby Road, Peterborough, PE3 8SB: email enquiries: pressoffice@thomas cook.com). These hold a wealth of information including handbooks, programmes and brochures from 1845 to the present that cover most holiday destinations in Britain and around the world. There are also copies of the two Thomas Cook newsletters, *Cook's Excursionist* (1851–1902) and *The Traveller's Gazette* (1902–39). These include detailed advertisements, itineraries, fares and lists of hotels and Cook's offices. The archives also hold a selection of travel diaries written by early holidaymakers with the company, as well as tickets, hotel coupons, luggage labels, menus and other ephemera. From March 1873, Cook's *Continental Time Tables and Tourist's Handbook* listed details of all the main railway, diligence (stagecoach) and steamship routes across Europe – incomplete records of this are held in the archives. For more on the Thomas Cook company archive see www.thomascook.com/about-us/thomas-cook-history/company-archives/.

Other nineteenth-century tour operators included Dean and Dawson, Henry Lunn, John Frame and Henry Gaze but their records are much more difficult to trace. Dean and Dawson merged with Thomas Cook in the 1950s and there are many Dean and Dawson travel brochures dating from 1904 onwards in the Cook archives as well as a few from Henry Gaze.

You should use the information that you glean from guidebooks, published travel accounts and tourist company archives as companion pieces to your ancestor's account. What aspects of these places did your ancestor select to write about? What did he or she unwittingly or knowingly miss out? How polite or fair is he or she when describing customs and cultures very different from his own? In these ways, published sources are an absolutely invaluable comparison to personal writings when travel is the topic.

QUESTIONS TO ASK OF YOUR ANCESTOR'S TRAVEL JOURNAL

1. Why do think your ancestor chose this particular destination at this particular time (historic happenings, business reasons, honeymoon, a family connection, to visit friends or relatives, to recuperate from an illness, for sport, or simply because it was 'the place to go')?
2. Did your ancestor leave any other corroborating evidence that he or she travelled to these places at these times (tickets, letters, postcards, photographs, souvenirs)?
3. How did your ancestor travel? What more can you find out about this?
4. Was the journal written 'on the hoof' or when your ancestor had returned from his or her travels? How do you know?
5. Do any guidebooks exist of the places to which your ancestors travelled at the time they travelled there?
6. Do any published accounts exist of travel to these places at these times? Are there any indications that your ancestor might have wanted to have his or her travel journal published at some point?
7. How does your ancestor preface his or her travel account? Are there apologies for anything? And, if so, are these justified?
8. What subjects did your ancestor cover in his or her travel journal (food, drink, sightseeing, customs, language, religion, politics, position of women)? What does this selection of detail tell you about your ancestor and his/her world?
9. What does the writing tell you about your ancestor's concept of his or her own national (British) identity?
10. What kind of writing does this travel journal most resemble (a diary, an adventure story, a novel, a political essay)? What features lead you to that conclusion?

FURTHER READING
Books

Black, Jeremy, *The British and the Grand Tour*, Croom Helm, 1985.
Brendon, Piers, *Thomas Cook: 150 Years of Popular Tourism*, Secker and Warburg, 1991.

Creaton, Heather, ed., *Victorian Diaries, The Daily Lives of Victorian Men and Women*, Mitchell Beazley, 2001.

Fjagesund, Peter, and Symes, Ruth A., *The Northern Utopia: British Perceptions of Norway in the Nineteenth Century*, Rodopi, 2003.

Foster, Shirley, *Across New Worlds: Nineteenth-Century Women Travellers and their Writings*, Harvester Wheatsheaf, 1990.

McAllister, Annemarie, *John Bull's Snakes and Ladders: English Attitudes to Italy in the Mid-Nineteenth-Century*, Cambridge Scholars Publishing, 2007.

Metcalfe, Frederick, *The Oxonian in Thelemarken; or Notes of Travel in South-Western Norway in the Summers of 1856 and 1857*, Hurst and Blackett, 1858.

Strong, Michele, *Education, Travel and the Civilization of the Victorian Working-Classes*, Palgrave Macmillan, 2014.

Withey, Lynn, *Grand Tours and Cook's Tours: A History of Leisure Travel, 1750-1915*, Aurum Press, 1998.

Youngs. Tim, *Travellers in Africa: British Travelogues, 1850-1900*, Manchester U.P., 1994.

Websites

www.bl.uk British Library catalogue

www.copac.ac.uk Copac Library catalogue

www.queenvictoriasjournals.org The digitized journals of Queen Victoria online.

www.thomascook.com/about-us/thomas-cook-history/company-archives The Thomas Cook Archives.

Chapter 8

SCRIBBLES IN THE MARGIN: ANNOTATION IN BOOKS

If you have inherited published books once owned by an ancestor, it's possible that you will find his or her handwritten scribbles here and there in the margins. Such personal markings found in published books can be irritating if you have no interest in the person who made them. Modern society no longer really values such 'defacement', and you might wonder why anyone wished to show such disrespect for the printed word. Once you sense that these are the jottings of an ancestor, however, it is likely that your annoyance will turn to fascination and even pleasure. It's worth remembering that scribbling in books was not always regarded as a vulgar act. Quite the reverse in fact, and rereading our ancestors' marginalia with more of an open mind might produce some interesting finds.

Journalist Mark O'Connell has remarked that, 'a book someone has written in is an oddly intimate object; like an item of clothing once worn by a person now passed away, it retains something of its former owner's presence' (Mark O'Connell, 'The Marginal Obsession with Marginalia', www.newyorker.com, 26 January 2012). When that 'former owner' is a past member of our own family the find is additionally thrilling. This is partly because, unlike with books annotated by just anybody, we might already know a little something of the scribbler's autobiography, their social class, education, family situation, employment and the like. These details can help us to interpret what might otherwise appear to be meandering jottings in productive ways. Likewise, jottings can sometimes tell us about aspects of the person who was our ancestor that we did not know before.

You should start by thinking a little about the kind of book(s) in which your ancestor has written. The type of book will depend very much on the owner's social class, income level and level of education. It's important to understand that with the proliferation of all sorts of new kinds of published reading material in the nineteenth century, our ancestors commonly rated books in a strict hierarchy of propriety with religious tomes and moral stories scoring highly, and novels, especially gothic horror stories and romances, rated very low. The 'value' placed by our ancestors' on different sorts of reading material in the past is an enormous subject, but, for the purposes of this kind of family history research, it is enough to know that some kinds of text were valued and others decried. Your ancestors' comments in the margin – positive and negative – will sometimes make this moral aspect of reading very apparent.

The Bible was one kind of book (owned by many families in the past even when there was no other literature in the house) that was particularly well-annotated by our ancestors (see Ruth A. Symes, 'He always had his nose in a book,' in my *Stories from Your Family Tree: Researching Ancestors Within Living Memory*, The History Press, 2008, and its updated reprint *Unearthing Family Tree Mysteries*, Pen and Sword Books, 2016). But, this section takes a look at the jottings made in some other popular kinds of reading material that might have graced your ancestors' shelves, namely cookery books, educational textbooks and novels.

When your ancestor jotted in a published book, he or she made a choice not to take the time required to get hold of a different notebook (or perhaps a commonplace book, see Chapter 9), and transfer his or her thoughts to it. Annotations on the printed text itself might, therefore, be considered more personal, more immediate and more intense – a better record of his or her thought processes than any other sort of notebook perhaps. As a recent commentator has pointed out, at its best, marginalia can be evidence of 'what a book actually *feels* like to the actively reading brain' (Sam Anderson, 'A Year in Marginalia' www.the millions.com). In keeping with this sense of immediate reaction, marginalia can seem startlingly abusive towards the printed material. A particularly funny example is that by Samuel Clemens (a.k.a. Mark Twain 1835–1910) in his copy of *Tacitus* (Vol II, 101), 'This book's English is the rottenest that was ever puked upon paper'(Cited in H. J. Jackson, *Marginalia: Readers Writing in Books*, Yale U.P., 2001, p. 91).

When our ancestors wrote in the margins of their books, they usually concerned themselves with the subject of the book itself. Thus, they might have added new handwritten recipes to published cookbooks, extra travel information to tourist guides, records of the sightings of particular wild birds or flowers in books which dealt with those subjects, and so on, but occasionally – and fascinatingly – they might have included a jotting of an entirely different kind. The poor availability of paper in the homes of many of our ancestors meant that the margins of printed books were used for doodles, notes, shopping lists, rudimentary diary entries or even further developed pieces of personal writing. And the most interesting bits of marginalia are, often, in fact, those that are the most unexpected and that seem to leap erratically off the page. In 1864, Charles Wentworth Dilke (at least it is presumed to be he) was heavily annotating a copy of a highly respected legal book, *Institutes of Justinian* (prob. 1853) when he decided to break off from his complex system of cross references and underlinings to write: 'Left off work at this point to row head of the river, 12th May 1864' (Jackson, *Marginalia*, p. 338). A descendant of the studious Charles would no doubt be thrilled to realise that he had a fun-loving side.

You might wonder how likely it is that you will find any marginalia by an ancestor. In fact, the older the book, the more likely it is. In the early nineteenth century, books were passed around and shared much more frequently than was later to be the case, and notes were frequently written in their margins as an aid to personal understanding and as a method of interacting with other later readers. A fascinating study of marginalia in two collections of children's books, the Hockliffe Collection, held at the Polhill campus of De Montfort University in Bedford in the UK (about 1,200 titles of all kinds of material), and the pre-1850 section of the Osborne Collection (held in Boys and Girls House, part of the Public Library Service in Toronto) revealed that of 1,722 books examined, 813 had some extra-textual marking (inscriptions, marginalia, sketches, scribbles, and so on). The complete findings of this survey are reported in Matthew Grenby, 'Early British Children's Books: Towards an Understanding of their Users and Usage,' *CW3 Journal*, Issue 3 Summer 2005, at www2.shu.ac.uk/corvey/CW3journal/issue three/grenby.html. You are less likely to find annotation in published books owned by your ancestors from the second half of the nineteenth century onwards. At this point, there was a growing public disapproval of the business of writing in books, inspired partly, at least, by the arrival of many more public libraries in Britain after 1850. As academic Leah Price puts it: 'Marginalia, valued earlier in the century as proof that reading involved strenuous production rather than idle consumption, was embargoed by the new public libraries which saw readers' hands as wandering, dirty or even capable of spreading diseases' ('Victorian Reading', *The Cambridge History of Victorian Literature*, C.U.P., 2012, p. 37).

On the plus side, however (as far as the likelihood of finding marginalia is concerned), in the late nineteenth century and early twentieth centuries, there was a much greater availability of books – about 325,000 separate items are known to have been published in the 1890s compared with 56,000 during the 1790s (figures from James Raven, Helen Small and Naomi Tadmor, *The Practice and Representation of Reading in England*, C.U.P., 1996, p. 5). At the same time, there is evidence that people had stronger feelings of personal ownership about their books from the late nineteenth century onwards, and that the practice of reading had, to some extent become more solitary and self-indulgent. In this period, the scribbles in the margin, it seems, became much more private to individual readers and more personal in content. In short, in our period of interest, there were more printed books in which our ancestors might write, and when they did so, their writings are potentially more interesting.

WHY DID YOUR ANCESTOR ANNOTATE HIS OR HER BOOKS?

Before you look at the content of an ancestor's marginalia, see if you can work out *when* it might have been made. Take a look at the date at which the book was published and any inscription at the front which might tell you when it arrived in the hands of your ancestor. Flick through the book to see if any of the notes are dated, signed or initialled. Try to see if there any clues to the gender of the scribbler. It's worth remembering that in a class-riven and male-dominated society, whilst middle and upper-class men were roundly encouraged to annotate their books, women and the lower orders were often heavily criticised for defacing texts in this way. Is there any indication of his or her age and also his or her country or place of origin, are any of the notes in another language, for example? Or does the wording include words or turns of phrases that indicate the class or regional background of the scribbler?

Next you should ask why your ancestor annotated this book. Here are some possibilities.

Penmanship

At the very least, the marginalia in an inherited book can tell you something about your ancestor's handwriting. Sometimes, indeed, our ancestors will have made jottings specifically as a means of improving their 'hand'. Indeed, if you visit any second-hand bookshop you will find countless examples of signatures being repeated over and over again in the flyleaves and endpapers of printed texts for just this purpose.

To Aid Understanding

But some of our ancestors who jotted notes and queries, references and witticisms had other, more sophisticated purposes in mind: to help in their own processes of learning, to enter into arguments with the writer, to try to improve upon the book in question, to compete with those who had annotated the text before, or to guide those who might read it later.

The early Victorians believed that reading ought to be an active rather than just a passive process. Thus, they often took out their pens and, as it were, engaged in a conversation with the books they were reading, to a degree that many modern readers might find uncomfortable. Readers sometimes created what might be called a 'personal geography' of their reading materials. Annotations in books might include all or any of the following: underlinings, circles, stars, highlighting, asterisks, vertical marks in the margin, numbers in the margin to indicate a series of points, numbers in the margin to reference other pages within the book (sometimes use of the abbreviation 'cf' to mean 'compare') and circling of information. Lengthier annotations might include writing in the margin in the form of questions (and perhaps also answers), and words or statements translated into a language with which the note-taker is more familiar. Your ancestor might have distilled a complicated discussion into to a simple statement, or added some aids to finding one's way around the book: a handwritten index at the back, or an outline of the book sketched onto the front papers, for example.

For Psychological Release

H. J. Jackson remarks of marginalia that 'every note entails a degree of self-assertion, if not of aggression,' on the part of the writer (*Marginalia*, p. 90), and she goes further, pointing to the possible psychological release that jottings might have provided, something of which our ancestors will probably have been unaware but which might be particularly striking to us as we encounter them: 'The outlet is given them for expressing their feelings – their joy when the author says exactly what they think, their dismay when their bond with the author is broken, and their fluctuating reactions to the course of an argument or a narrative. It is a cheap and convenient form of therapy' (Jackson, *Marginalia*, p. 92).

To Record the Writing Event

One modern writer on marginalia has commented, 'the marks and scrawls help me to recall the text – and crucially, the person I was when reading it: how I was feeling, where I was sitting, whom I was with' (Toby Lichtig, 'Defacing Books: The Effluence of Engagement', *The Guardian*, 5 February 2010). Some of our ancestor's marginalia might help to convey the same sort of contextual information. One Samuel Maude, for example, moaned into the white spaces of his copy of Samuel Johnson's *Plan of a Dictionary* (1747):

> August 1st 1792: I awake, chilly and cold, in the night: this complaint affects me at times, at others, fussy, tho too warm, my wife being engaged, cannot walk with me with convenience this forenoon? She has shaved me: I think I will dress me: why save my cloaths? Perhaps I may not be much longer here: perhaps a Good Providence in his Mercy, may release my Mind from its uneasy State of Anxiety, and care, and permit my spirit, to enter the realms of Peace: Homeside Cottage in the 31st year of my persecution (cited in Jackson, *Marginalia*, p. 92).

It is rare indeed that we get this sort of insight into exactly what was going on around our ancestors as they lived their everyday lives, but an enormous pleasure to have even a tiny glimpse. Another good example of this almost 'photographic' aspect of writings in the margin is an entry in the so-called 'Diary Papers' of writer Emily Brontë (1818–48) (these are in fact loose sheets of paper upon which she has also doodled and drawn):

Emily Jane Brontë, July the 30th. 1841

It is Friday evening – near 9 o'clock – wild rainy weather. I am seated in the dining room alone having just concluded tidying our desk-boxes – writing this document. Papa is in the parlour. Aunt upstairs in her room. She has been reading *Blackwood's Magazine* to papa. Victoria and Adelaide [the geese] are ensconced in the peat-house. Keeper [the dog] is in the Kitchen. Hero in his cage. We are all stout and hearty as I hope is the case with Charlotte, Branwell, and Anne, of whom the first is at Mr White Esqre., Upperwood House, Rawden; the second is at Luddenden Foot; and the third is, I believe, at Scarborough – inditing [*sic*] perhaps a paper corresponding to this (Emily Brontë, *Diary Papers*, 1841).

Emily's use of the present tense, 'I am seated,' 'Papa is in the parlour,' is striking – different from the retrospective past tense of most diary entries. Here we are seeing the writer in action, undertaking her task, almost as if she is filming herself. Emily's words are accompanied by a drawing of herself at her desk which actually includes the piece of paper upon which she is writing!

For Posterity

Marginalia can be a private exchange between the reader and whatever book they happen to be talking to, or it may have been written specifically with another later audience in mind. You should always ask yourself how much effort your ancestor has put into making the content of his or her personal annotations intelligible to others (i.e. do you think the scribbles were written for the benefit of other later readers and – if so – whom, or not?). Ask yourself also whether repeat readers have returned to their own notes, and commented on them? And, if the annotations are by one hand only, or by more than one? If there are two annotators, can you establish what the relationship is between them? Does the earlier annotator anticipate the later one? Does the later annotator ignore the first, or is he or she drawn to the passages the other one has marked?

ANNOTATION IN DIFFERENT KINDS OF BOOK

Here are some ideas of what to look for in inherited books which might contain marginalia by an ancestor.

Notes in Cookery Books

An inherited cookery book might include many different kinds of indication of its previous owners including newspaper cuttings or recipes cut from other books, but also, a variety of methods for marking important recipes and handwritten annotations. Published cookery books may be one of the few places where you might find evidence of a female hand amongst your family papers, one of the few places indeed where you might find any indication of a female ancestor's independent existence at all. As a bonus, marginalia might include handwritten remarks by members of many different female generations within a family.

The nineteenth century saw a greater tendency for middle-class women to devote themselves to the domestic environment rather than the public world of work, and plenty of published material existed to guide in them in the development of their housewifery skills (see Leonore Davidoff and Catherine Hall, *Family Fortunes: Men and Women of the English Middle-Classes*, 2nd ed. Routledge, 2002). Cookery books – as well as books of other sorts of household advice – were also increasingly necessary in an industrialized age when many young married women found themselves living in towns and cities a long way from their mothers and the older generations of their families. These published how-to books were part of an enormous shift in the transmission of domestic knowledge from oral to print sources.

But, whilst published books aimed to instruct the modern housewife, many of them did not see themselves as the last word on a topic. Indeed, the very structure of some published cookery books actually encouraged women to add annotation, with blank pages for expressly that purpose being included at the ends, in the middle or at the end of each section, or even after each recipe. Our female ancestors sometimes used these pages to add new recipes, record the successes and failures of certain dishes, alter recipe measurements (to suit the size and composition of real families), and make substitutions of ingredients, or tools (to suit their geographical location and their access to new kitchen technology). Some women made more drastic emendations to their cookery books. *The Aberdeen Cookery Book* (1931), for example, had rather high-falutin' recipes which were not necessarily appropriate for the tastes or pockets of its readership. Marginalia included in one copy of this book kept in the National Library of Scotland includes a handwritten recipe for 'Milk and Macaroni soup', a dish more suited to the family of the woman who once owned it than some of the printed material.

Recent scholarship on the matter of annotation in cookbooks by Janet Theopano (*Eat My Words: Reading Women's Lives Through the Cookbooks They Wrote*, St Martin's Press, 2002) suggests that most of the annotation in published cookbooks tended to be written alongside the *special* recipes, and especially those for sweets and pastries. These were the new-fangled dishes requiring advanced culinary skills which belonged to the middle-class world of entertaining to which some of the users of cookbooks aspired. To ensure that they had a better chance of replicating a culinary success, women added glosses to their recipes which included changes in ingredients (for example, recognizing that different seasons and locations required different kinds of meat or fish), or more specific ingredients (for example, the addition of herbs and spices to which they had access), and tweaks to method (for example, adding flavourings to an omelette just before it left the pan rather than at an earlier stage in the cooking). The more usual everyday recipes received less annotation. Presumably this is because women already felt comfortable with what to feed their families on a daily basis and read the ordinary recipes less often. Other marginalia in cookbooks deals not so much with the food itself but with the etiquette of how it was to be served, what important occasions it might be brought out to celebrate, how the table might be set and just occasionally (but most fascinatingly), the names of those who had partaken of the meal the last time it was cooked.

Cookbook annotation could be empowering for our great-grandmothers. They were not simply on the receiving end of domestic advice, but able to take the printed word to task and, correct, alter or otherwise shape it to suit their own particular ends. The domestic world, whilst by no means as liberating as the public world of paid work, was an important state in its own right and one which women were increasingly making their own.

Notes in Educational Textbooks
Old school textbooks are often the first kinds of book to be sent to the charity shop or the rubbish tip when sorting out inherited family possessions, but you really should pause a short while before doing so.

In the nineteenth century, books used in the classroom and other books used for educational purposes at home were often annotated, revealing something not only of our ancestors themselves but also of their relationships with those who taught them: teachers, governesses, tutors and parents.

Since schooling for many was a regular activity taking up a great deal of time, annotation in this sort of book ends to be more plentiful, and potentially more interesting than that in other kinds of book. In the past, parents and teachers were encouraged to intervene heavily in a child's reading activity. The markings in their textbooks often confirm that much of what was read was supposed to be learnt off by heart. This regimen particularly applied to poetry, but it could also be applied to all manner of other subjects including science, history and religion. Some textbooks might have particular passages marked in some way to show progress in learning (e.g. with a cross or a tick, or with the word 'learnt' [or similar] written in the margins). Some books have dates written next to the entries showing exactly when they were committed to memory. In the M. O. Grenby study mentioned earlier, the chapter 'On Monsters' in a copy of *The Pantheon of Ancient History of the Gods of Greece and Rome* (1814) by Edward Baldwin (a pseudonym for the famous writer William Godwin), for example, has the annotation, 'This chapter to be read until the proper names have been memorized.' Textbooks might also include lists, written by the teacher or the pupil, of questions or catechetical exercises to test knowledge and these might be ticked or dated when the lessons have been learned.

Dates jotted in the margin of educational books might show just how much of the book has been read in a certain time period, allowing you to follow the user's rapid or slow, steady or erratic, progress from one lesson to the next. A book (again in the Grenby study) inscribed by 'E. Newport' on 3 March 1812 (Richard Valpy's *Elements of Mythology; or an easy and concise history of the Pagan Deities*, 1810), includes various dates written into the margin, presumably by either Newport or his teacher. The sequence begins 3 March 1812, and continues through 10 March 1812, 17 March 1812, and so on – one day each week in other words. By checking on a perpetual calendar (www.5a.biglobe.ne.jp), it has been possible to see that these dates, in the Spring of 1812, were all Tuesdays. Gaps in the dates indicate that E. Newport had a month's holiday from 25 March to 28 April, and then another break from 16 June to 16 August. The final lesson appears to have taken place on 3 September 1812, with the pupil reading only a couple of pages in each lesson and only eventually reaching as far as page 22!

Victorian teachers and parents were not simply there to test children and to make sure that lessons had been completed. Look out for annotations in children's books and educational textbooks that show them in action in all sorts of other ways: explaining the language, clarifying analogies and pointing out the morals of stories. In some books with extracts from drama, the names of the real children given the different parts in the school or home classroom might be written in by hand. Sometimes pupils are praised in the margin for having learnt something very well, or encouraged to repeat the exercise. On other occasions, parents have made every attempt to personalise the text: 'your mama' appears next to the description of a loving fictional mother in a copy of John Aikin and Anna Laetitia Barbauld's *Evenings at Home* (1804), and in a copy of Maria Edgeworth's *Early Lessons* a sham 'errata' section has been included, insisting 'For "Rosamond" read "Alicia"' – presumably the name of the real child reading the book. Indeed, in many early children's books certain words or passages have been corrected, or sometimes bowdlerised (excised of material that might have been considered offensive or objectionable) by adults.

Rude words might be scored out, salacious passages underlined, difficult words glossed, foreign words translated, typological errors corrected, syllables broken up to aid pronunciation and meaningful passages underlined. In a copy of *Don Quixote* (from the Grenby study) for instance, the phrase 'ladies of pleasure' has been inked out. Later, the word 'virgins' has also been scored out with the word 'ladies' substituted and written above the line. Children's books may have been more substantially annotated by adult readers. A copy of *The Geographical Guide: a Poetical Nautical Trip round the island of Great-Britain* (1805), though evidently meant for children, is covered by neat marginal notes, exhibiting a substantial knowledge of the sea, and indicative that the main reader of this copy of this book was an adult.

Elsewhere, religious concerns appear to have excited parental disquiet: in a copy of Mary Hughes' *Pleasing and Instructive Stories* (1821), the word 'meeting' has been deleted by hand from the following sentence, '. . . and on Sunday, we ought to go to church, or chapel, or meeting, to join with our friends and neighbours in thanking and praising Him who is the Father of us all', Presumably this is because the word 'meeting' had connotations of Quakerism which the parents of the owner of this book did not want to encourage.

The most thrilling findings amongst annotation in educational works might indicate a pupil's state of mind. We get a shockingly brilliant insight, for example, into the young William Makepeace Thackeray's boredom from a scribble in his copy of *Collection of English Poems* (1820), here he counts down the days until his holidays 'Only 2 weeks, only 13 days, only 12 days' and so on down to one (Jackson, *Marginalia*, p. 24). Other exciting finds might allow us an insight into what was actually being said between teachers and pupils in the nineteenth or early twentieth-century classroom. On the verso of the title-page of the Richard Valpy book mentioned above, for example, a child has delightedly scribbled a remark just made by the teacher: 'Madame said Eliza Lomas prononced [*sic*] like an owl and could trace the sound of every animal in her lesson!'

Notes in Novels

Our ancestors apparently scribbled less in novels than in other kinds of published writing. As H. J. Jackson puts it, 'works of fiction and imaginative literature – plays, poems, novels and romances – seem, perhaps surprisingly, to have been the least attractive to annotators . . . The absorbed state of mind normal for reading fiction seemed to be incompatible with the practice of annotation, unless the reader is a teacher or fellow writer' (*Marginalia*, p. 77)

But, there are, of course, exceptions to this generalisation. A certain British Lieutenant-General Coote Synge-Hutchinson (1832–1902) scribbled notes on sixty-nine out of the 372 pages of his copy of a novel by Benjamin Farjeon, *Great Porter Square: A Mystery* (1885). This meant that about a fifth of the text was covered with marginalia, but if all the lines, question marks and squiggles are taken into account, 'scarcely a page is left unscathed' (http://thepassingtramp. blogspot.co.uk/2012/04/bosh-marvelous-marginalia-of-lieutenant_ 10.html.).

Synge-Hutchinson's robust marginal interjections are intoned in the upper-class slang of the late Victorian period. He uses words such as, 'Bosh', 'Rot' and 'Stuff', for example. Some of his expostulations are directed at the kind of novel he is reading – a sensational story with a great deal of narrative improbability. When two of its characters meet accidentally in London, he scribbles, 'How is it all these convenient things happens in novels?' At another point he despairs of the characterisation, 'the author appears to have collected about the greatest lot of idiots I have ever come across'.

But the marginalia goes further than this, giving us a good insight into Synge-Hutchinson's opinions of certain aspects of the society in the book and thus also, presumably, of his opinions on those subjects in real life. Topics in his sights include the rights of women, the status of America in world politics, the value of the press and the virtue of poverty. When a character in the novel remarks that a certain woman is 'a daughter of Eve and, therefore, the equal of a queen', for example, he rails against the emergent democratic movement in general, 'What utter rot: I suppose the author goes in for manhood suffrage!' When another character refers sycophantically to the United States as 'the wonderful country which is one day to rule the world', he scribbles: 'Bah!, Stuff! Nonsense!' When the author writes approvingly of the press, 'Such is the power of the newspaper. To convey to remote distances, into village and city, to the resides of the poor and rich, the records of ennobling deeds,' Synge-Hutchinson retaliates with, 'papers, I should say, have been a far greater curse than a blessing'. And when it is suggested that 'more happiness is to be found amongst the poor than the rich', he cannot resist adding sardonically, 'Oh really?'

In their entirety, all these interjections in the margin give us quite a lot of clues about the character of Synge-Hutchinson, which might never have been gleaned from more conventional historical documents. He was evidently outspoken, unsentimental, conservative, misogynist and unafraid of expressing his – somewhat bigoted – opinions. Fascinatingly for the family historian, a descendant of the General has commented on the blog about his marginalia and suggests how it has made her re-evaluate her ancestor a little:

I am Coote Synge-Hutchinson's great-great-granddaughter (granddaughter of Patrick Synge-Hutchinson, 1912–98, great niece of Joan Synge-Hutchinson Wilson, 1911–2004). I have a number of his other books – all adorned with his florid signature and some with a name stamp – but none of them have marginalia. This is perhaps because they are all more serious reference books or in Latin! I have some of his military regalia too. I enjoyed reading your blog – I can just imagine my grandfather saying, 'What utter rot!'

QUESTIONS TO ASK OF YOUR ANCESTOR'S ANNOTATIONS

1. In which kind of book do the jottings appear? What kind of moral or practical value would this kind of book have had as reading material at the time of the jottings, do you think?
2. Who made the annotations and for whose benefit has the annotation in this book been done?
3. When were the jottings made (compare this with known events in the family and historical events)?
4. Are all the annotations made by the same person and at around the same time? Or is more than one annotator involved?
5. Are all sections of the main text evenly marked? If not, why not, do you think? What kind of ideas/sections receive the most annotations? In a cookbook, what kind of recipes are annotated more commonly than others?
6. How connected are the annotations to what is being said in the text, and how much are they about other things?
7. What appear to be the purpose (s) of the annotation? To learn? To let off steam? To create humour? To correct? To take a writer to task?
8. Can you deduce anything about an ancestor's viewpoint on important issues (such as politics, religion or women's role) from the jottings?
9. Can you glean anything about the environment your ancestor was writing in from the jottings?
10. Are there any clues in the language used to the time-period, social or geographical status of your ancestor?

FURTHER READING
Books
Bennett. Andrew, ed., *Readers and Reading*, Longman, 1995.

Fadiman. Anne, *Ex-Libris: Confessions of a Common Reader*, Penguin, 2000.

Jackson, H. J., *Marginalia: Readers Writing in Books*, Yale University Press, 2001

Manguel, Alberto, *A History of Reading*, Flamingo, 1997.
Raven, James, Small, Helen, and Tadmor, Naomi, eds, *The Practice and Representation of Reading in England*, C.U.P., 1996.
Theopano, Janet, *Eat My Words: Reading Women's Lives through the Cookbooks They Wrote*, St Martin's Press, 2002.

Websites
www.bl.uk/collection-items/emily-brontes-diary-1837 – Brontë, Emily, *Diary Papers* (1841)
www2.shu.ac.uk/corvey/CW3journal/issuethree/grenby.html. Matthew Grenby, 'Early British Children's Books: Towards An Understanding of Their Users and Usage,' CW3 Journal, Issue 3: Summer 2005.
http://thepassingtramp.blogspot.co.uk/2012/04/bosh-marvelous-marginalia-of-lieutenant_10.html. – On the marginalia of Lieutenant-General Coote Synge-Hutchinson.

Chapter 9

'COLLECTIONS OF SAD CRUDITES': COMMONPLACE BOOKS

Some of the most interesting examples of personal writing that turn up in archives are simply notebooks (originally blank) containing miscellaneous handwritten bits and pieces by our ancestors. Occasionally these books might have been bought with the printed title 'Commonplace Book'. If not, they might have been given that title by the writers themselves. Some writers used the alternative terms, 'Miscellanies', 'Memoranda' or 'Scrapbooks'. More often than not, however, especially in the twentieth century, the haphazard entries (of what shall hereinafter be called 'commonplace books') were made in cheap, unexceptional-looking notepads, anything from pocketbooks with ruled lines to ring-bound loose-leaf pads.

'Commonplace books' (rather like the late twentieth-century Filofax or some early twenty-first century social networking websites such as Facebook www.facebook.com or Pinterest www.pinterest.com), allowed the compiler to put together disparate fragments of information that might have taken his or her eye over a period of time. The substance might be copied from elsewhere or it might be material that was original to the writer. A commonplace book is generally not organized chronologically and is, on the whole, not introspective in the way that a diary might be. All of the material within it will, however, have had some significance to the ancestor who compiled it. The term 'commonplace' is a translation of the Latin '*locus communis*' which means 'a theme or argument of general application', and many traditional commonplace books did include fragments of advice and pithy aphorisms, recorded so that the compiler might apply them more

A manuscript commonplace book, compiled by Emma Knight of Dodington, Gloucestershire, containing mainly extracts from English poetry, c. 1830. The cover is made from goatskin dyed purple and is tooled blind and in gold. (Part of the Charles Ramsden Collection of Signed Bindings. Provided by the British Library from its digitized bookbindings collection. Wikimedia Commons)

generally to situations at appropriate times. But the word 'commonplace' might more usefully be interpreted as the idea of a single location or 'common place', in which a miscellany of material might be collected. As Elizabeth Sykes (1775–1853), wife of Wilbraham Egerton of Tatton, put it, the commonplace book which she started in

1791 at the age of 16 was 'for keeping in remembrance observations made in reading, reflecting, conversing and travelling' (Cheshire Archives and Local Studies Centre) – in short a holdall for scraps of knowledge acquired in the course of her daily activities.

Commonplace books have a long history. First used as an educational tool aiding powers of argument and reason in antiquity, they later developed into reference books for snippets of knowledge and wisdom during the Renaissance (fourteenth to the seventeenth centuries). In the nineteenth and twentieth centuries, however, the practice of commonplacing became far more common and was practised by ancestors in every walk of life, from grocers and clockmakers to young married women, nurses and scientists. Commonplace books found amongst your family papers might include copied items such as recipes, remedies, prayers, passages from literature, lines of verse, whole poems of all kinds, proverbs, prayers, legal and mathematical formulae, tables of weights and measures, accounts, observations, definitions, jokes, cyphers, riddles, drawings, moral aphorisms, songs, epigrams, transcriptions of speeches, ideas and lists of all manner of things from household plate to livestock or ships. Original items might include drafts of letters sent (like letter-books described in Chapter 2), poetry, and pen-and-ink sketches. Some commonplace books also include loose enclosures such as pages from magazines, parish circulars, newspaper cuttings and photographs.

A commonplace book is likely immediately to reveal an ancestor's gender, class background, and (possibly, also), his or her religious persuasion. In the distant past, few women wrote commonplace books but as paper, writing materials, and even time, became more available to them in the nineteenth century, more and more women at all stages in their lives started to write in notebooks. Often the contents of commonplace books by women include recipes, remedies, prayers and morally edifying sentences – items suited to their domestic lives caring for others. In general, however, the practice of commonplacing was most popular amongst educated men with some leisure time on their hands. Their books might have included excerpts from their reading – classical poetry in translation, other poetry in French or Italian, and extracts from ancient and contemporary philosophy and literature. Those further down the social scale such as merchants and artisans included in their commonplace books material on more practical topics, weights and measures, drawings of how things worked and lists of their possessions, for example. In terms of religion, a commonplace book might include information taken from parish circulars, extracts from sermons enjoyed, passages from the Bible, records of monumental inscriptions, and even hymns, all of which might provide clues as to whether they were Anglican, Nonconformists of some kind, Catholic, or of some other faith.

Three very different examples will give an idea of the kind of variety of commonplace book that might be found amongst family papers:

A. A young girl approaching marriage, Ellen Norman, received a commonplace book, 'as a gift from her dear father 13th [14th deleted] November 1885.' It includes not only sentimental, religious and didactic poetry which she had painstakingly copied out, but also handwritten recipes for cakes, biscuits, puddings, sauces, pastry, haricot mutton, cheese straws and lemonade, and knitting patterns mostly for baby clothes. Since the book is also inscribed with the name 'Ellen Gingell, April 7th, 1897', one might imagine that this young woman took the book with her when she left her father's home and made the transition from her single state to her role as a wife and mother (Berkshire Record Office D/EX1538/1).

B. In the 1840s and 1850s, classically-educated Warrington wire-manufacturer Thomas Glazebrook Rylands (1818–1900), used his commonplace book as a repository for a diverse set of personal musings on life which he described as 'sad crudites'). Some of his entries take the form of drafts of letters, others are lengthy prose entries on such thought-provoking matters as 'the peculiarities of younger sisters', 'what an ideal wife should be', and 'random thoughts on what is and what is not a home.' There are also some entirely off-the-wall inclusions such as something he has seen written on a sign 'at an inn in Stirling on March 27th 1857', and a humorous poem of his own creation written by way of explanation for why he could not go for a ride in the country one day. He was suffering 'at the time from the infliction of a blister on [his] back' (Cheshire Record Office D4298).

C. In the 1960s, railway engine driver G. W. who had left school at 12, kept a small leather notebook in which he recorded a few addresses, the tablets which his sick wife needed to take every day, his forthcoming doctor's appointments, and programmes that he had enjoyed listening to on the wireless with the odd comment (Author's collection).

THE KEEPERS OF COMMONPLACE BOOKS AND WHY THEY KEPT THEM

Try to establish how many contributors there might have been to your family commonplace book and what their relationship to each other might have been. It might, for instance, have been kept by one ancestor over a long period of time – a whole lifetime in fact. In other cases, many hands might have been at work. The commonplace book of James Murie, Naturalist (1832–1925), for example, kept by him from his youth and – as the catalogue entry tells us – 'considerably added to in his old age' (Wellcome Library), also includes evidence of many other compilers. Other books were started by one compiler and then completed by another. In 1836, Edwin Clark (1814–94), an inventor and engineer, was taken by the sight of a commonplace book (for sale at a booksellers in Cambridge) which already included entries by 'Mitford of Jesus College'. Undeterred, he purchased the book for five shillings and proceeded to add all sorts of material of his own, including epigrams, riddles, charades, quotations, autobiographical and family notes, lists of pupils and teachers, lists of books and a great deal more besides (Centre for Buckinghamshire Studies).

More satisfying for the family historian are the books that have quite evidently been passed from one owner to another down through the generations of a family, either with a deliberate idea of continuity in mind, or simply as a way of saving paper. The process of compilation in these cases might have gone on for decades or even longer. Such is the case of a commonplace book kept by the Whitmore family of Gloucestershire, between 1786 and 1908. The front of the book contains notes in French and Italian, poetry and copied letters probably entered in the book's earlier period, whilst the back (quite differently) records notes on various shrubs and flowers which appear to have been planted at the family home of Lower Slaughter between 1903 and 1908 (Gloucestershire Archive).

Other commonplace books are evidently compilations put together by several members of a family at around the same time. In the Edinburgh Archive, for example, there are two volumes of a

One of my grandmother's albums, in her handwriting throughout. Given to me by my father 20 Sept: 1899.

Frontispiece to the commonplace book of Mrs Mary Rylands (compiled 1835–6) with a bookplate. The caption reads 'One of my grandmother's albums, with her handwriting throughout. Given to me by my father, 20th September, 1894.' My own archival research suggests that Mary was, in fact, J.P. Rylands' step great-grandmother, third wife of his grandfather John Rylands of Bewsey Hall. (Document D4299 held in Chester Record Office and reproduced with the permission of Cheshire Archives and Local Studies and the owner/depositor to whom copyright is reserved)

commonplace book, the first dated 25 December 1852 is titled, 'Mother's Christmas Book' and the second is undated, but titled 'A Christmas Offering for our Mother'. It would seem that either one or both of these volumes has been compiled by a group of children for their (unfortunately anonymous) mother. The books include lines from poetry with titles such as: 'The Elswick Villains', 'To A Soot Flake', 'A Legend of Marsden Rocks', 'A Paragraph on Poetry', 'The Hanoverian Brothers', 'The Policeman's Soliloquy', 'A Dream', 'Sketches of a Journey through Dreamland', 'Lines written in the Vatican: A

Fragment', 'The Letter Box', 'King Cole', 'The Philosophers', 'The Devil's water', 'The Sea', 'Music' and 'New Year's Eve.' The pages are decorated with original sketches of mistletoe, plants, birds and children some of which are initialled 'HP'.

In some cases, the compilers of a commonplace book might be acquaintances, colleagues or fellow aspirant writers rather than relations. Thomas Rylands (mentioned earlier) copied into his book many original pieces written by a friend, 'Stephen Kirkby Somerset esquire of Manchester', claiming that he has done this because he hates 'monopoly' and will therefore include contributions from various sources. Other books still include entries from many contributors who might not be either family or friends but who might be members of the same community. A striking example is that of a commonplace book recently discovered in Warrington, Cheshire. It had been compiled by many different people between 1848 and 1866. Here is part of its archival catalogue description, which ends with a useful explanation of how the book came to be preserved:

> This recently discovered book, a sort of journal, was written between 1848 and 1866. It seems to have been open to anyone who wished to record their thoughts, and about anything. Items range literally from the sublime to the ridiculous; some are crude, others of a high style of literacy; some are in copperplate, others in scribble. Many entries are political and anti-establishment. There are twenty poems and thirty songs – with mostly topical words to contemporary airs. It is likely the book was kept in one of the many inns in Warrington, one which was frequented by those who supported the Tory Party, for most of the political items attack those who were Liberals. There are a number of Election Addresses mostly by Anon; some to be printed give the name of the printer, the number of copies and the cost – the book no doubt being handed to the printer and later returned to its lodging house. Almost half of the pages are unused, the entries ceasing in about 1866. There are, however, two interesting items hidden away. Some two-thirds of the way through the book are six pages of remedies for hush-hush diseases, and right at the back are forty-two aphorisms relating to the evils of drink. After 1866 the book may have been kept by a local printer and may, by

the end of the century, have come to the proprietors of the 'Sunrise Press' and thus to the well-known Arthur Bennett, Accountant. In the mid-20th century he had a partner Philip Gandy who kept the book which was found among his possessions when he died in 2002' (Warrington Library).

Your ancestor's commonplace book might have had multiple compilers, but it is even more likely to have had multiple readers. People would sometimes lend their commonplace books or miscellanies to their friends, who could then flick through the entries and copy anything of interest into their own books.

Given the miscellaneous nature of commonplace books, it is likely that there might have been more than one reason why your ancestor undertook to keep one. Whatever else you find out, you should consider that any ancestor who devoted time and energy to compiling such a book must have had a high degree of self-awareness (although not perhaps the degree of introspection held by diary writers). A commonplace book could simultaneously act as a record of reading, an information management system, a moral or spiritual reference point, a practical self-help book, a record of family, local or national history, an educational textbook, a practice book for various kinds of creativity, or a sort of unacknowledged autobiography. Here are some elements to look out for.

Information About the Family

Some commonplace books will reveal direct and satisfying information about a family in the past. One Margaret Bateson used her commonplace book, dated 11 October 1884 to 1926 (and now kept in the Women's Library at the London School of Economics, University of London) as a journal of key domestic happenings. Into this she recorded the deaths of friends and family as well as poems she had copied out. Other commonplace books might contain surprising information about family events such as the wordings of funeral addresses, lists of those attending a funeral, and even potted biographies of the writer's nearest and dearest. In another rewarding genealogical example, the commonplace book of Laura Calmady (1844–85), includes a copy of the will of Charles Biggs Calmady (1853) and details of the wedding of Honora Calmady and John A. Boyd extracted from the *Plymouth Journal*, 1850 (Plymouth and West Devon Record Office).

The Locality

It's worth bearing in mind that commonplace books produced in the locality where your ancestor lived, even if not actually written by him or her, might provide fascinating information about the area that simply does not exist anywhere else. This is particularly often the case, where the writer is a vicar or other person of note. John West of Trevorder, St Breock, Cornwall, kept a fascinating commonplace book which included details of the winter and summer weather of 1839, local epitaphs, death and marriage notices, a note of the local population of St Breock in 1831, a 'cure' for cholera and an account of the sheep sheared at Trevorder in 1833–44 (Cornwall Record Office).

Cultural Tastes

A commonplace book might alert you to the cultural tastes of your ancestor, especially where it included a list of books that he or she had read or wanted to read. As the writer Virginia Woolf (1882–1941) put it:

> [L]et us take down one of those old notebooks which we have all, at one time or another, had a passion for beginning. Most of the pages are blank, it is true; but at the beginning we shall find a certain number very beautifully covered with a strikingly legible hand-writing. Here we have written down the names of great writers in their order of merit; here we have copied out fine passages from the classics; here are lists of books to be read; and here, most interesting of all, lists of books that have actually been read, as the reader testifies with some youthful vanity by a dash of red ink (Virginia Woolf, 'Hours in a Library', *Granite and Rainbow: Essays by Virginia Woolf*, Harcourt, Brace and Co., 1958, p. 25).

Lists of reading material were supplemented in more modern 'commonplace books' by lists of films seen, theatres visited, radio and television shows recorded and watched. Bear in mind, however, that lists of such cultural activity, are likely to be more of an indication of an ancestor's aspirations – what they intended to watch, read and see – than what they actually experienced.

Practical Information

Commonplace books are also a reminder that there was far less available in the way of published material on a number of professional and practical subjects in the nineteenth and early twentieth centuries than there is today. Look out for information connected to an ancestor's employment or special interest. Fictional detective Sherlock Holmes kept commonplace books with notes and newspaper cuttings about old murders, for example (see *The Veiled Lodger*, 1927). Nurse Florence Nightingale's Commonplace Book (1836) is evidence that she was taught the rudiments of geography, astronomy, chemistry and physics as an adolescent. Scientist Charles Darwin (1809–82) filled fifteen pocket notebooks while sailing as a naturalist aboard HMS *Beagle*,

Double-page spread (pp.118–19) from the commonplace book of Mrs M. Rylands. The entries are densely written in ink and separated by ruled horizontal lines. No space is wasted and small areas are filled with short epigrams or extracts from longer poems. ((Document D4299 held in Chester Record Office and reproduced with the permission of Cheshire Archives and Local Studies and the owner/depositor to whom copyright is reserved))

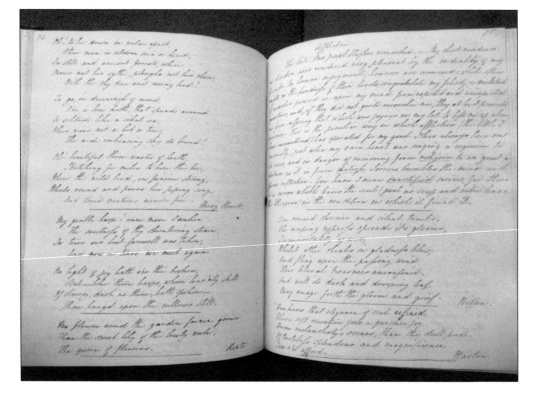

(1832–6). As one commentator has noted, 'unlike many other documents that Darwin created during the voyage, the field notebooks are not confined to any one subject. They contain notes and observations on geology, zoology, botany, ecology, weather notes, barometer and thermometer readings, ethnography, archaeology and linguistics, as well as maps, drawings, financial records, shopping lists, reading notes and personal entries' (www.core.sc.uk/download/files /197/10198592.pdf)

HOW DID MY ANCESTOR MAKE USE OF HIS OR HER COMMONPLACE BOOK?

The compilation of a commonplace book was not a passive or an idle process. Even where entries were taken from elsewhere (rather than original) the compiler had to exercise choice and judgement in his or her selection: 'The advantages of making a Commonplace Book are many; it not only makes a man read with accuracy and attention, but induces him insensibly to think for himself' (*Encyclopaedia Britannica*, cited in *The Royal Cornwall Gazette*, 27 November 1835).

The very act of copying out pieces of information served various educational purposes that might not be immediately obvious to us in our twenty-first century digital age. First, a compiler had to make sure that copied passages were understood and then that they were faithfully transcribed. Commonplacing provided handwriting practice, and an opportunity to encounter, understand and learn new vocabulary. Items that had been copied out in languages other than English allowed the scribe to familiarize him or herself with that language. If a poem was translated, the act of doing so might have sharpened his or her language skills. When poetry of certain kinds was copied out, the copier might come better to understand the stylistic rules of the different poetic forms. Victorian commonplacer Thomas Rylands, for example, included the well-known verse forms of a published sonnet, valentine and reverie in his commonplace book before trying out his own versions.

Filling up a commonplace book sometimes involved even greater intellectual skill. Your ancestor might have summarized or condensed long works, might actively have commented upon the entries, recording perhaps why he or she had included them, his or her response to them, questions the material might have made him ask, and parallel or extended thoughts. Items on similar themes might have been placed alongside each other by way of constructing an argument. At other times, commonplace books were a medium for giving vent to anxiety or puzzlement created by any issues that were currently preoccupying the compiler. Louie Crisp of Willowfield, Whittington and Pipe Hall, Lichfield, for example, kept a commonplace book between 1880 and 1886 that tackled such issues as 'The Science of Kissing', 'Pocket Handkerchiefs', 'Flirtation', 'The History of the Poor' and 'Husbands' (Staffordshire and Stoke-on-Trent Archive Service).

Interested compilers might have learned the collected material by heart. The extracts stored could be used as authorities on particular subjects. Some writers used commonplace books as a repository of information which could then be drawn upon if they needed to give a speech or write an article on a particular subject. Similarly, commonplace books served as a trove of information for would-be professional writers. Armed with the valuable reference tool of the commonplace book, anyone could imagine themselves an author ready to produce original work of their own. And indeed, many famous published writers, including Samuel Taylor Coleridge (1772–1834) and Thomas Hardy (1840–1928), did use commonplace books as a holdall and threshing pot for their ideas.

WHERE DID THE MATERIAL COME FROM?

You should consider how your ancestor set about collecting his or her material for the commonplace book. It's possible that he or she stored items (for example, letters, sketches and printed material) away until sufficient numbers could be added en masse to the pages of the commonplace book. An interesting insight into such techniques of composition is provided by an item kept by the Yorkshire Archaeological Society described as a 'Lettercase (probably belonging to one Margaret Bolland) c. 1820–1838 with collected items for a commonplace book'. It is described as follows:

> Leather covered portfolio containing articles, poems, small sketches, cartoons of two men playing chess, rough ink sketch of a lady in ball dress addressed to Pudsey Dawson, rough design for stable gateway, historical notes on Giggleswick. Printed items: subscription list for building work at Settle church, 1837, illustrations from journals including Torpoint Floating Bridge;

Facts on the character of Popery (printed at Leeds); subscription list for building work at Christ Church, Chatburn, 1838 (Yorkshire Archaeological Society).

Next, you should try to ascertain what proportion of your ancestor's commonplace book is copied from other sources and what proportion is original material. Think about the different genres represented, (poetry, fiction, sermons, political speeches, humorous overheard remarks and the like). A pedantic commonplacer will have given the details of where he or she has taken the piece from, but, of course, this information might not be complete. To say that a poem is by 'Shelley' does not tell us which poem it is, or which edition it has been taken from.

And some items will not have been attributed at all. The task then is to find out just where these particular lines came from. There are a number of places in which you can investigate the material in your ancestor's commonplace book in more detail. Begin by simply typing a line of a poem or prose piece into an internet search engine such as Google. If it is pretty well-known, it is possible that it will immediately be referenced. In the commonplace book of Mary Rylands (1760–1836), started 29 April 1835), kept in Chester Record Office (D4299), for example, the lines, 'I know/That oft we tremble at an empty terror;/ But the false phantasm brings a real misery', are attributed to Coleridge but a quick search on the internet for this line reveals that it is in fact from the German writer Schiller. Commonplacer Mary Rylands did not know that Coleridge had only translated it.

It is increasingly easy to find lines from literature online in this way, especially as more and more published books from the past are constantly being made freely available in digital editions (e.g. at Googlebooks: www.books.google.com). Other more directed ways of finding the origins of a line from literature are large poetry databases such as www.firstlines; www.folger.edu/; www.poetryfoundation.org.; www.quodlib.umich.edu (English Poetry Database); www.bartleby.com; www. poetry.com; and www.poetrylibrary.org.uk. For lines from prose or drama, search the databases at www.earlymodernweb.org which includes the text of 1,600 plays by more than 350 authors from the Renaissance to the end of the nineteenth century, or the nineteenth-century fiction, eighteenth-century fiction, and twentieth-century databases at www.proquest.com (for a fee).

Once you have found the relevant line, double-check the whole poem or piece of prose to see how faithfully your ancestor copied it out. If there are any differences between the two versions, there are various possible reasons why. Your ancestor might have been copying from a different edition of the poem or prose piece, he or she might have been a sloppy transcriber, or he or she might have deliberately altered a word or a line to make the piece better reflect what he or she wanted to say.

Mary Rylands' commonplace book mentioned above, is unusually full of entries, so densely covered in fact that not even the smallest space is left blank. The compiler's sentimental life is portrayed through the poems she has chosen. These include many on nature, infancy and death. Perhaps these references have some autobiographical import. Mary died a year after starting the book. Perhaps she sensed her impending end. The book includes samples from well-known and lesser-known poets of the first half of the nineteenth century and earlier, such as Rogers, Wordsworth, Blair, Beattie, Pomfret, Wilson, Thomson, Scott, David Garrick, Shelley, Fawcett, Campbell, Rowe, Spencer, Thomas H. Bailey, Grahame, Young, Fitzgerald, Pickering, Hogg, Schiller, Langhorne, Burns, Southey, Cooper and Cunningham. Rylands also interestingly includes poems by contemporary female poets from both sides of the Atlantic such as Americans Lydia Huntley Sigourney (1791–1865) and Nancy Maria Hyde (1792–1816), and Caroline Bowles (1786–1854). The contemporaneity of the entries in commonplace books is something that should not be missed. Nineteenth-century compilers in particular wanted to record the flux of the here and now in their new fast-paced society, not necessarily words of wisdom from the distant past. Thus, a compiler might record the latest poetry by a famous poet, or a recent quotation from a statesman. So do check the dates of publication of printed works with the dates at which the commonplace book was probably written.

Of course, some writers used commonplace books at least partly to create their own original works. In this way, such books were a vehicle for creative expression for people in society who were not likely ever to have their own works published. Branwell Brontë, for example, wrote four manuscript poems in his commonplace book (1817–48). You can view this material at www.blog.hrc.utexas.edu/2015/06/09/social-media-nothing-new-commonplace-books. There is more on our ancestors' original poetry in Chapter 11.

WHAT CAN I LEARN FROM THE WAY IN WHICH THE BOOK IS ORGANIZED?

One useful way of thinking about a commonplace book is to ask how truly miscellaneous it is and what, if any, attempts your ancestor has made to bring it closer to the look of a published book. Since commonplace books were miscellaneous and added to at intervals, many will be simply a hotchpotch of information with items crammed in to any blank space that they might fill.

Some commonplace books, however, were very deliberately organized in one way or another. They might have revolved round a theme or an area of life – medical, spiritual, literary or agricultural, for example – or around an experience such as travel to a foreign country. The commonplace book (1828–39) of William Oldham, a London hatter, for example, focuses on issues related to philosophy and mesmerism (The Contemporary Archives Medical Centre, Wellcome Institute for the History of Medicine, London). Another, by surgeon Charles Irving Smith (1809–71), in the same archive, relates specifically to his time in Bangalore, India (MS 7367). Such books, where items have been added strictly in the order in which they were acquired, provide useful information about the growing tastes of the compiler on a particular theme over a period of time.

In some cases, an ancestor will have tried to organize the material in another way, bringing the commonplace book a little nearer in appearance to a published book. Pages might have been numbered and an index created, for example, Simon Lloyd Evans, of Bridge Street, Chester, started what he described as a 'theme book' on 27 January 1837. The book included some original writings by Evans himself, copied out passages of scripture, moral homilies and translations. He listed the contents in a handwritten index at the back as follows:

1. Leaving home
2. Ode on Isaiah
3. Good Manners
4. Destruction of Sidon and Gomorrah
5. Viewing the scenes of Christ's Life and Death
6. Death of J. Williams
7. Importance of Forming Good habits in Growth
8. Death of J. Williams corrected

9. Hannibal Crossing The Alps
10. Revelations 7
11. Contrast between the Worldly and the Christian Hero
12. Ezekiel 32
13. The Poor Gentleman
14. Heaven Transferred
15. Course of Time (midsummer theme)
16. Virgil translation

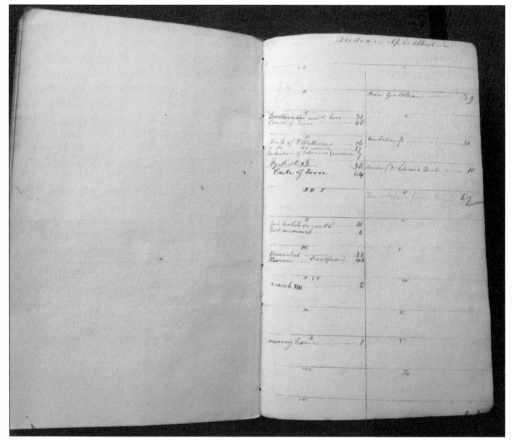

Alphabetical index to the commonplace book of Simon Lloyd Evans, 1837. One of two indexes added to this book by the writer. ((Document D4334/1-3 held in Chester Record Office and reproduced with the permission of Cheshire Archives and Local Studies and the owner/depositor to whom copyright is reserved))

Not entirely satisfied with this index, Simon Lloyd Evans also drew up a second one (placed a page behind the other) which listed the same themes in alphabetical order (with page numbers), for easy retrieval.

There was also a significant historical precedent for the correct organizing of commonplace books, though few of our ordinary ancestors will have been aware of it and even fewer will have bothered to use it. The philosopher John Locke's method was set out in his *A New Method of a Common-Place Book*, first published in French in 1687 and then, posthumously, in an English translation in 1706. Here, Locke gave specific advice on how to create an index for commonplace books. It need not be longer than two pages and material was to be arranged by subject and category, using such key topics as love, politics, or religion. The index was to be organized as a table at the front of the book in which key words were listed according to their first letter and then by the first vowel immediately following:

> When I meet with anything, that I think fit to put into my commonplace-book, I first find a proper head. Suppose for example that the head be EPISTOLA, I look unto the index for the first letter and the following vowel which in this instance are E. i. If in the space marked E. i. there is any number that directs me to the page designed for words that begin with an E and whose first vowel after the initial letter is I, I must then write under the word Epistola in that page what I have to remark (John Locke, 'A New Method of a Common-Place Book (1687)' in *An Essay Concerning Human Understanding*, Gale Echo Print Editions, 2010, Vol II).

Locke's method of indexing used Latin headers but, a later great advocate of his system, Ephraim Chambers in his *Cyclopedia* of 1751, advocated that the headers should be in English. This method – which was in fact the precursor of all modern indexing methods – was widely used by the writers of some commonplace books for at least a hundred years. Locke's system was, in fact, difficult to put into practice since it required a compiler to leave gaps in the book for prospective material of the same kind. The system was, however, favoured by some more erudite commonplacers right into the twentieth century. Lord David Cecil, a British biographer, historian and academic, for example had, under the letter 'C', in his commonplace book, the following categories of information: Change of Key, Child in the House, Colour Sense, Comedy, Class System, Classics, Commitment, Complaints, Comparative, Conservation, Content, Contrasts, and Criticism (David Cecil, *Library Looking Glass: A Personal Anthology*, HarperCollins, 1977).

Many commonplace books by our ancestors will exhibit no signs of organization at all. An unattributed commonplace book from c. 1805 kept in Nottingham University Library, Department of Manuscripts and Special Collections, for instance, includes 'genealogical notes about the Dutton and Biddle families, various recipes for preserves and dyes, accounts and miscellaneous notes'. Other commonplace books might turn up surprising information about a family member where you least expect to find it. The commonplace book of the Rev. Thomas Lloyd (1745–1813), rector of South Walsham, for example, gives details of his son's education at Eton and King's College Cambridge amongst other details of his investments and property and trips to his native Carmarthenshire. In these examples, there is what might appear to us to be a strange blending of information about family life and work life. But do bear in mind that this admixture might actually be typical of the way life was lived by many middle-class families at the beginning of the nineteenth century, with domestic and business concerns often taking place under the same roof, rather than in the very separate spheres of home and office as they were to do later in the nineteenth century.

Of course, as you read through your ancestor's commonplace book, you might find all sorts of connections between items which have not necessarily been placed side-by-side. Your ancestor might have been aware of some of these even where the connections are not articulated. The items might be connected, for example, by content, or by the quality of the emotion they summon up, or by the geographical location that they describe. Such connections should not really surprise you. An individual commonplace book has, after all, one overarching linking factor: the consciousness of your ancestor him or herself.

QUESTIONS TO ASK OF YOUR ANCESTOR'S COMMONPLACE BOOK

1. Who is the compiler of this book? Is it an individual, various members of a family at one time, various members of a family over

time? Friends or other group? Who was the book written for, if anyone?

2. Are there any clues about family members or events in this book? Were any entries made on special days, birthdays, or other family occasions? Is there any evidence that the book was taken to different locations where material was added?

3. What might have been your ancestor's motive(s) for keeping this commonplace book? Look, particularly to see if there are any opening comments suggesting possible reasons.

4. Does this commonplace book have a key theme or themes, or is it a true hotchpotch?

5. What are the main genres of writing included in this book and what does this tell you about your ancestor's education and probable reading material?

6. What is it about each individual piece in the commonplace book that caught your ancestor's attention do you think? Has your ancestor annotated or commented on any of the entries in any way? How? What does this tell you about your ancestor?

7. Where are the copied items in this book taken from? How contemporary are published items with the compilation of the commonplace book?

8. What proportion of the entries are entirely the work of your ancestor? How, if at all, is this originality indicated?

9. How close is this commonplace book to a published book (i.e. has your ancestor organized it by themes, using page numbers, an index, or by other means)

10. What, if anything, can you glean about the processes of collection and compilation of material?

FURTHER READING
Books

Allan, David, *Commonplace Books and Reading in Georgian England*, C.U.P., 2014.

Cecil, David, *Library Looking Glass: A Personal Anthology*, HarperCollins, 1977.

Chancellor, Gordon, and Whythe, John Van, eds, *Charles Darwin's Notebooks from the Voyage of the Beagle*, C.U.P., 2009.

Locke, John, 'A New Method of a Common-Place Book (1687)' in *An Essay Concerning Human Understanding*, Gale Echo Print Editions, 2010, Vol. II.

Moss, Ann, *Printed Common-Place Books and the Structuring of Renaissance Thought*, Oxford, 1996.

Woolf, Virginia, 'Hours in a Library,' *Granite and Rainbow: Essays by Virginia Woolf*, Harcourt, Brace and Co., 1958.

Websites

www.bartleby.com – includes free access to the works of featured authors online.

www.books.google.com – full text books online.

www.core.sc.uk/download/files/197/10198592.pdf – A. Sedgwick's review of Gordon Chancellor and John van Whythe, eds, *Charles Darwin's Notebooks from the Voyage of the Beagle*, C.U.P., 2009.

www.earlymodernweb.org – early modern drama database.

www.facebook.com – social networking site.

www.firstlines.folger.edu – database of the first lines of English verse.

www.ocp.hul.harvard.edu/reading/commonplace.html – digitized commonplace books in the Harvard University Library Open Collections Programme.www.pinterest.com – online catalogue of ideas.

www.poetryfoundation.org – site which discovers and celebrates the best poetry in our culture.

www.poetrylibrary.org.uk – major library for modern and contemporary poetry.

www.proquest.com – fiction databases.

www.quodlib.umich.edu – English poetry database.

Chapter 10

RAMBLING REMINISCENCES: AUTOBIOGRAPHIES AND MEMOIRS

A few, just a few, of our ancestors had the inclination, time, materials and skill to write a longer piece about their own lives. Autobiographies (generally the story of a whole life) and memoirs (generally a carefully chosen section of a life) were written by all kinds of people from the early nineteenth century onwards. The increased publication rate of self-histories (as both of these kinds of writing shall be known forthwith in this chapter) by well-known and obscure people in the nineteenth century might be one reason why some of our more ordinary ancestors started upon their own life stories in manuscript form in the Victorian period. Lords, ladies, politicians and bishops wrote their autobiographies deliberately for publication, and so too did members of the middling sorts, ministers, missionaries, school inspectors and headmistresses, doctors, scientists and social reformers. There are also published and unpublished examples by nurses, cabinet makers, railway signalmen, hat shapers, housemaids, crane-drivers, machinists and agricultural labourers – to name but a few surprising sorts of writer. As a recent commentator, Jonathan Rose, has acknowledged, 'Autobiographies were produced in every one of the several British working classes, ranging down to tramps and petty criminals, but a disproportionate number were written by skilled workers and especially the self-employed' (Jonathon Rose, 'Rereading the English Common Reader: A Preface to a History of Audiences', in David Finkelstein and Alastair McCleery, *The Book History Reader*, Routledge, 2006, p. 324).

At the beginning of the twentieth century, various historical events around the First World War conspired to make it more likely that your

*'Reading a Memoir – It Carried Her Back Into The Past.' Memoirs of famous people such as politicians or military men made popular reading in the Victorian period and, through them, many ordinary Victorians were encouraged to try their own hand at writing a self-history. (*The Girl's Own Paper *Vol. VI, No. 276, 11 April 1885)*

ancestor might have put pen to paper in a sustained rather than a piecemeal fashion. As Martin Lyons has put it, 'the trauma of separation, the experience of combat, the pain of imprisonment, all produced a multitude of memories which could not be retained without a written record' (Lyons, *The Writing Culture of Ordinary People*, p. 53).

Many of our ancestors' attempts at self-history have remained forgotten in manuscript form amongst family papers, or in archives or specialist repositories of one kind or another – just waiting to be discovered. One particular project to retrieve and preserve these deserves special mention. Between the 1960s and the 1980s, the social historian John Burnett gave a series of talks on Radio 4's *Woman's Hour* on the subject of working-class autobiographies. As a result many handwritten or typed manuscripts were sent to him. Some of these are now stored in the Burnett Archive of Working-Class Autobiographies at Brunel University Library (which now includes over 230 manuscript autobiographies). The three-volume annotated bibliography by John Burnett, David Vincent and David Mayall, *The Autobiography of the Working Class* (Harvester Press, 1984–1989) identifies not only the large numbers of printed works scattered in various local history libraries and record offices, but also extant private memoirs, many of which remain hidden in family attics, known only to the author and a handful of relatives' (Introduction to *The Autobiography of the Working Class*, Vol. 1, p. xxix). The criteria for inclusion in these volumes were that the writers were working-class for at least part of their lives, that they wrote in English, and that they lived for some time in England, Scotland or Wales between 1790 and 1945. To consult the material in the Burnett Archive, you will need to specify the author, title and volume number of each autobiography that you wish to consult. A complete list of the holdings with their volume numbers is available in the index to the Burnett Archive of Working-Class Autobiographies (www.brunel. ac.uk/ services/ library/research/special-collections/collections/burnett). Excerpts from some of the autobiographies have been published in *Destiny Obscure: Autobiographies of Childhood, Education, and Family from the 1820s to the 1920s*, edited by John Burnett (Routledge, 1994). Some of these self-histories have now been made available to a wider public by the fascinating 'Writing Lives Project' set up by Dr Helen Rogers of Liverpool John Moore's University (www.writinglives.org). Many of the texts have been digitized and cogently analysed by students. If you

Born Mary Anne Hearn (1834–1909), Marianne Farningham took the name of her local village in Dartford, Kent. She was a Sunday school teacher, editor and journalist, and published her autobiography in 1907. (Marianne Farningham, A Working Woman's Life: An Autobiography, *James Clarke, 1907, frontispiece)*

autobiography by someone else who worked in the same employment at a similar time; John Smith's *The Autobiography of a Chimney Sweep Past and Present By One of the Trade* (1877) and *The Autobiography of William Farish: The Struggles of a Handloom Weaver* (1890) are two such examples. The Copac and British Library websites mentioned above are so extensive that you are almost bound to find something relevant there. Such books can give you invaluable first-hand information about what working life was really like for your family member. Don't forget that even if your ancestor didn't publish his or her own life story, he or she might be mentioned in somebody else's memoir. Additionally, some nineteenth-century published autobiographies mention the name of the town from which the writer came in the title, for example *The Autobiography of Thomas Wright of Birkenshaw, in the County of York, 1736-1797,* (John Russell Smith, 1864: available online at www.archive. org/details/ autobiographyoft00wrig). If you find such a volume with the name of your ancestral town – it's worth having a look at it, just to see if your family appears.

WHY MIGHT MY ANCESTOR HAVE DECIDED TO WRITE A MEMOIR OR AUTOBIOGRAPHY?

If a life-history or fragment of a life-history exists, your ancestor must have thought his or her life worth writing about for some reason. Additionally, it's worth bearing in mind that he or she will have spent a considerable amount of time putting the piece together, even if it is unfinished. Bear in mind also that a common ingredient in working-class autobiographies is a sense of the writer's intellectual superiority over his or her peers. Mary Holinrake (b. 1912) (from the Writing Lives project) wrote, typically, of her education, 'I enjoyed the school and felt rather superior, as only five children from my area had gained entry to grammar school' (p. 54). Some autobiographies were, as it were, commissioned (or at least encouraged) by interested middle-class mentors who might have been involved in the same social and political causes as the autobiographer. Your ancestor's autobiography may include several different kinds of clue as to why he or she wrote it.

Titles

Whilst some self-histories adopted neutral titles such as 'Recollections' or 'Retrospect', others were carefully considered and highly indicative of what the autobiographers thought their purposes in writing were – whether it was to emphasize how hard their lives had been, to highlight the geographical location from which they came, to point out the role that God had played in their life histories, or some other reason. Consider the impact of the following autobiography titles, taken from the Writing Lives project: Florence Powell (no date), *An Orphanage in the Thirties*; Mary Hollinrake (b. 1912), *Lancashire Lass*; Elizabeth Rignall (b. 1894), *All So Long Ago*; Winifred Relph (b. 1912), *Through Rough Ways*; Charles L. Hansford (b. 1902), *Memoirs of a Bricklayer*; and Ernest Martin (b. 1907), *The Best Street in Rochdale*.

Dedications and Genealogies

Many autobiographers wrote – or purported to write – their life stories for the attention of a certain designated person or persons, for family members in younger generations, for friends, or simply for their own self-satisfaction. The Lancashire governess Ellen Weeton (1776–1849), for example, claimed that she was writing what she called her 'Retrospect' (1824) – a score of pages about her life history – specifically for her daughter Mary:

> It is for my little Mary principally that I write this. When she is older she will undoubtedly feel a great an interest in everything relating to her mother. To others, it is of little consequence who I am, or who were my ancestors; to her, it will be a matter of importance. My father, Thomas Weeton, was born at Scale Hall near Lancaster. His father then farmed that estate. Either he, or some of his ancestors had, as I think I have heard my mother say, possessed that estate and many more, but from dissipation had lost them all and were now only tenants. My father was the second of three sons. Both their parents dying when they were very little, and their father without making any will, the two youngest were left wholly destitute, a small estate at Sunderland, near Lancaster, devolving to James, the eldest (Ellen Weeton, *Journal of a Governess Vol 1 1807-1811*, edited by J. J. Bagley, David and Charles, 1969, pp. 3–4).

The quality of Weeton's writing suggests that she perhaps had some ambition of being published at some point, though her life story didn't actually appear in print until some one hundred years after her death following the discovery of the handwritten 'Retrospect' and other material in a Wigan bookshop by book collector Edward Hall in 1926.

Weeton's opening comments are very important both in terms of the factual information they provide and because they create the mood for the rest of the 'Retrospect'. She positions herself (and by implication her daughter Mary) as the impoverished descendants of one-time wealthy farmers; the following pages resound with a yearning for the family to return to its previous financial stability and position of social superiority. To the great delight of family historians, many autobiographies (of the middle and upper classes at least) open up with some sort of genealogical summary like Weeton's. This is how the nineteenth-century writer Harriet Martineau, for example, began her (albeit published) autobiography: 'Our French name indicates our origin. The first Martineaus that we know of were expatriated Huguenots who came over from Normandy on the Revocation of the Edict of Nantes (Harriet Martineau, *Harriet Martineau's Autobiography with Memorials by Maria Weston Chapman* (1877), Virago, 1983, Vol. 1, p. 36).

This sort of information can be invaluable since it often involves a record of the movements of a family that are distant in time and geography and that would be difficult to locate from any other source. Look carefully at the way in which the author tries to draw conclusions from these genealogical pathways. He might explain how the fact that his grandfather was Scottish, his great-grandmother a Catholic or his uncle a wayward soldier, has had a bearing on his own progress through life. Note that working-class autobiographies characteristically tend not to have access to such genealogical information, with the writer often unable to go back further than a couple of generations, if at all.

Public Purpose

Some of our autobiographer ancestors – even those who remained unpublished – wrote with a sense of public purpose. They might have wanted to rectify some perceived injustice that they had suffered in their life (perhaps because of their gender, their geographical location, their class, their religion or their particular type of employment). Thus, the story might simultaneously be an account of an individual life and the history of a repressed group of people (consider, for instance, the title

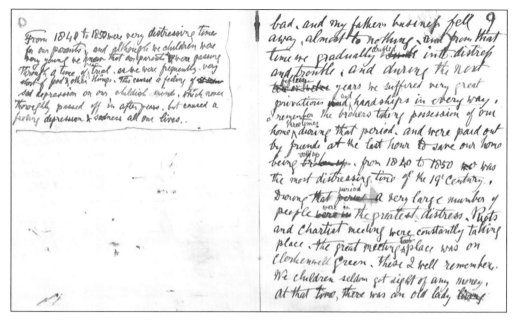

Page from a working-class autobiography in which the hardships faced by the poor in the 1840s and 1850s are described. (John Shinn b. 1837, A Sketch of My Life and Times*, www.writinglives.org). (With permission from the Special Collections at Brunel University, London)*

of an autobiography from the Writing Lives Project by Joe Eyre (b. 1910) – *The Socialist*). Many autobiographers wrote very much in the knowledge that they were breaking an historical silence, for the first time putting the world of ordinary people – millworkers, railwaymen, soldiers and the like into the public (of not the published) arena. Indeed some emerging political groups such as the Labour Party and the Suffragettes at the beginning of the twentieth century encouraged their members to put pen to paper and tell their life stories for these reasons.

Other autobiographers wrote as an education or warning to others. Burglar William Parker, for example, felt the need to tell his life story in the form of a book and explained his motives for doing so at the Central Criminal Court in 1909 thus: 'The chief object of me writing this book and entitling it "*Fallen Among Thieves*" is to give you a little idea that how[ever] well a son or daughter might be brought up by his parents. If it is in his mind to go the wrong road, he will go' (*Derbyshire Chronicle*, 1 May 1909).

Gesture to Posterity

Yet other autobiographers wrote with a degree of self-importance and self-assurance that indicated, even if they did not state it – and many did – that they would like to create a lasting testimonial to posterity. Like published novelists and poets they saw their writing as a way of defeating the oblivion of death, as a method of remaining, in some way, immortal.

WHEN WAS THE MEMOIR OR AUTOBIOGRAPHY WRITTEN?

Your ancestor's manuscript will cover a certain period in his or her life. Make sure you are clear about these dates, but also about the date at which the manuscript is likely to have been written or, at least, started (the date of composition might be included at the beginning or end of the piece). Some self-histories will cover almost an entire life and some just a salient part of it. The autobiography of Writing Lives autobiographer Lottie Martin (b. 1899), mentioned above, for example, covers just her first twenty-one years from 1899 to 1920.

It's also important to remember when reading a life history that you are dealing with at least two different incarnations of your ancestor: the one who lived the experiences and the one who (with the benefit of hindsight but perhaps also the disadvantages of failing memory) set it down on paper at a later date. You should ask yourself why your ancestor started to write his or her life story exactly when he or she did? Was it written, for example, as a kind of therapy after a major family event such as the death of a parent, spouse or child, for example? Did it mark the beginning of a period of retirement or a geographical move? Did it come at the end of a war, or a period abroad, or after serving in the armed forces?

It is fairly likely that your ancestor will have been in late-middle or old age when he or she started to write his or her life history. Ask yourself, therefore, whether it was written through the lens of illness or loneliness? What physical space did your ancestor occupy as she or she wrote? Sometimes autobiographies are painfully forthcoming on these matters. Elizabeth Rignall wrote her life story at the age of 79 and commented openly on the difficulties that this presented, 'I am practically incapacitated physically by arthritis, blood pressure and diverticulitis. Beside all these considerations I did want to complete this little chronicle while I still have my mental faculties' (Writing Lives writer Elizabeth Rignall, (b. 1894), *All So Long Ago*, p. 129).

CONTENT
Historical Events

Whether or not your ancestor is overtly aware of it, his or her self-history will be inflected by the more public history of the times through which he or she was living. Charles V. Skargan (b. 1900) from the Writing Lives Project (*From Boy To Man The Hard Way*) was unable to find work as a seaman out of Liverpool in the years after the First World War and was forced to return to his native city of Southampton where he found employment on a troopship sailing to Bombay and back. He might not fully have understood the political and economic reasons why this change was forced upon him, but he certainly felt its repercussions keenly. Once you know the (approximate) dates covered by the piece of writing, use the internet to work out what the historical circumstances of its composition might have been. The British History timeline at http://www.bbc.co.uk/history/ british/launch_tl_british .shtml might be one starting point – but there are also timelines available on the internet for just about every kind of history you can think of from medical history to legal history to political history and much more besides.

Key moments in our recent ancestors' life histories might have been the introduction of compulsory elementary education in 1870, the expanding welfare state in the early twentieth century (including state pensions from 1909), and the formation of the NHS and social security system after 1945. Some self-historians were well aware that they were living through a particularly unusual time in history, the soldiers of the First and Second World Wars, for example, or women who were involved in the fight for women's emancipation. These writers might have seen their whole lives in terms of these external events and forces, making their own stories subservient to the wider history of the times in which they lived. Others might refer to historical events only in passing, or not at all. Yet others such as Writing Lives autobiographer, Emily Gertrude Lee (b. 1902), *Reflections in the Setting Sun: I Remember After Fifty Years*, began their life stories by recounting intimate personal details but then shaded off into accounts of much more public events such as the coronation of Queen Elizabeth II in 1953.

It is worth taking time to consider the proportion of general to personal history in any piece written by your ancestor. A particular delight can be when a well-known historical phenomenon is given new

First page from the manuscript autobiography of working-class writer, Adeline Hodges (b. 1899) I Remember. *Daughter of a miner from Dawdon, County Durham, Adeline went on to become a teacher. (Hodges www.writinglives.org. (With permission from the Special Collections at Brunel University, London)* life through the eyes of an ancestor as in this case by Writing Lives autobiographer, Adeline Hodges (b. 1899). Born in Dowdon, County Durham, Hodges recounts how some people in the neighbourhood did not properly black out their windows during the First World War, 'It was very surprising how suspicion spread amongst the neighbours about those little streaks of light in the blackout. For no reason at all, they were looked upon as spies and the stories grew more and more alarming. Everybody was looking with suspicion at each other and delving into backgrounds to find the smallest connection with the Germans' (*I Remember*, n.p.).

Class Status

Crucial to an autobiographer's portrayal of him or herself will probably be an appreciation of his or her class status. If your ancestor came from the working class, he or she is likely to have started his or her memoir or autobiography with an apology for ordinariness. This was a common trope. You should pay particular attention to just how your ancestor builds up a sense of his or her class status and just how central it is to the story. Is a sense of class created through a description of education, through youthful contacts and influences, through a description of foods eaten or something else? In her autobiography, Emily Gertrude Lee (b. 1902), mentioned above, comments, ' Of course, I was never lucky enough to have white shoes and socks and a white jap silk dress like some children had' (p. 9). This is a small but telling detail of fashion that immediately places Lee at the more disadvantaged end of the class spectrum. Ask yourself if the writer embraces his or her class status or rails against it? Does he or she feel any agency or power over the course his or her life took? Or were matters dictated more by an external force, such as God, bad luck or social circumstances? Does your ancestor's perception of his or her class status change over the course of his or her lifetime? Why and how? How does the author see him or herself in class terms in relation to the rest of his or her family or community? In this respect it is interesting to note where an autobiography might occasionally deviate into local or regional dialect. Does your ancestor write in Standard English in the narrative but drop into colloquialisms when he or she is recounting what other people said, for example?

Family Matters

One of the reasons that memoirs and autobiographies are such prized finds amongst family historians is the weight given (in terms of number of pages and amount of detail) to the matters of birth, marriage and death of the autobiographer and their close family members. Relationships that are represented merely by a line on your family tree might start to come to life in the reminiscences of an ancestor. Writing Lives autobiographer Frank Goss (b. 1896), *My Boyhood at the Turn of the Century*, for example, described the closeness he felt with his brother Ralph who was two years older, 'we might have been identical twins held together by an invisible cord' (p. 98).

Memoirs and autobiographies might also alert you to all sorts of other information about your family members, anything from the schools they attended to the names of their cousins and grandparents, from their yearly income to the property they owned, from their public duties to their personal prejudices. You should think of an ancestor's autobiography as a potential repository of leads of many different sorts into your family history. Look out particularly for the names of social and work groups (chapels, working-men's clubs, cycling clubs, or unions, for example) to which your ancestor belonged and about which there might be further records. Read more about this in Ruth A. Symes, *Family First: Tracing Relationships in the Past* (Pen and Sword Books, 2016). Once you have a name for any of these organizations, search for it at the Discovery part of the website of the National Archives www.discovery.nationalarchives.gov.uk to see if any archival records exist. If your ancestor worked for a big company that is still around, check to see if that company holds any archives. It's just possible that further research will reveal mentions of your ancestor in these records. You might also find that books have been published on some of these clubs, associations, places of work and the like. Search for these by keyword at some of the big commercial internet booksites such as www.abe.com or www.amazon.co.uk.

Other people mentioned in your ancestor's memoir or autobiography (neighbours, schoolteachers, employers and the like) are usually included because the writer considers them important in some way or another to the way his or her life developed. They might have affected your ancestor's life by providing a job opportunity, giving money, creating romance or in some other way. The details provided about these people in an autobiography should be considered as starting points for further research. Look them up in the ordinary records for family history (censuses and birth, marriage and death certificates) as you would do your ancestors. It is very likely that their life histories will tell you something more about your ancestor's.

STYLE

Since there were no hard and fast rules about how to write a life history, memoirs and autobiographies can vary greatly in terms of writing style. Here are a few pointers as to what to look for.

Narrative Shape

What is the shape of your ancestor's autobiography? Is it chronological or does it jump back and forth in time? Is there the same amount of space devoted to all parts of the life, or is there a particular focus on one time period such as early childhood or the early years of marriage? If so, why is this, do you think? In Thomas Raymont's *Memories of an Octogeneraian*, 1864–1949 (the Writing Lives Project), a single paragraph only is devoted to his two marriages and the status of his children, whilst the main thrust of the narrative is clearly on his developing career. Evidently he wished to be remembered for his public rather than his private life.

Many autobiographical writings are focused around a narrative of improvement, that is they chart the betterment of the writer in one way or another, either through education, marriage, career or geographical move. Your ancestor's story might involve a personal fight to overcome hardship of some sort, or a struggle that relates to a wider social group, working-class women, Indian immigrants or the like. Often an autobiography will be a rags-to-riches story with an embedded moral along the lines of 'if you live your life the way I have done, you are likely to share the same rewards'. For most autobiographers, the narrative arc is an upwardly moving one, with life somewhat better at the end of the story than it was at the beginning. If your ancestor's autobiography deviates from this model, you should consider this to be rather unusual.

Selves and Others

As you read your ancestor's life story, it may come as something of a surprise to you that a piece of writing that purports to be about the self is actually about everything but. Sometimes (especially, it has been suggested, in self-histories by women) the writer spends far more time describing the activities of other people with whom they were connected (their mothers, their husbands, their children) rather than themselves. Some autobiographers might take this trope to its fullest extent by writing about groups of people or even whole communities using the collective personal pronoun 'we' rather than the individuated 'I'. Look out also for the degree to which the story presents the opinions of other people as well as the author alone.

Turning Points
Look out for moments in the life story which the writer flags up as turning points of one sort or another: the move from one country to another, the moment at which a partner was first met and married, the first job and the like. Manchester-born Thomas Waddicor (b. 1906), another Writing Lives autobiographer, spent his early years worrying about money. On moving to London and taking up an advertising job, however, he found he had both more cash and more spare time. He joined an elite sporting group for employees of his company. When he returned to Manchester his family felt that he had become 'so la di da' and he himself points to the London move as the major turning point in his life history.

Other autobiographies might be structured around a moment of religious enlightenment (for example, having a prayer answered, taking communion for the first time) or an educational success of some sort (for example, getting a place at a grammar school or university). Turning points might be wars in which the ancestor fought, or dreadful illnesses from which he recovered. Of course, these are also the moments in which you – as a family historian – are likely to be most interested. From other records, you might already have the date at which your ancestor emigrated to America or converted to Catholicism, but an autobiography can explain the *reasons* why your ancestors made these decisions and their consequences.

Mood
What emotional notes are struck by your ancestor's autobiography? Some life-histories, are almost deliberately unemotional, full of facts rather than feelings in deference to what the writers felt their later

audience might most want to hear. But you might pick up threads of nostalgia, romance, patriotism or self-congratulation, which will give you some idea of your ancestor's personality and what mattered to him or her. Ask yourself what the historical reasons might be for these moods. An ancestor writing in the aftermath of the First World War, but looking back on his or her Victorian childhood, for example, might be far more open, but also less sentimental, than one writing thirty years earlier.

Ask yourself if your ancestor's life history is accepting of his or her life conditions or expresses discontent, anger and even rebellion against them? Is there a consciousness of God's overarching goodness that keeps the mood resigned and calm? Does the mood become more critical of social circumstances as the narrative progresses? Of the majority of working-class self-histories that he encountered, John Burnett stated, 'One of the most remarkable characteristics is the uncomplaining acceptance of conditions of life and work which to the modern reader seem brutal, degrading and almost unimaginable – of near-poverty and, sometimes, extreme poverty, of overcrowded and inadequate housing, of bad working conditions, periodic unemployment and generally restricted opportunities, and of the high incidence of disease, disablement and death. Yet most of those who experienced such conditions are not, in their writings at least, consciously discontented, let alone in a state of revolt' (John Burnett, 'Working-Class Attitudes: Stoicism and Acceptance' www.victorianweb. org/history/work/burnett 6.html).

Genre
Consider what other kinds of writing your ancestor's memoir resembles. It is more like a religious treatise or an adventure novel? The autobiography of Thomas Wright of Birkenshaw (1864), for example, was originally written, he claimed, solely for the instruction and amusement of the author's children and descendants, though it was later published. *The Lincolnshire Chronicle* commented not altogether approvingly that it 'sometimes resembles a novel, at other times a sermon, but more frequently it is an uninterrupted flow of reminiscences chiefly of a sorrowful and lugubrious character' (28 May 1964). No doubt Wright's own reading material is to some degree reflected in the style of his life history. Later autobiographers might have

borrowed structure and language from whatever cultural material they were most familiar with, films from the big screen, radio drama, and even television scripts.

In terms of genre there are many different aspects of an autobiography that might remind you of other kinds of writing, but one of the most useful questions to ask yourself is how close this story is to a novel. A sophisticated writer (one who has usually read a great deal of fiction) will build up his characters carefully through descriptions of small aspects of dress, speech, mannerisms and activity, will develop plotlines which include suspense and drama, and will create realistic settings from telling detail. He or she might adopt literary techniques, for example, using descriptions of weather that are timed to reflect human misery or happiness. Be aware, however, that in an effort to tell a pleasing story, an autobiographer might distort the reality of his or her past experience. And too much striving for literary effect in any kind of writing can appear clumsy, clichéd and contrived.

Omissions and Distortions

Remember that an autobiography is just *one* story of an ancestor's life and not *the* definitive story. On the subject of working-class autobiographies, David Vincent comments, 'At first glance the most striking characteristic of the autobiographer's treatment of their family experience is not what is said but what is not said' ('Love and Death and the Nineteenth-Century Working Class', *Social History*, 5.2, 1980, p. 226). When reading, look out for the gaps in the narrative – the family events or experiences which are missed out completely, glossed over lightly or skewed in some way. Autobiographies can also be distorted because they are emotionally intense, written in the aftermath of a loss or a disruption of some kind. Once you have identified where these under- or over-emphases might be, put your mind to the task of working out why this is the case.

It might simply be that through illness or old age, the writer's memory is faulty. More commonly, however, autobiographers will sketch over episodes in their family life that have been disagreeable or which they feel might show them in a bad light. These include failed marriages, changes of career or job losses, and periods in prison, for example. Details of education are commonly described in such a way as to positively emphasise the writer's social status, intellectual capacity or moral worth. In general, in self-histories, writers try to make themselves look as respectable as possible. Bear in mind also in cases where a memoirist or autobiographer has included information about the family tree, this is particularly unlikely to be comprehensive. Rather the writer will probably have provided merely the best spin on his or her family history by picking out significant ancestors in the past and extrapolating something significant. His or her conclusions about the family based on this will, of course, not always be correct.

QUESTIONS TO ASK OF YOUR ANCESTOR'S MEMOIR OR AUTOBIOGRAPHY

1. For what reason(s) did your ancestor apparently write this self-history?
2. What historical time period does the self-history cover (which historical events might have had an impact on this writer's life, e.g. World Wars, suffrage, conscription, closing of the railways)?
3. Although this piece of writing is supposed to be the life story of the writer, is this in fact how it reads (or is it the story of a relationship, a family, a group of workers, a community)?
4. Which aspects of the author's identity are most important to him/her and what is the order of priority (gender, class, religion, employment, place in the family pecking order)?
5. Taking each of the above areas in turn, how does the author build up a picture of that facet of his or her life (e.g. for class status consider education, details of food, clothing, language, and books read)?
6. What time period in the author's life is covered (at what point in his or her life does he/she choose to start and end)? How is the material organized (is it structured around a particular turning point or turning points)?
7. What leads can be followed up through other historical records (names of people and the relationships between them, places of employment, addresses, dates of important family events)?
8. Is there anything important missing from the story (family life, work life, certain relationships, periods of illness, unemployment)? Why might this be, do you think?
9. What kind of writing does this seem closest to (a novel, a political treatise)? What features lead you to that conclusion (viewpoint,

shape of the story, language)? Why do you think your ancestor might have written in this way?

10. Are there any features of this autobiography that make you think that your ancestor might ever have considered that it would be published at some point? Have you checked whether or not it was published?

FURTHER READING

Books

Baggerman, Arianne, Dekker, Rudolf, and Mascuch, Michael, eds, *Controlling Time and Shaping the Self: Developments in Autobiographical Writing Since the Sixteenth Century*, Brill, 2011.

Benson, John, *The Working Class in Britain, 1850-1939*, Tauris, 2003.

Burnett, John, *Destiny Obscure: Autobiographies of Childhood, Education, and Family from the 1820s to the 1920s*, Routledge, 1994.

Burnett, John, *Idle Hands: The Experience of Unemployment, 1790-1990*, Routledge, 1994.

Burnett, John, ed., *Useful Toil: Autobiographies of Working People from the 1820s to the 1920s*, Penguin, 1977.

Burnett, John, David, Vincent, and Mayall, David, eds, *The Autobiography of the Working Class. An Annotated Critical Bibliography, Vol.1, 1790-1900*, Harvester, 1984.

Gagnier, Regenia, *Subjectivities: A History of Self-Representation in Britain, 1832-1920*, O.U.P., 1990.

Martin, Lottie, *Never Let Anyone Draw the Blinds* (1899) (125 Bramcote Lane, 1985).

Martineau, Harriet, *Harriet Martineau's Autobiography with Memorials by Maria Weston Chapman (1877)*, Virago, 1983.

Peterson, Linda H., *Victorian Autobiography: the Tradition of Self-interpretation*, Yale U.P., 1986.

Rose, Jonathon, *The Intellectual Life of the British Working Classes*, Yale U.P., 2001.

Rose, Jonathon, 'Rereading the English Common Reader: A Preface to a History of Audiences', in Finkelstein, David and McCleery, Alastair, *The Book History Reader*, Routledge, 2006, pp. 324–39.

Sanders, Valerie, *The Private Lives of Victorian Women: Autobiography in Nineteenth-Century England*, Harvester Wheatsheaf, 1989.

Symes, Ruth, A. *Family First: Tracing Relationships in the Past* (Pen and Sword Books, 2016).

Vincent, David, *Bread, Knowledge and Freedom: A Study of Nineteenth-Century Working-Class Autobiography*, Methuen, rpt, 1982.

Vincent, David, 'Love and Death and the Nineteenth-Century Working Class,' *Social History*, 5.2, 1980, pp. 223–47.

Waters, Martin Chris, 'Autobiography, Nostalgia, and the Changing Practices of Working-class Selfhood', in Behlmer, George K., and Leventhal, Fred Marc (eds), *Singular Continuities: Tradition, Nostalgia, and Society in Modern Britain*, Stanford U.P., 2000, pp. 178–95.

Websites

www.archive.org/details/autobiographyoft00wrig – Thomas Wright, *The Autobiography of Thomas Wright of Birkenshaw, in the County of York, 1736-1797* (1864), John Russell Smith, 1864.

www.bbc.co.uk/history/british/launch_tl_british.shtml – BBC British History Timeline.

www.bl.uk – British Library catalogue.

www.brunel.ac.uk/services/library/research/special-collections/collections/burnett – Burnett Archive of Working-Class Autobiographies at Brunel University Library.

www.copac.ac.uk – UK and Irish library catalogues.

www.victorianweb.org/history/work/burnett6.html. John Burnett, 'Working-Class Attitudes: Stoicism and Acceptance'.

Chapter 11

LITERARY LEANINGS: POETRY

A surprising number of our ancestors turned their thoughts, at one time or another in their lives, to original poetry, or what they might more humbly have regarded as 'verse'. Having the time and leisure to produce non-essential kinds of writing purely for pleasure indicates probably that an ancestor had the financial means and lifestyle which occasionally allowed him or her the time and space to think deeply and to be creative. Nevertheless, unpublished poetry from men and women of *all* classes of society does turn up occasionally in family papers, private collections, libraries and archive holdings. Poems were written by Cambridge dons in their spare time, by professional men and aristocratic women, but also by factory workers and itinerant weavers, by midwives and milkmaids.

Poetry is traditionally seen as an elevated rendition of human emotion, quite separate from and above the times in which it was written. By these criteria, your ancestors' attempts at poetry might fall short. You might find it dull, unimaginative, meandering, and too rooted in the realities of their everyday lives. Poems by a family member might not reach the highest states of consciousness or expression; rather they might be clichéd, grammatically inaccurate, poorly spelt, carelessly punctuated, and lacking in 'poetic development'. They might show evidence of being composed in haste and never revised. Yet, even if they are artistically wanting, our ancestors' poems are still of potential interest as historical artefacts. They might seem an oblique route into your family history, but in fact there are many different ways in which, they might provide an insight into the material conditions of your ancestor's life, his or her education, work and living conditions. Additionally, the techniques of poetic composition themselves have a history which can be researched and analysed to further elucidate the genesis of a verse by an ordinary person. Finally, but most strikingly of all, poems might give you a much more powerful insight into your ancestors' *feelings* about their world in ways that no other evidence – official or personal – ever could.

Your ancestor might have left a couple of lines of poetry, a single poem or a whole oeuvre. And he or she might have been a prolific writer of other genres or not much of a writer at all. Charles Robert Ashbee (1863–1942), for instance, a designer, entrepreneur and former Cambridge student who led an artistic and literary life and had several novels published, wrote seven poems between 1920 and 1941 which ended up in a single envelope and are now stored in King's College Archive Centre. They are entitled, 'The Two Roses', 'Love and Give', 'Come What May', 'Three in One', 'King Intef's Harper Sings Again', 'Desert Sandstorm' and 'I never saw the Parthenon at Nashville, Tennesee' – a spread of titles which reflects numerous emotions, poetic styles and historical moments. A poet with a very different background was Lancashire coalminer Jack Daniels (1900–67), whose previous efforts at writing had comprised only a very sparsely-written diary (see Chapter 5). His single marvellous handwritten fourteen-verse poem 'Down There' (reproduced at the end of this chapter), on the dangers of working underground, was eventually donated by an interested relative to the National Coal Mining Museum in Wakefield. These two examples, from opposite ends of the social spectrum show just how indicative the titles of poems can be of their writer's class background. Amateur poets from an upper or middle-class background, such as Charles Ashbee, embrace a wide range of cultural references (religious, classical, geographical or historical) in their titles. Working-class writers like Jack Daniels tend to be more direct and prosaic.

Some of your ancestor's manuscript poetry will be self-described as 'fragmentary', 'unfinished' or 'partial'. Other amateur poets labelled their efforts with characteristic self-deprecation as 'juvenilia', 'doggrel', 'little songs' or 'boyish compositions'. With poetry, our ancestors felt their own inadequacies as writers more deeply than with any of the other kinds of material that we have investigated so far. They knew that 'real' poetry belonged very firmly to a world into which they could not – for the most part – claim entry, the world of published literature, with all its scaffolding of editing and reviewing. Warrington wire manufacturer Thomas Rylands (1818–1900), for instance, modestly describes his own poetry in his commonplace book as 'a fragment that was never anything else' and 'pseudo-poesy', and remarks at one point with typical self-effacement, 'is it not commonplace indeed, and worthy of the room it occupies?' (*Commonplace Book of Thomas Rylands*, Chester Archives, frontispiece and p. 41).

Miscellaneous unpublished poetry, since it is a genre that requires little space and which may have been created at odd times and in odd places, was often written on whatever scrap of paper came to hand when the muse struck. Unlike some of the other kinds of personal writing in this book, however, poetry is likely to have gone through a process of revision and transcription before being preserved. You might come across earlier drafts scored through or scribbled out, but what you are most likely to find preserved in family papers or archives are 'fair copies' – the best version that your ancestor might have produced.

A single poem might appear on a loose sheet of paper, and is quite likely to be accompanied by hand-drawn illustrations. Emily Brontë (1818–48) tore pages down to fit the exact size and shape of her manuscript poems after she had penned them and doodled volcanic landscapes, and energetic-looking animals and birds around them – symbols, as it were, of the fierce creativity that had gone into her compositions. Individual poetic efforts also turn up in the archives on the backs of letters or might be included within a letter, some appear in autograph books or visitors' books (although here they are less likely to be original). Sometimes several loose sheets of poetry are bundled together, or a number of poems might be found together in a single book. In these cases, you can assume that your ancestor had a need to think of them as a body of work. Whether or not they were ever sent to a publisher, the collection is the poet's own version of a published anthology. A collection of mid-twentieth century poetry by Laura Ward of Airmyn, for example, kept in the East Riding of Yorkshire Archives and Local Study Centre appears written on the backs of postcards and Christmas cards, inside a Letts Diary for 1955 and in three small exercise books, each one dedicated to a different person (presumably family members – 'Ann', 'David' and 'Lynn'). Ward has also created an index of titles for the poetry recorded in the diary.

OUR ANCESTORS' KNOWLEDGE OF PUBLISHED POETRY

When first confronted with verse apparently authored by a member of your family, you might wonder if your particular ancestors had any exposure to the published poetry of their day, particularly if they lived far from urban centres. In fact, from the mid-Victorian period, it's fair to say that poetry was enjoyed by many people in all classes and from all the different parts of Britain.

Chief amongst the reasons for this was the developing national system of education, which has been discussed in the introduction and Chapter 1. Poetry was a convenient tool in the nineteenth and early twentieth century classroom. Short and easily learnt, it provided a body of text that could be quickly written up on a blackboard so that everyone could see and study it at the same time, thus obviating the need for expensive textbooks. In 1870, the Elementary Education Act (Forster's Act) introduced compulsory state-sponsored education across England and Wales for children between the ages of 5 and 12 (with a few exceptions). At the same time, new rules were laid down about the learning of poetry with each standard from 4 (roughly aged 8 years) being required to learn a certain number of lines by heart. This was deemed to teach discipline, morality, elocution and grammar..

It's interesting to speculate upon which famous poems our ancestors might have been expected to rote learn, or copy out at school. Some of our knowledge of such matters might come down to us through oral history, with elderly relatives remembering lines that they learnt and lines learnt by earlier generations of their families. Diaries, letters and significant autobiographies often mention what literature was learnt at school. School log books (mentioned in the Introduction) are sometimes frustratingly unforthcoming on the content of what was actually imparted in the classroom. Our ancestors from privileged backgrounds might have been treated to the whole gamut of English poetic history with young public schoolboys (and later girls) learning classical poetry in Latin and Greek with a view to emulating it in their own productions. But our ancestors in ordinary village and urban schools would have concentrated on far more recent works in English. This kind of poetry was more accessible to those with only elementary education, being easier to read and understand, and easier to memorise and recite. Bear in mind that there will have been something of a gap in time between a poem being published and it finding its way into your ancestor's school. Poems written at the end of the eighteenth century were popular in classrooms in the late

Victorian period and would have been remembered in old age by those who had been pupils right up until the middle of the twentieth century.

A second vehicle through which many of our ancestors might have gained knowledge of poetry was the press, especially since an explosion of new magazines and journals were printed from the mid-nineteenth century onwards. In 1852, the company W. H. Smith set up a chain of railway bookstalls across the country where magazines and journals could be purchased cheaply and other shops followed suit. The short length of poems, and particularly sonnets, meant that poetry from well-known poets, but also submissions from more minor or occasional writers, could be used to fill up small, otherwise empty spaces, in a paper. In some exceptional cases in the Victorian period, the appearance of a poem that particularly resonated with the public could be the sole reason for which a paper sold well. Thomas Hood's 'Song of the Shirt' (1843), for example, about the plight of poor seamstresses, tripled sales of the magazine *Punch* in the month it appeared and was soon appearing in popular ballad form on the streets of London. And the infamous phrase from Tennyson's 'The Charge of the Light Brigade', 'someone had blundered' (which the poet himself had taken from a newspaper article about the mismanagement of the Crimean War) had become common parlance by the end of the nineteenth century. In short, for many of our ancestors, poetry was everywhere.

Some of the most popular poetic works in the late nineteenth and early twentieth centuries were: Thomas Gray's 'Elegy in a Country Churchyard' (1751), Felicia Heman's 'Casabianca' (1826) (with its ultra-famous first line, 'The Boy Stood on the Burning Deck'), Wordsworth's 'Sonnet Composed on Westminster Bridge' (1802), Elizabeth Barrett Browning's 'Lady Geraldine's Courtship' (1844), and Tennyson's 'Locksley Hall' (1842), 'Ode on the Death of the Duke of Wellington' (1852) and 'The Charge of the Light Brigade' (1854). Other nineteenth-century favourites were 'Dover Beach' (1867) by Matthew Arnold, 'Goblin Market' (1862) with its abundance of rhyme, sound and colour by Christina Rossetti, Gerard Manley Hopkins, 'The Child is Father to the Man' (1862), and, most popular of all, Rudyard Kipling's 'If' (1895). Later favourites, bridging the Victorian to the Edwardian period, included Thomas Hardy (1840–1928) and W. B. Yeats (1865–1939). A. E.

Houseman (1859–1936), who wrote poetry about the Boer War and the First World War, appealed to a new generation which had been through the horrors of combat. In the mid-twentieth century, British school pupils studied the war poetry of Wilfred Owen (1893–1918), Siegfried Sassoon (1886–1967), and Rupert Brooke (1887–1915), and later the verses of D. H. Lawrence (1885–1930), Dylan Thomas (1914–53), T. S. Eliot (1888–1965), W.H. Auden (1907–73), and John Betjeman (1906–84), to name but the most obvious.

Certain poems by these poetic greats (and others) might have remained in the consciousness of your family for generations and you might wonder why specific lines, in particular, remained firmly embedded in their memory. Poems were generally chosen for use in classrooms because of their 'formal regularity, thematic transparency and cultural centrality' (Catherine Robson, *Heartbeats: Everyday Life and the Memorised Poem*, Princeton, 2012, p. 25). Whilst schoolteachers had a certain amount of leeway in which poems they chose to offer their students, there were some restricting factors. In 1875, for example, government guidance suggested that only poems with lines of certain lengths should be learnt. Our ancestors' lifelong relationship with poetry (positive or negative) was often shaped by their early experiences of rote learning. Many derived deep pleasure from the lines they had been forced to commit to memory, either at the time, or later in life in times of struggle when the touchstones of remembered phrases and verses helped to keep their spirits buoyant. It's worth bearing in mind that British state schools between 1882 and 1900 sometimes faced monetary penalties if their students did not meet rote-learning standards at inspection. Remember too that physical punishments were meted out to children who were deemed not to have learned their lines fluently enough. Little wonder then that our ancestors were able to remember some of those poems learned in childhood later in life.

It's more than likely that your ancestor will have sat down to compose his or her poem with a memory in mind of some poem learnt at school or encountered in a book or magazine. Indeed, he or she might have deliberately set out to imitate such a poem using the themes, language or rhythms of one better-known. As the aforementioned Thomas Rylands points out on the frontispiece of his commonplace book:

A manufactured, self-spun, so-called Poet, is an object to feel pity for. The spirit of his soul is plagiary not poesy; he steals and strangles thoughts; ('November 4, 1843.' (*Commonplace Book of Thomas Rylands*, Chester Archives, frontispiece).

It would seem that plagiarism was the name of the game as far as amateur poets were concerned. Certainly it is something to look out for, particularly where you have evidence of the kinds of reading material to which your ancestor might have been exposed.

AUDIENCE

Armed with an ancestor's poem, ask yourself first and foremost who the audience for this manuscript might have been. Was it simply a personal outpouring meant for the eyes of the poet only? Or was it expressly created to be read out to family and friends, or even to a wider audience of work colleagues or political associates? In the absence of music halls, cinema, radio and television in the past, much poetry was written to entertain others in the family or wider social circle at times of celebration or commemoration. On the other hand, some amateur poets will have written furtively, embarrassed, perhaps, of a talent which others might have considered self-indulgent, flighty, or even, in the case of the efforts of working-class men, shamefully 'feminine'.

Most poems are the work of one consciousness, but it's worth noting that a few collections of manuscript poetry kept in archives are the joint efforts of a group of people rather than an individual. For instance in Norfolk Record Office, there is a collection of poems, songs, riddles and party poems written by the Partridge family of King's Lynn between 1860 and 1869. It is more than likely that your ancestor's poem(s) remained handwritten and left in an envelope, box or file, to be pulled out and read occasionally, or never looked at again. However, it is worth considering whether the poem was ever intended for publication. It is always possible that it was published in a journal, newspaper or magazine. The British Newspaper database can be searched online (www.british newspaperarchive.co.uk or via www.findmypast.co.uk) by keyword or sentence, for example. Of course not all newspapers yet appear on this database, and it is likely that your ancestor's poem, if published at all, will have appeared in a low-circulation local publication which is not yet part of the database (see www.hobbb.tumblr.com. – the local press as poetry publisher 1800–1900). These local publications however, can be searched in local archives and record offices where many have been helpfully indexed. Other nineteenth-century periodicals which include poetry, such as *Household Words* (1850–9) (www.djo.org.uk) edited by Charles Dickens and *The Gentleman's Magazine* (1731–1922) (www.bodley. ox.ac.uk – *a digital library of 18th and 19th century journals*) can be searched by keyword online. Internet poetry databases (including www.poetry foundation.org, and others mentioned in the bibliography to Chapter 9) can also be searched by titles and individual lines. If your ancestor's poetry was published in book form or as part of a collection of poetry, you might continue your research by trying to find out how that eventuality came about. Did he or she, for example, perhaps have a patron (someone who could see his or her literary potential and who thought he or she was worthy of financial backing)? For working-class poets of this sort, see www. lcpoets.wordpress.com (The Database of Labouring Class Poets Online) which identifies groups of published poets in the big British cities and other areas, 1700–1900.

Doing such a search for a title or line of poetry online is also imperative if you are to establish whether the poem or poems in question are indeed the original production of your ancestor (and not simply some obscure work by a published poet which took his or her fancy at some point and which he or she simply copied out). Chapter 9 on commonplace books has shown how readers in the past often copied out poetry and bits of prose as handwriting practice or for their own edification and pleasure. Another possibility is that an educated ancestor might have translated a poem from another language into English merely as an exercise. If a line of your ancestor's poetry is not exactly the same as that in a published poem but very similar, it may simply have been misremembered or miscopied from the original.

Assuming that your ancestor's poem is an original production by his own hand, you are now ready to begin your more detailed analysis. Here are some preliminary ways of thinking about poetry from the past.

DEDICATIONS

Although many original manuscript poems remain frustratingly untitled, undated and unsigned, sometimes would-be poets went to great lengths to frame their work with the details of its composition, giving dates, times and even the place where the poem was composed or where a fair copy was made. Ken Bowen, for example, who later had his poetry published, accompanied some of his manuscript poems (now stored in the Second World War Experience Centre, Walton, Near Wetherby, Yorkshire) with the useful information that he wrote them, 'when on firewatching duty' during the Second World War.

An ancestor's poem might be ascribed or dedicated to particular people, often in the most obsequious of ways (e.g. 'humbly inscribed to . . .' or 'politely addressed to. . .') Many were written 'to my wife', 'my

Pages showing two drafts of an original Valentine's Day poem (one pasted in and the other written) from the commonplace book of Thomas Rylands (1829– 64) written c. 13 February 1844. (Document D4298 held in Chester Record Office and reproduced with the permission of Cheshire Archives and Local Studies and the owner/depositor to whom copyright is reserved)

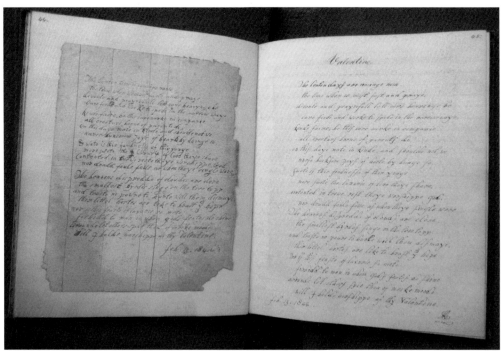

brother', 'my daughter' and the like, others simply bear the initials of the person to whom they were written, 'to A. W.' for example. When analysing your family poem, you should have a copy of the family tree at hand, to see if any relationships, names or initials mentioned possibly indicate family members already known to you.

Some poems start with an indication of an event by which they have been 'occasioned'. They might, for instance, have commemorated an historical event. One Ann Stevens, **for example**, wrote a sixteen-verse poem on the death of the Duke of Wellington dated 19 November 1853, a year after the Duke's death and after the publication of Tennyson's poem dedicated to the same event (Northamptonshire Record Office). Military and royal events too brought forth the muse in ordinary people with amateur poems on the French Revolution in 1789, the Battles of Waterloo in 1814 and of Gallipoli in 1915, and the coronation of George V in 1911. An anonymous poem of 1871 (kept in Herford Museum) was entitled 'Poem Mourning Charles D.', not a family member but, the famous novelist Charles Dickens, who had died that year.

CONTENT

Our ancestors' poems of the nineteenth and early twentieth centuries could be about anything and everything. By the middle of the Victorian period, the abstract and imaginative flights of fancy endorsed by the Romantic poets of the earlier part of the nineteenth century had largely disappeared and a new more down-to-earth, 'realistic' kind of verse was being produced. Typically poems by those lower down the social scale also tended to be more rooted in the real world, and include fewer fantastical elements than those written by the upper echelons of society.

Some manuscript poems were written to celebrate a new happening in the poet's life: seeing the sights of London, hearing a certain birdsong for the first time, the coming of a ball, the departure for foreign shores and the like. Unnatural weather events might inspire poetry as in the case of a poem by John Owens written 'somewhere in Northern England' to commemorate 'The Storm of 9th February of 1861: Regarding its dreadful consequences in the Bay and Rocks of Hartlepool' (Canterbury Cathedral Archives). Well-known mid-Victorian poets entered into debates on all manner of matters (social issues, religion, morality, industrialization, marital relations and the position of women in society, for example) in ways unfamiliar in earlier centuries. These were topics that an interested but ordinary poet of the Victorian period and beyond could also feel inspired to tackle with his own pen.

Other amateur poets took up their pens for political reasons, to champion a particular candidate in a local or national election, to support women's suffrage or describe appalling working conditions, for example. Foxhunting was a topic which occasioned poems both to commemorate its celebration of country life and in criticism of its cruelty. The unfairnesses of capitalism were also a popular topic in the nineteenth century. A coarsely but strongly voiced poem entitled 'Doggrel for Dupes', by one Ebenezer Elliott, from Great Haughton Common near Barnsley, together with a covering letter was sent to a Sheffield railway company (Messrs. S. Ironside) in August of 1847 as a protest at the way in which the company was 'buying and running down' canals.

Doggrel for Dupes by Ebenezer Elliott

Who's a dead canal to sell,
Worth a skinn'd cat's clothing?
Who will buy a dead canal,
Dog cheap, and worth nothing?
Rig off hand your dead canal,
Worth a skinn'd cat's clothing:
Rig off hand, and lump the lot,
Dog cheap, and worth nothing;
At five hundred thousand pounds,
Where pluck'd geese are cry it;
Wink at Railway Shareholders!
And the dolts will buy it.
Then, reward with fete and plate
Railway Secretary;
Don't forget to print your Do [Ditto?],
Just to make folks wary.

[Original punctuation retained]
August 21, 1847, Great Houghton Common near Barnsley (Sheffield City Archives).

Some poets, on the other hand, wrote more morosely and introspectively, tackling that grand new topic of nineteenth- and early twentieth-century poetry, the 'landscape of the mind'. Their themes – love, separation and death, for example – are universal and poems will be hard to date (unless actually dated by the writer him or herself). Others will be very much the product of the times and you might be able to guess a possible date of composition from the content. Many soldiers tried their hand at poetry after the First World War, for example.

To the great advantage of the family historian, more personal family matters might also have been commemorated by amateur poets. Poems entitled, 'Advice to Grandchildren' or 'Mother's Love' can throw open a window on a family relationship in a way that no other source perhaps can. In Northamptonshire Record Office, a nineteenth-century poet referred to as PAPILLON LUBENHAM composed a fifteen-verse poem entitled, 'to a poetical friend on his birthday' (undated). One Harriett Browne composed a poem, 'To a Beautiful Arbor for My Mother's Birthday 22nd May 1807' (Liverpool Record Office). And Mary Eliza Haweis (evidently a child since the record is labelled 'Juvenalia') wrote a poem 'On grandmother Joy's marriage' in 1865 which has found its way into the Women's Library at the London School of Economics. Deaths in the family are frequently commemorated in amateur poetry with verse being considered one way in which to immortalise the deceased person. Poems written at a death have the added advantage to the family historian of often including the date of death in their titles. A poem, for example, written on the death of Mrs Sarah Roberts of East Bergholt who died on 2 December 1811 is kept in Northamptonshire Record Office. A more sombre example is the poem written on the deaths of three young men of the Grenville family, Julian, Gerald William (Billy) and Auberon Thomas Herbert (Bron) in the First World War. This poem, (kept in the Hertfordshire Archives and Local Studies Centre), is beautifully decorated or 'illuminated', suggesting that it once took pride of place on some parlour wall.

And other more poignant family experiences are recorded in manuscript verse. A long poem in the Upcher of Sherringham Collection (Norfolk Record Office), and possibly written by the Reverend Geo Burges Halvergate (whose name is inscribed upon the back of it), describes itself as 'Lines on Visiting the Sherringham Woods in 1814'. Amongst the papers of the Strange and Hart families in London Metropolitan Archives are anonymous verses composed in 1833, 'On the recovery of a sick mother'. In The East Riding of Yorkshire Archives are drafted lines by one Peter Sibree to his 'dear brother John' on the 'departure of [their] beloved sister Hannah, June 12th, 1856'. It's possible that she had died, but she could have been emigrating. And the occasion for poetry inspired by family did not have to be momentous. Gerald Upcher (in the Upcher collection at Norfolk Record Office mentioned above) drafted a poem on 6 December 1857 that was simply in praise of his family being together again after a long period of separation. It began 'O happy day that thee again/Beholds us all assembled here.' Evidently this was written for (and sent to) his mother, Caroline, because there is also a letter in the collection from her thanking him for his effort. A later similar example, pleased by a tiny moment in family life is that written in August 1921 by Alan Rawsthorne from Birkdale, Southport. So pleased was this young man by a trip to the cinema with his sister, Barbara, that he wrote her a poem spread out between two sheets of paper, one a piece of headed notepaper and the other a ruled sheet from a notebook. He described it as 'an amusing burlesque to mark the occasion' and posted it to her in Kendal without further explanation (Royal Northern College of Music Archives).

STYLE
The issue of poetic style in history is an enormous one, which requires a book to itself, but four matters in particular (verse form, humour, point of view and sound) might make useful starting points for your investigation of your ancestor's poem.

Verse Form
By comparison with earlier kinds of verse, poetry from the Victorian period and beyond was more experimental in structure and (although some fixed verse forms were enthusiastically used), there was also a great deal of leeway for experimentation on the part of poets, a freedom that filtered down to amateur poets as well. There are a vast array of possible verse forms which might have been used by your nineteenth or early twentieth century ancestor. Indeed the poem might have been written specifically as an exercise in learning how one poetic form or

another worked. In the nineteenth century, look out for sonnets, Petrarchan sonnets, villanelles, ballades, sestinas and rondeaus (each with their own structure and rhythm). Look out also for types of poetry such as epics, odes and elegies, lyrical, pastoral and sentimental poems. In the twentieth century, many poets abandoned poetic structures altogether. Look out for amateur examples of symbolist, modernist and concrete poetry. All of these forms of poetry are fully described and exemplified on the internet (e.g. www.poetryfoundation.org) and in dedicated books such as Linda K. Hughes, *The Cambridge Introduction to Victorian Poetry*, C.U.P., 2010.

Humour

Amateur writers who wrote mainly for pleasure tended to choose non-elevated poetic forms with which they were comfortable. One way around the embarrassment of producing poetry that self-evidently failed to meet the standards of the literary establishment was to produce verse with a comic element to it. A great deal of this kind of verse abounded in satirical magazines such as *Punch* (read by the educated classes), and no doubt much more exists amongst family papers and in archives. The Northamptonshire Record Office, for example, includes an acrostic poem (where the first letter of each line is taken from a key word) on the name of Miss Sally Fagg signed by one William Young. The papers of John Tressider Sheppard, classicist and later College Provost, in King's College, Archive, Cambridge, include poems which sound like limericks and which may have been written in jest to be read out at a party to celebrate a Founder's Feast.

Viewpoint

Don't assume that a manuscript poem necessarily speaks your ancestor's mind. Whilst earlier poetry had tended to embody a single viewpoint, the poetry of the Victorian period and later was often 'multi-vocal'. Readers could no longer be sure when reading a poem exactly which lines were the poet's own opinions and which voices came from characters he or she had created. Our ancestors who were amateur poets revelled in the possibilities created by this trend, inventing all sorts of different mouthpieces for different views in their poetry.

Sound

If the rhymes in your ancestor's poems are not completely perfect don't assume that this is lack of expertise on the part of the writer. Half-rhymes, other rhyming variations and no rhymes at all were enthusiastically endorsed by published poets and seemed to be symptomatic of a society that was growing less certain of itself as the nineteenth century moved into the twentieth. Bear in mind that literary devices might seem clumsier in poetry written by ancestors with less education. Alliteration (where several words appearing together begin with the same letter) and onomatopoeia (where words sound like the sound they describe), have been identified as more common, and less subtle, in the poems of self-taught writers than in the poems of those in the mainstream tradition (Julie Prandi, *The Poetry of the Self-Taught: An Eighteenth Century Phenomenon*, Peter Lang, 2008, p. 10).

Whilst these few areas are by no means comprehensive, they will provide you with some simple techniques for opening up an ancestor's poem and starting to work out why and exactly how it was composed.

* * *

The last words in this chapter (and indeed in this book) must go to my ancestor, Lancashire miner Jack Daniels (mentioned earlier). Here in its entirety is his fourteen-verse poem, 'Down There', penned under the pseudonym Jay Dee, in 1929 when he was 29. The poem is a passionate polemic against the dangers of mining – made on behalf on some of the illiterate mining community – at a time soon after the impassioned and literate Jack himself had suffered an accident underground. It is expressed through the vigorous, sinewy language of the mines and pounds to a relentless beat that calls to mind the soundtrack of coal being hewed. It is a poem with some infelicities of vocabulary and punctuation, and the occasional misplacing of rhythm, but one which in its entirety – far better than in any detailed exposition of its constituent parts – shows just how sophisticated and powerful our ancestors' personal writing had become by the interwar period. And it is a reminder that all their many efforts with the pen fully deserve to be read and understood.

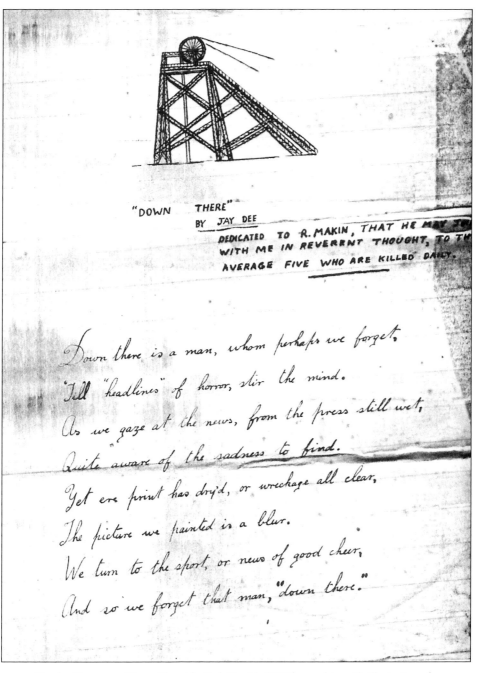

"DOWN THERE"

BY JAY DEE

DEDICATED TO R. MAKIN, THAT HE MAY J...
WITH ME IN REVERENT THOUGHT, TO TH...
AVERAGE FIVE WHO ARE KILLED DAILY.

Down there is a man, whom perhaps we forget,
'Till "headlines" of horror, stir the mind.
As we gaze at the news, from the press still wet,
Quite aware of the sadness to find.
Yet ere print has dry'd, or wreckage all clear,
The picture we painted is a blur.
We turn to the sport, or news of good cheer,
And so we forget that man, "down there."

Handwritten poem 'Down There' by Jack Daniels (1929) complete with illustration of a pit head. (Author's collection)

'Down There' by Jay Dee

Dedicated to R. Makin that he may join with me in reverent
thought, to the average five who are killed daily

Down there is a man, whom perhaps we forget
Till 'headlines' of horror stir in the mind
As we gaze at the news from the press still wet,
Quite aware of the sadness to find!
Yet ere print has dried, or wreckage all clear,
The picture we painted is a blur.
We turn to the sport, or news of good cheer,
And so we forget that man, 'down there'.

He went there and swung on that line yesterday
He's gone again today risking 'snap.'
Tomorrow he'll go, though fate can bid him stay,
There's confidence and trust in that chap.
He sends us the heat we're dependent upon,
But we're blind to the blood in its glare.
The price that is paid for the coals that are won.
By the man who is slaving 'down there'.

At earth's gaping mouth, he's to enter a cage
A conveyance not worthy of note.
Where a few pulsing seconds seem quite an age,
As he's swallowed deep down that black throat.
His eyes are affected, as down, down, he swings,
By a darkness that's felt 'as it were.'
His safety-lamp glows but on distorted things,
Till his sight is accustomed 'down there'.

Dropping so swiftly, through a void black as night,
Imprisoned by the bars of a fence.
He'll sigh when the cages have passed by allright.
It relieves concentrated suspense.
Till around his ears, a slackness he feels,
In the foul-smelling uprushing air.

He hardly needs the soft thud under his heels,
To signal he's landed 'down there'.

Into the workings, he's a distance to tramp,
But not along a smooth, concrete road.
Obstructions on the way, plus drink, tools and lamp,
Give the start to a day's heavy load.
A stumble and a bruise, as he plods along,
May give cause for an unconscious swear.
That suddenly turns to the hum of a song,
For it's a part of the day 'down there'.

The end of that journey means 'something achieved,'
As he lays on one side drink and food,
Strips off his sticky rags, and 'how he's relieved',
It's a comfort to be in the nude.
The temperature has risen rather high,
There's a trickle from under his hair,
Have you ever thought as you gaze at the sky,
That there's a man and a 'hell' 'down there?'

His place he will test before starting a hew,
By scrutiny and tapping around.
A strong pocket of gas may need moving through,
And the roof give a deep hollow sound.
Supports badly broken, or tilted askew,
Will call for some dangerous repair.
It may mean a death, but does it trouble you,
A lost husband or laddie, 'down there?'

A cracking he hears and down falls some rock,
If fortunate, he's scrambled clear.
He'll move it away at the risk of a knock
Without any heart throbs of fear.
'Tis only a sample of fate's many tricks
With more inconvenience to bear.
There is no surprise where the earth is on sticks,
The unforeseen's expected 'down there'.

He'll pause for a breath, ease his limbs from a cramp,
Listening that everything's quiet.
He'll go find his food by the aid of his lamp,
The usual bread and jam diet.
Little time is allowed for him to break fast,
And [he] must squat on the floor anywhere.
With some filthy odours travelling past,
And the presence of 'vermin, 'down there'.

Sanitation is nil, there's no white-tiled sink,
A grimy cave, is that man's canteen.
Filth smears his food, unless he washes in drink,
But his thirst can't give way to hygiene.
Illiterate we brand him, lacks etiquette,
But are we not a little unfair?
He's caught in the strands of environment's net,
That are woven around him, 'down there'.

Accidents to him, are numbered by the score,
The daily little 'cuts' never fail.
A few broken ribs, a crushed finger or more,
How his blue mottled flesh tells the tale.
Yet under the scars, his rippling muscles dance,
Portraying the energy to spare,
Should the voice of a comrade be heard by chance,
In the call for assistance 'down there'.

He gives his heart and soul, for a pittance to get
As away in that treacherous hole
Steam shrouds his body from rivulets of sweat,
Dripping down onto that 'bloody coal'
There's no scene to cheer him, no sun to shine,
In his lungs, gassy dust-laden air
But his constitution comes from a long line,
Of the fathers who have been 'down there'.

Few are his pleasures, the sacrifice is great,
For a spark there can wrap him in flame.

248

Yet we cast him aside, when youth is of late,
And we don't put a 'sir' to his name.
When our fire is low, and the room has got chilled,
We think those black jewels incompared,
But what of the man who has gone to be killed,
Cutting that 'bloody coal' from 'down there'.

That man's memorial would reach in the sky,
If we built it as to honour due.
It would cover the ground, that we could not pass by,
Without memory stirring anew.
Won't you remember, when the glow's in your room?
Won't you try giving one little prayer
For the man who has gone down in the gloom,
For the man who is 'all man' 'down there'?

QUESTIONS TO ASK OF YOUR ANCESTOR'S POETRY

1. Is this, in fact, an original poem by your ancestor? If not, how can you find out where it comes from?
2. Who was the likely audience? Is this poem a one-off, part of a collection, written on a greetings card or embedded in a letter? What might be the significance of this?
3. Is this a first draft or fair copy, do you think? What can you learn from any apparent revisions?
4. Are there any aspects of the poem that might help you date it (ascription, date, historical reference, verse form, unusual word)?
5. Was the poem written to commemorate a special family occasion, the birth of a baby, a marriage, or even a visit somewhere? Can the event be corroborated by other family history evidence (certificate of birth, baptism, marriage, death, diary entry)?
6. What exposure to published poetry (of any sort) is your ancestor likely to have had?
7. Are the poem's themes and general mood typical of the times in which it was written?
8. Does the poem fit into any recognized poetic structure (sonnet, limerick, ode, etc)? What might this tell you about your ancestor's purpose in writing it, (and his or her educational background and reading experiences?)

9. Are there any aspects of the poem that suggest it was written to chime in with an historical event?
10. Is the poem likely to have been published anywhere? How can you find out?

FURTHER READING
Books
Boos, Florence S., *Working-Class Women Poets in Victorian Britain: An Anthology*, Broadview, 2008.

Prandi, Julie, *The Poetry of the Self-Taught: An Eighteenth Century Phenomenon*, Peter Lang, 2008

Robson, V. Catherine, *Heart Beats: Everyday Life and the Memorized Poem*, Princeton, 2012.

Tonks, David, *My Ancestor was a Coalminer*, Society of Genealogists' Enterprises Ltd, 2003.

Websites
www.bodley.ox.ac.uk – *The Gentleman's Magazine* (1731–1922) and other digitized eighteenth and nineteenth-century periodicals.

www.britishnewspaperarchive.co.uk – Digitized copies of British newspapers online.

www.djo.org.uk *Household Words* (1850–9) – digitized magazine edited by Charles Dickens.

www.findmypast.co.uk – Commercial genealogical website that gives access to the British newspapers online archive.

www.gerald-massey.org.uk – minor Victorian poets and authors.

www.hobbb.tumblr.ocm – research blog by Andrew Hobbs and Claire Januszewski on 'The local press as poetry publisher 1800–1900'.

www.lcpoets.wordpress.com – Labouring Class Poets online.

www.poetryfoundation.org – includes useful glossary of literary terms.

See also Bibliography of websites to Chapter 9.

BIBLIOGRAPHY

Aldis, Marion, and Indler, Pam, *The Happiest Days of Their Lives? Nineteenth-Century Education Through the Eyes of Those Who Were There*, Chaplin Books, 2016.

Allan, David, *Commonplace Books and Reading in Georgian England*, C.U.P., 2014.

Anon, *The Birthday Motto Book and Calendar of Nature*, Frederick Warne and Co., 1871.

Anon, *The Beaconsfield Birthday Book*, Longmans, Green and Co., 1884.

Anon, *The Christian Birthday Souvenir*, London, 1878.

Anon, *The Scott Birthday Book*, London, 1879

Aylmer, Felix, *Dickens Incognito*, Rupert Hart-Davis, 1959.

Ayto, John, and Simpson, John, *The Oxford Dictionary of Modern Slang*, O.U.P., 2010.

Baggerman, A., Dekker, R., and Mascuch, M., eds, *Controlling Time and Shaping the Self: Developments in Autobiographical Writing Since the Sixteenth Century*, Brill, 2011.

Bagley, J.J., ed., *Miss Weeton's Journal of a Governess* Volumes 1 and 2, Orig. published Augustus M. Kelley, David and Charles Reprints, 1969.

Barra D., and Papen, U., eds, *The Anthropology of Writing: Understanding Textually Mediated Worlds*, Continuum-3PL Reprint, 2011.

Batts, John Stuart, *British Manuscript Diaries of the Nineteenth Century: An Annotated Listing*, Rowman and Littlefield, 1976.

Bennett, Andrew, ed., *Readers and Reading*, Longman, 1995.

Benson, John, *The Working Class in Britain, 1850-1939*, Tauris, 2003.

Black, Jeremy, *The British and the Grand Tour*, Croom Helm, 1985.

Blodgett, Harriet, *Centuries of Female Days: Englishwomen's Private Diaries*, Rutgers U.P., 1967.

Boos, Florence S., *Working-Class Women Poets in Victorian Britain: An Anthology*, Broadview, 2008.

Bourke, Joanna, *Working-Class Cultures in Britain, 1890-1960: Gender, Class and Ethnicity*, Routledge, 1994.

Bradford, Emma, ed., *Roses are Red: Love and Scorn in Victorian Valentines*, Albion Press, 1986.

Brendon, Piers, *Thomas Cook: 150 Years of Popular Tourism*, Secker and Warburg, 1991.

Briggs, Asa, *Victorian Things*, Penguin Books, 1990.

Burnett, John, ed., *Useful Toil: Autobiographies of Working People from the 1820s to the 1920s*, Penguin, 1974.

Burnett, J., *Destiny Obscure: Autobiographies of Childhood, Education, and Family from the 1820s to the 1920s, Routledge, 2nd edit., 1994.*

Burnett, J., David, V., and Mayall, David, eds., *The Autobiography of the Working Class. An Annotated Critical Bibliography, Vol.1, 1790-1900*, Harvester, 1984.

Campbell-Smith, Duncan, *Masters of the Post: The Authorised History of the Royal Mail*, Penguin, 2012.

Cecil, David, *Library Looking Glass: A Personal Anthology*, HarperCollins, 1977.

Coe, Richard N., *When the Grass was Taller. Autobiography and the Experience of Childhood*, Yale University Press, 1984.

Creaton, Heather, ed., *Checklist of Unpublished Diaries by Londoners and Visitors*, London Record Society Publications, 2003.

Creaton, Heather, *Victorian Diaries: The Daily Lives of Victorian Men and Women*, Mitchell Beazley, 2001.

Cullwick, Hannah, *The Diaries of Hannah Cullwick, Victorian Maidservant*, Rutgers U.P., 1984.

Damiani, A., *Enlightened Observers: British Travellers to the Near East, 1715-1850*, American University of Beirut, 1979.

Davidoff, Leonore, and Hall, Catherine, *Family Fortunes: Men and Women of the English Middle-Classes*, 2nd edition, Routledge, 2002.

Dickens, C., and Wills, W. H., 'Valentine's Day at the Post Office,' *Household Words: A Weekly Journal* (30 March 1850), pp. 7–12.

Dolan, Brian, *Ladies of the Grand Tour*, Flamingo, 2001.

Earle, Rebecca, ed., *Epistolary Selves: Letters and Letter-Writers, 1600–1945*, Warwick Studies in the European Humanities. Ashgate, 1999.

Fadiman, Anne, *Ex-Libris: Confessions of a Common Reader*, Penguin, 2000.

Faulks, S., and Wolf, Dr H., *A Broken World: Letters, Diaries and Memories of the Great War*, Vintage, 2015.

Fjagesund, Peter, and Symes, Ruth A., *The Northern Utopia: British Perceptions of Norway in the Nineteenth Century*, Rodopi, 2003.

Flowers, Kitty Burns, *Script and Scribble: The Rise and Fall of Handwriting*, Melville House Publishing, 2009.

Foster, Shirley, *Across New Worlds: Nineteenth-Century Women Travellers and their Writings*, Harvester Wheatsheaf, 1990.

Gagnier, Regenia, *Subjectivities: A History of Self-Representation in Britain, 1832-1920*, O.U.P., 1990.

Gillen, Julia, and Hall, Nigel, 'The Edwardian Postcard: A Revolutionary Moment in Rapid Multimodal Communication', Paper presented at the British Educational Research Association Annual Conference, Manchester, 2–5 September 2009.

Gilmartin, Sophie, *Ancestry Narrative in Nineteenth-Century British Literature: Blood Relations from Edgeworth to Hardy*, C.U.P., 2008.

Golden, Catherine J., *Posting It: The Victorian Revolution in Letter Writing*, University of Florida Press, 2009.

Hallay, Amanda, *The Popular History of Graffiti: From the Ancient World to the Present*, Skyhorse Publishing, 2013.

Harrison, Brian, *Drink and the Victorians: The Temperance Question in England, 1815-1872*, Keele U. P., 1994.

Hemeon, Joseph Clarence, *The History of the British Post Office*, Bibliobazaar, 2009.

Higgs, Edward, *Life, Death and Statistics: Civil Registration, Censuses and the Work of the General Register Office, 1837-1952*, Hatfield, 2004.

Higgs, Michelle, *Christmas Cards: From the 1840s to the 1940s*, Osprey Publishing, 1999.

Hill, Rowland, *Post Office Reform: Its Importance and Practicability* (1837), Kessinger Publishing, 2008.

Holt, Tonie, and Holt, Vakmai, *Till the Boys Come Home: The Picture Postcards of the First World War*, Pen and Sword Military, 2014.

Horn, Pamela, *The Victorian and Edwardian Schoolchild*, Sutton Publishing, 2013.

Horner, Craig, ed., *The Diary of Edmund Harrold: Wigmaker of Manchester 1712-1715* Routledge, 2008.

Huff, Cynthia, *British Women's Diaries: A Descriptive Bibliography of Selected Nineteenth Century Women's Manuscript Diaries*, AMS Press, 1985.

Inglis, Fred, *The Delicious History of the Holiday*, Routledge, 2000.

Jackson, H. J., *Marginalia: Readers Writing in Books*, Yale University Press, 2001.

Jones, Kaye, *The Case of the Chocolate Cream Poisoner: The Poisonous Passion of Christiana Edmunds*, Pen and Sword, 2016.

Kieve, J. L., *Electric Telegraph: A Social and Economic History*, David and Charles, 1973.

Linklater, Andro, *The Code of Love: A True Story*, Phoenix, 2001.

Lister, Anne, and Whitbread, Helena, *I Know My Own Heart: The Diaries of Anne Lister, 1791-1840*, Virago, 2000.

Lister, Raymond, *Private Telegraph Companies of Great Britain and Their Stamps*, The Golden Head Press, 1961.

Locke, John, 'A New Method of a Common-Place Book, (1687)' in *An Essay Concerning Human Understanding*, Gale Echo Print Editions, 2010, Vol. II.

Lowe, Sheila, *The Complete Idiot's Guide to Handwriting Analysis*, Alpha Books, 1999.

Lutz, Deborah, *The Brontë Cabinet: Three Lives in Nine Objects*, W. W. Norton and Co., 2015.

Lyons, Martin, *The Writing Culture of Ordinary People in Europe, c. 1860-1920*, C.U.P., 2014.

Mackay, James A., *British Stamps*, Longman, 1965

Mancoff, Debra N., *Love's Messenger: Tokens of Affection in the Victorian Age*, Art Institute of Chicago, 1997.

Manguel, Alberto, *A History of Reading*, Flamingo, 1997.

Martineau, Harriet, *Harriet Martineau's Autobiography with Memorials by Maria Weston Chapman (1877)*, Virago, 1983.

Marvin, Carol, *When Old Technologies Were New: Thinking about Electric Communication in the Late Nineteenth Century*, O.U.P., 1988.

Matthews, William, *British Diaries: An Annotated Bibliography of British Diaries Written Between 1442 and 1942*, California UP, 1992.

McAllister, Annemarie, *John Bull's Snakes and Ladders: English Attitudes to Italy in the Mid-Nineteenth-Century*, Cambridge Scholars Publishing, 2007.

Metcalfe, Frederick, *The Oxonian in Thelemarken; or Notes of Travel in South-Western Norway in the Summers of 1856 and 1857*, Hurst and Blackett, 1858.

Millim, Anne-Marie, *The Victorian Diary: Authorship and Emotional Labour*, Ashgate, 2013.

Moss, Ann, *Printed Common-Place Books and the Structuring of Renaissance Thought*, Oxford, 1996.

Peel, Mark, *The New Meritocracy: A History of UK Independent Schools 1979-2014*, Elliott and Thompson, 2015.

Peterson, Linda H., *Victorian Autobiography: the Tradition of Self-interpretation*, Yale U. P., 1986.

Poster, Carol, and Mitchell, C. Linda, eds., *Letter-Writing Manuals and Instruction from Antiquity to the Present: Historical and Bibliographic Studies*, Studies in Rhetoric/Communication, University of South Carolina Press, 2007.

Potter, Beatrix and Linder, Leslie, *The Journal of Beatrix Potter from 1881-1897*, Kindle Edition, April 2012.

Prandi, Julie, *The Poetry of the Self-Taught: An Eighteenth Century Phenomenon*, Peter Lang, 2008.

Raven, James, Small, Helen and Tadmor, Noami, eds., *The Practice and Representation of Reading in England*, Cambridge U.P., 1996.

Roberts, Andrew, *Postcards from the Trenches: Images from the First World War*, Bodleian Library, 2008.

Robson, V. Catherine, *Heart Beats: Everyday Life and the Memorized Poem*, Princeton, 2012.

Roes, Nelson E., *How to Write Telegrams Properly: A Small Booklet*, 1928.

Rose, Jonathan, 'Rereading the English Common Reader: A Preface to a History of Audiences' in Finkelstein, David and McCleery, Alastair, *The Book History Reader*, Routledge, 2006, pp. 324–39.

Rose, Jonathon, *The Intellectual Life of the British Working Classes*, Yale U. P., 2001.

Sanders, Valerie, *The Private Lives of Victorian Women: Autobiography in Nineteenth-Century England*, Harvester Wheatsheaf, 1989.

Schofield, Roger, 'The Measure of Literacy in Pre-Industrial England' in Goody, J., ed., *Literacy in Traditional Societies*, C.U.P., 1968, pp. 311–35.

Singh, Simon, *The Code Book: The Secret History of Codes and Code-breaking*, Fourth Estate, 2010.

Standage, Tom, *The Victorian Internet: The Remarkable Story of the Telegraph and the Nineteenth Century's On-line Pioneers*, Phoenix Reprint, 1999.

Standage, Tom, *Writing on the Wall: The Intriguing History of Social Media, from Ancient Rome to the Present Day*, Bloomsbury, 2014.

Steinitz, Rebecca, *Time, Space and Gender in the Nineteenth-Century British Diary*, Palgrave Macmillan, 2011.

Stephens, W. B., *Education, Literacy and Society, 1830-70: The Geography of Diversity in Provincial England*, Manchester U. P., 1987.

Strong, Michele, *Education, Travel and the Civilization of the Victorian Working-Classes*, Palgrave Macmillan, 2014.

Taine, Hippolyte, *Notes on England*, Translated from the French *Notes Sur L'Angleterre* by Hippolyte Taine, 1860-1870 with an introduction by Edward Hyams, Thames and Hudson, 1957,

Theopano, Janet, *Eat My Words: Reading Women's Lives through the Cookbooks They Wrote*, St Martin's Press, 2002.

Tonks, David, *My Ancestor was a Coalminer*, Society of Genealogists' Enterprises Ltd, 2003.

Van Hulle, Dirk, and Mierlo, Wim Van, eds, *Reading Notes*, Rodopi, 2004.

Victoria, Queen, *Highland Journals*, Hamlyn, 1997.

Vincent, David, 'Love and Death and the Nineteenth-Century Working Class', *Social History*, 5.2, 1980, pp. 223–47.

Vincent, David, *Bread, Knowledge and Freedom: A Study of Nineteenth-Century Working-Class Autobiography*, Methuen reprint, 1982.

Vincent, David, *Literacy and Popular Culture: England, 1750-1914*, C.U.P., 1993.

Walker, Julian and Doyle, Peter, *Trench Talk – Words of the First World War*, The History Press, 2012.

Ware, J. Redding, *The Victorian Dictionary of Slang and Phrase*, The Bodleian Library, 2015.

Waters, Martin Chris, 'Autobiography, Nostalgia, and the Changing Practices of Working-class Selfhood', in Behlmer, George K., and Leventhal, F. M., eds, *Singular Continuities: Tradition, Nostalgia, and Society in Modern Britain*, Stanford U. P., 2000, pp. 178–95.

Wehman, Henry J., *The Mystery of Love, Courtship and Marriage Explained*, Wehman Bros, 1890.

William, D. H., *Lyric Birthday Book: Snatches of Song for Every Day in the Year*, P. Nimmo, 1883.

Willoughby. A., *A History of Postcards*, Bracken Books, 1994.

Withey, Lynn, *Grand Tours and Cook's Tours: A History of Leisure Travel, 1750-1915*, Aurum Press, 1998.

Woolf, Virginia, 'Hours in a Library,' *Granite and Rainbow: Essays by Virginia Woolf*, Harcourt, Brace and Co., 1958.

Youngs. Tim, *Travellers in Africa: British Travelogues, 1850-1900*, Manchester U.P., 1994.

Useful Websites

@eVIIpc Twitter account Breathing new life into the Edwardian postcard by retweeting messages from between 1901 and 1910.

www.abe.com American online bookstore specializing in second-hand and out-of-print books.

www.amberskyline.com/treasuremaps/oldhand.htm Online help with understanding your ancestor's handwriting

www.archive.org/details/autobiographyoft00wrig Thomas Wright, *The Autobiography of Thomas Wright of Birkenshaw, in the County of York, 1736-1797* (1864), John Russell Smith, 1864.

www.bartleby.com Internet publisher of literature, reference and verse with free access.

www.bbc.co.uk/history/british/launch_tl_british.shtml BBC British History Timeline.

www.bristol.gov.uk/ccm/content/Leisure-Culture/Libraries/central-library-reference-library.en Bristol Central Reference Library which contains a collection of slave diaries.

www.bl.uk British Library catalogue

www.britishtelephones.com/histuk.htm The history of telephones in the UK

www.bl.uk/collection-items/emily-brontes-diary-1837 – Brontë, Emily, *Diary Papers* (1841)

www.brunel.ac.uk/services/library/research/special-collections/collections/burnett Burnett Archive of Working-Class Autobiographies at Brunel University Library

www.copac.ac.uk UK and Irish library catalogues

www.distantwriting.co.uk *Distant Writing: A History of the Telegraph Companies in Britain between 1838 and 1868* by Steven Roberts.

www.cam.ac.uk/research/features/the-un-limited-edition Cambridge Scriptorium Project – a digital archive of early commonplace books from the fifteenth to the eighteenth centuries.

Commonplace Books, Harvard Open Collections Digitized commonplace books

www.diarysearch.co.uk Diary search website. These are the digital texts of published diaries.

www.earlymodernweb.org Includes the text of 1,600 plays by more than 350 authors from the Renaissance to the end of the nineteenth century.

www.firstlines.folger.edu/ Union First Line Index of English Verse.

www.firstworldwar.com/diaries/index.htm Diaries by soldiers in the First World War.

www.gerald-massey.org.uk minor Victorian poets and authors.

www.hobbb.tumblr.com research blog by Andrew Hobbs and Claire Januszewski on 'The local press as poetry publisher 1800–1900'.

www.iwm.org.uk Imperial War Museum which houses a large collection of personal war diaries written by British and Commonwealth servicemen

www.ir.library.oregonstate.edu Review by John C. Briggs, of Chancellor, Gordon and Whythe, John Van, eds., *Charles Darwin's Notebooks from the Voyage of the Beagle* (C.U.P., 2009).

www.massobs.org.uk/index.htm The Mass Observation archive recording everyday life in Britain from 1937 to the present day (at the University of Sussex)

www.poetryfoundation.org Independent literary organization committed 'to a vigorous presence for poetry in our culture.'

www.poetrylibrary.org.uk Collection of poetry in Britain from 1912.

www.proquest.com Digitized fiction of the eighteenth, nineteenth and twentieth centuries, for a fee

www.postalheritage.org.uk/collections/stamps/postalstationery/ The British Postal Museum and Archive.

www.proquest.com Databases of eighteenth, nineteenth and twentieth century fiction for a fee.

www.queenvictoriasjournals.org The digitized journals of Queen Victoria online.

www.quodlib.umich.edu English Poetry Database.

www.royalmailheritage.com/accessible.html#t_1500 – A visual tour through the history of the British Postal Service.

www2.shu.ac.uk/corvey/CW3journal/issuethree/grenby.html. Matthew Grenby, 'Early British Children's Books: Towards An Understanding of Their Users and Usage,' CW3 Journal, Issue 3: Summer 2005.

www.sussex.ac.uk/broadcast/read/17135 On Virginia Woolf's appointment diaries.

www.telegraph-office.com A tribute to Morse telegraphy.

www.thegreatdiaryproject.co.uk The Great Diary Project

www.thomascook.com/about-us/thomas-cook-history/company-archives/ Information about the Thomas Cook company archive.

www.victorianweb.org/history/work/burnett6.html, Burnett, John, 'Working-Class Attitudes: Stoicism and Acceptance'

www.victorianweb.org/victorian/technology/letters/works.html Examples of Victorian letters.

www.wikihow.com/Write-in-Your-Diary-in-Secret-Code Practical advice on how to write your own diary in code which may be of help in deciphering other codes.

www.writinglives.org Collaborative Research Project on Working-Class Autobiography.

INDEX